Adolescence and Health

Adolescence and Health

edited by

John Coleman

Leo B. Hendry

Marion Kloep

John Wiley & Sons, Ltd

Other Wiley Editorial Offices

John Wiley & Sons Inc., 111 River Street, Hoboken, NJ 07030, USA

Jossey-Bass, 989 Market Street, San Francisco, CA 94103-1741, USA

Wiley-VCH Verlag GmbH, Boschstr. 12, D-69469 Weinheim, Germany

John Wiley & Sons Australia Ltd, 42 McDougall Street, Milton, Queensland 4064, Australia

John Wiley & Sons (Asia) Pte Ltd, 2 Clementi Loop #02-01, Jin Xing Distripark, Singapore 129809

John Wiley & Sons Canada Ltd, 6045 Freemont Blvd, Mississauga, ONT, L5R 4J3

Wiley also publishes its books in a variety of electronic formats. Some content that appears in print may not be
available in electronic books.

Anniversary logo design: Richard J. Pacifico

Library of Congress Cataloging-in-Publication Data

Adolescence and health / edited by John Coleman, Leo B. Hendry, Marion Kloep.
        p. ; cm. – (Understanding adolescence)
   Includes bibliographical references and index.
    ISBN 978-0-470-09206-4 (hb: alk. paper) – ISBN 978-0-470-09207-1 (pbk.: alk. paper)
   1. Adolescent medicine.   2. Health behavior in adolescence.   3. Teenagers–Health and
hygiene.   I. Coleman, John C., Ph. D.   II. Hendry, Leo B.   III. Kloep, Marion   IV. Series.
    [DNLM: 1. Adolescent Medicine.   2. Adolescent Behavior.   3. Adolescent.   4. Attitude to
Health.   5. Health Promotion. WS 460 A23913 2007]

RJ550.A32 2007
616.00835–dc22   2006100394

British Library Cataloguing in Publication Data

A catalogue record for this book is available from the British Library

ISBN 978-0-470-09206-4 (HB)   978-0-470-09207-1 (PB)

Typeset in 10/12 pt Times by Thomson Digital
Printed and bound in Great Britain by Scotprint, East Lothian
This book is printed on acid-free paper responsibly manufactured from sustainable forestry
in which at least two trees are planted for each one used for paper production.

Contents

Preface

The health care needs of young people are increasingly on multiple agendas in the UK, and the time is right for a comprehensive textbook on adolescent health. *Adolescence and Health* is well-placed to be highly influential in promoting the health of young people at the same time as being of great value to clinicians, public health professionals and those in social care and education.

Adolescents are the only age-group in the population in which every priority health indicator (e.g. mental health, obesity and cardiovascular risk, smoking, alcohol use, drug use, sexual health) is either adverse or static. The health of adolescents has changed little in the past 40 years, in striking contrast to the dramatic strides made in the health of children and the elderly.

This is currently being recognized as a major deficit in UK health care. We certainly have seen a stronger emphasis on adolescent health in governmental, clinical and public health arenas in the last five years, together with an increased recognition of the need for training of all health professionals in basic adolescent health issues.

To my mind, the great error of UK approaches to adolescent health has been to focus on single issues in isolation – for example, teenage pregnancy, sexually transmitted infections, drug use or mental health. Otherwise excellent programmes, such as the government's Teenage Pregnancy Programme and the various governmental drug and alcohol or sexual health strategies, while recognizing the importance of young people's health, fail to look beyond their narrow silo and beyond their traditional medical or public health remit.

However, the striking feature of health in adolescence is the interconnection of physical and mental health and health behaviours, more so than at any other age. Those who drink, smoke, take drugs or have unprotected sex are between 6 to 15 times more likely to engage in other exploratory or risky behaviours. Indeed, there is substantial evidence that what appear to be separate behaviours may form what has been called a 'single syndrome', with common ætiology factors related to emotional well-being, deprivation and connectedness to family, community and peers.

Indeed, it can be argued that the unique health and social care needs of young people are driven directly by the developmental nature of adolescence. Problems as diverse as exploratory behaviours, sexuality, adaptation to chronic conditions, violence, accidents and mental health problems are directly related to the interplay of biological, psychological and social elements of adolescent development, and the interface of this development with peers, family and the wider community.

Adolescence and Health provides a welcome corrective to single issue approaches, enthusiastically embracing the wider perspectives and providing a refreshing challenge to prevailing myths about adolescent health and health service use. The editors are national figures in the field and have recruited an impressive panel of experts to contribute individual chapters. The book meets the common challenge seen in adolescent health of being sufficiently 'big picture' while providing the detail needed to be useful to the practising clinician or public health professional.

Importantly, it avoids the usual problem-saturated view of adolescence and gives a strong sense of the resilience and strengths of young people and the rewards of working with them. Adolescent health is not a speciality but a generality. The knowledge and skills outlined in *Adolescence and Health* are needed by, and will be welcomed by, professionals who regularly, or even occasionally, have responsibility for caring for, or organizing health services for, young people.

Russell Viner
Consultant in Adolescent Medicine
Hospital for Sick Children, Great Ormond St., London

Chapter 1

Understanding Adolescent Health

John Coleman

Department of Educational Studies, University of Oxford

Leo Hendry and Marion Kloep

Centre for Lifespan Research, University of Glamorgan

- ■ Introduction
- ■ What is Health?
- ■ The Young Person's View of Health
- ■ The Lifespan Developmental Model
- ■ Influences on Adolescent Health
- ■ Conclusion

Learning Objectives

After reading this chapter you should:

1 Understand adult concerns about adolescent health.
2 Be aware that health can be defined in a number of different ways.
3 Have an understanding of the contrast between adult and adolescent views of health.
4 Have learnt how the lifespan developmental model can help us to understand adolescent health.
5 Be aware of the different influences on adolescent health.

Introduction

It is often said that adolescents are the healthiest group in society. They make less use of health services than other age groups, and they appear to show less interest in health concerns than adults. However, the health of young people is a source of major anxiety to adults. This is what Professor Andrew Copp says in his introductory remarks on health in *Working with children 2006/2007*:

> *Many of our concerns about long-term health arise in adolescence. On many indicators, such as mental health, suicide and self-harm, obesity and lack of exercise, smoking, drinking and drugs, sexually transmitted diseases and teenage pregnancy, adolescents are getting less healthy, or at least giving cause for concern. As young people assume responsibility for their own health, they can become harder to reach with traditional health services. Yet, especially in an aging society, we need healthy, motivated and well-educated young people to keep our society vibrant, flourishing and productive. (Copp, 2005)*

Professor Copp is not alone in expressing these concerns. In the recent past, the British Medical Association published a major report on adolescent health (Nathanson, 2003) which had a predominantly gloomy tone, and Viner and Barker (2005) in their article 'Young people's health: the need for action' pointed out that adolescence is the one age group where there has been no discernible improvement in health over the last 20 years. For both children and older people there have been major health gains, and yet for adolescents there have either been adverse trends (as, for example, in obesity, sexually transmitted infections and so on) or there has been no change. As these authors argue, this has to be set in the context of a situation where the prevalence of diseases in children and young people such as asthma and diabetes is on the increase. Furthermore, over the last two decades mortality among adolescents has fallen much less than in children, primarily because the numbers of deaths resulting from injury and suicide have not decreased in this period.

Is this pessimism justified? It is certainly true that some of the indicators of health risk, such as substance use and problematic sexual behaviour, do show a deteriorating situation. It is also the case that young people in Britain have higher rates of drinking, illegal drug use, and teenage pregnancy than their peers in other European countries. However, the health of adolescents cannot be completely divorced from the health of children or adults. Obesity, for example, is a problem that applies to all age groups, and the increased incidence of mental health problems and of sexually transmitted infections are trends that can be seen in adults as well as in young people.

Another factor of significance here is that health services for young people have a long way to go before they address the needs of this population. Professor Copp, in his remarks quoted above, makes reference to the fact that young people are harder to reach with traditional health services than other age groups. There are many problems that are associated with the provision of appropriate services, including the need for confidentiality, the problem of access to services for those who attend school or college during normal clinic opening times, and transport for those who do not live within easy distance of health centres. There is little doubt that the medical profession has been slow to address these issues. While there are some encouraging trends in health care for adolescents, there is still far too little energy and too few resources going into the provision of effective services for this age group.

It is also the case that, contrary to popular mythology, young people are in fact as concerned about health as adults. However, their concerns are slightly different. They do not necessarily worry about long-term health risks. A message about the consequences of smoking on life expectancy is not likely to have much of an impact. Yet they do worry about their appearance, their hair and skin, and about various aspects of their bodies. They are particularly concerned about how they compare with other young people of a similar age. They want health information, whether it is about sex, mental health or healthy eating. Good quality teaching on PSHE (personal, social and health education) is valued highly, and they make good use of books and web sites, as is demonstrated by the popularity of publications such as *The diary of a teenage health freak* (Macfarlane and McPherson, 2002).

In considering adolescent health it is important to point out that young people do go to the doctor, as has been shown in numerous research studies (Coleman and Schofield, 2005). They may be healthier than other groups, but they do get infections and injuries, and they do of course suffer from the same common complaints as adults. Also there are major health inequalities that affect young people as much as they do other age groups. The health of young people growing up in poverty and deprivation is significantly poorer than the health of less disadvantaged adolescents, so that it is essential to keep in mind that the health of young people is not the same across the social spectrum. As we shall see, adolescent health is a complex topic, yet one of profound importance to us all. In the following sections of this chapter we will explore some of these complexities.

What is Health?

One of the factors which contribute to the complexity we have just mentioned is that there are many different definitions of health. We will look at some of these here.

Population Health: a Demographic Approach

From a demographic point of view, the health of a population is measured by objective criteria, such as the mean life expectancy of the inhabitants of a country. Other measures considered in demographic research include malnutrition levels, the number of patients per doctor, distance to hospital or health centre, access to water and other services, housing conditions and so on. The latter ones are not measures of health per se, but rather factors which affect health. Nonetheless from this perspective one could state that the population of Britain (mean life expectancy at birth: males 75.7, females 80.7 years) is healthier than the population of Zimbabwe (mean life expectancy at birth: males 37.9, females 35.1 years) (Index Mundi, 2004).

This raises the question of whether health is equated with longevity. Is health calculated by the number of years added to the life course? Modern technology enables us to keep people alive for longer. If we keep terminally ill people alive with the help of complicated machines that artificially sustain only the most vital life functions, are we maintaining health? Such a question leads us on to another way of defining health.

Objective Biomedical Assessments of Health

A second possible approach to health is to say that health is the absence of illness. A normally healthy person who comes down with flu for a fortnight would, according to this definition, be ill during the period of infection. There are measurable criteria against which to estimate an individual's health status. Such criteria include blood pressure, body temperature, amount of red and white blood cells, heart rate and cholesterol level. If all bodily functions are within the normal range and no infections or other negative medical evidence are apparent, then the doctor may consider the patient's health to be 'good'.

Of course it is possible that the individual may not agree with this diagnosis. The patient might be experiencing aches and pains, yet these can go undetected as they do not affect the criteria mentioned above. The doctor may believe that the individual is healthy, and yet the personal experience of the patient contradicts this. They do not feel 'healthy'. Alternatively, the doctor might identify some bodily malfunction that has not previously troubled the patient at all. In such a case the doctor might have difficulty convincing the person concerned that they are not healthy, and that they need medical treatment. This mismatch of perceptions takes us on to another possible definition of health.

Subjective Feelings and Well-Being

The perspective that considers subjective feelings is one that says: "if I feel healthy, then I am healthy". As Blaxter puts it:

> *The predominant concept of health in oneself (is) a psychological one. To feel good, happy, able to cope …. (Blaxter, 1987, p. 141)*

Of course feelings of well-being and life satisfaction are not unconnected with objective health assessments, but they are not necessarily highly correlated either. In a study by Herzog (1991) only 6% of respondents reported that they were not satisfied with their life, in spite of the fact that a high proportion of this particular sample (62%) suffered from at least one chronic medical condition.

It may be the case that people showing symptoms of minor physical conditions suffer subjectively more than people with serious illnesses. Whether this occurs will depend on the individual's coping skills, the social support received, personal resilience, and the impact of the condition on daily functioning. Interestingly it has been found that an individual's subjective perceptions of health predict longevity more strongly than health assessments carried out by medical personnel (e.g. McCamish-Svensson et al., 1999). It is also of interest to consider what people regard as healthy. Asked to describe someone they know who is 'very healthy', the majority of people in a British study (Blaxter, 1987) described a physically active, sporty, adult *male* figure. This finding suggests that masculinity, activity and fitness are the basic essentials of health in the eyes of the general population!

The World Health Organization (WHO) Definition

The best-known definition of health is perhaps that put forward by the World Health Organization:

> *Health is a state of complete physical, mental and social well-being and not merely the absence of disease or infirmity. (WHO, 1946)*

This definition is interesting, in that it emphasizes health as a positive force, defined by something more than the absence of illness. Indeed it adds other dimensions to a solely medical perspective on health. Yet there are problems with this definition:

* It is somewhat static, and rather too idealistic as a working model. Logically from this definition few, if any, can be completely healthy, because total well-being cannot be achieved.
* The notion of well-being is as difficult to define as the notion of health. Do we mean objective or subjective well-being?
* What does social well-being involve? Is it conformity to community/societal norms, or individualism and independence?

For these reasons commentators in the health field have tried to develop a new definition of health, the so-called 'open notion of health'. Admitting that a definition of health can never be completely objective, or value free, Wackerhausen (1994) proposes health to be:

> *The ability to realise one's goals (both in daily life and in the long term planning of one's life) under given life conditions.*

This definition allows for individual differences. For example, a young woman who is a cross-country runner will have different goals from another who has no sporting interests but has recently entered into her first sexual relationship. The first young woman may regard a pain in her foot as being of serious concern, whilst the second may hardly notice her foot, being preoccupied with different types of contraception.

This definition differs significantly from a strictly medical one, since it is relative. It also takes the focus away from solely physical conditions, and encompasses anything that prevents us from reaching our goals. Such features of health may include lack of competence, lack of confidence, poor psychomotor judgement, lack of knowledge about the task we are undertaking and so on. Also, there is a question as to whether health as defined here is synonymous with the ability to reach one's goal, or whether it is a means, or an obstacle to it. To what extent would young people consider their health as one of the factors which limits the activities in which they participate?

We have explored here a number of ways of defining health. Perhaps all these definitions are relevant and have their place, depending on what we need the definition for. It might be required for deciding about medical treatment, for measuring the quality of life, for prevention, for investing in new services, or for creating possibilities for positive personal development. Additionally, it is important to recognize that any definition is only looking at one part of the puzzle. Possibly this is all that can be achieved. Systemic theory (e.g. Lerner, 1998) proposes that we take account of multi-level, two-way interactive factors from the gene to the cellular level, through biological and perceptual-motor individual factors, to the cultural and historical macro-level factors, all of which affect the individual's development. Yet realistically, in professional practice or in research, it seems likely that one cannot look at everything at once. We should be aware of the limitations of any one definition or analytical approach. The most important thing to realize is that there are many definitions of health, and we need to be careful about which one we use.

The Young Person's View of Health

Up to this point we have been considering adult definitions of health, but how do young people see this? We have stated that young people see health differently, and we can now look at this in more detail. Firstly, young people generally show less interest in discussing smoking, alcohol or drugs with health professionals, as these are seen as adult concerns. In the study carried out by Hendry et al. (1998) the opinion was expressed frequently that adults, and this included parents, teachers and adults in the community, did not necessarily understand what adolescent health concerns were. As evidenced by Backett and Davison (1992) these concerns related to fitness, appearance, attractiveness and peer acceptance. In this study, adolescents expressed the view that to be overly worried about health and lifestyle was 'boring' and 'middle-aged'.

In a school-based questionnaire survey of teenagers aged between 13 and 15 in London, young people indicated that their main health concerns were about weight, acne, nutrition and exercise (Epstein et al., 1989). A series of interviews carried out by Aggleton and colleagues (1996) with young people between the ages of 8 and 17 support the view that young people's health worries extend beyond issues to do with smoking, drugs and sexual health. Rather, adolescents express concerns about their developing bodies as puberty progresses. The following quotes are taken from Shucksmith and Hendry (1998):

> "Oh God, where did all this fat come from? It never used to be there or I never noticed it. I used to be able to eat loads of sweets and the only thing that grew were my feet!" (Girl, 15)
> "I worry a bit about health – well, quite a bit. I'm trying to keep a constant weight, making sure I'm not overweight. I don't want to look fat and horrible, and have people making jokes about me." (Girl, 15)

Young people not only mention differing health concerns, but they often consider that adults overestimate the risks that are associated with behaviours such as drinking and smoking. This is particularly the case where the focus is on behaviour that is seen as normal in adulthood.

> "Your father says don't smoke, and yet he has a cigarette in his hand. He says don't drink, when the following weekend he's out in the bar getting drunk!" (Girl, 14) (Shucksmith and Hendry, 1998)

One important difference between the age groups is that young people do not see health in abstract terms. For adolescents health is very much about the here and now, and their needs are to do with having the best information, and also having the skills to manage the situations in which they find themselves, such as at a party where alcohol and possibly illegal drugs are available. Some commentators have made the point that health for young people is best seen as a trade-off between knowing what is good for you and dealing with pressure from peers and family. As Kalnins *et al.* (1992) put it:

> *They [young people] perceive health in terms of conflict situations in which courses of action are pitted against pressure from friends and family.*

Thus adolescents tend to adopt a subjective definition of health – in contrast to their parents – and give preference to learning skills that might enhance their well-being rather than simply avoid risks.

Where the provision of health information is concerned, a fine line has to be drawn between basic knowledge and social skills. Teenagers are not necessarily interested in receiving even more information about such things as alcohol and drugs, especially as they are often quite knowledgeable already. However, they are open about the fact that they lack the skills to manage the social pressures and to implement what they know in their daily lives. To take the example of smoking, most young people are aware of the risks of smoking, and many would like to give up, and yet they do not know how to achieve that goal in the face of peer encouragement. Long-term goals, such as the avoidance of lung disease in the future, do not seem sufficiently potent at the age of 14 (Turtle *et al.*, 1997).

To take another example, Hendry and Singer (1981) found that adolescent girls have positive attitudes to physical activity for health reasons, but assign low priority to their actual involvement in these pursuits because of conflicting interests. These interests are usually social,

involving spending time with friends and thus, it could be said, sacrificing long-term goals for the needs of the moment. As Coffield (1992) noted, teenagers find it difficult, if not impossible, to worry about the health of a 50-year-old stranger, that is, themselves 35 years in the future. However, a warning note needs to be sounded here. Are adults any better at making personal sacrifices for long-term health goals? If we think of our own behaviour, our weight, our lack of physical fitness, our use of alcohol at the weekends, we can recognize that some caution is needed before we make value judgements about a generation younger than ourselves.

This raises the interesting question of whether young people are more likely than adults to engage in health risk behaviour. An argument could be advanced that a certain amount of learning is inevitable for young people, and that risks are taken in order for this learning to take place. In the case of alcohol many young people describe their early experiences as being ones of losing control, but then finding ways to manage their behaviour better as they grow older. The following quotes are from Shucksmith and Hendry (1998):

> "Yeah, I know about limits now, but not when I first started. I was drinking far too much, and I was just totally 'over the top'. I want to be able to control what I am drinking now...and be sensible." (Boy, 15)
>
> "You must do this, you must find your own limits. Try to, because if you are going to drink it is essential. It is part of growing up." (Girl, 14)

Hendry and Reid (2000) found that having the basic skills to 'get along with others' is seen by young people as an essential component to a sense of health and well-being. Adolescents also believe that they should receive what they call 'emotional education' (how to cope with anger, recognize emotions and so on) if their health needs are to be addressed. We shall have more to say about this in the chapter on 'Emotional Health and Well-Being'. It is the view of young people that few adults appreciate the nature of teenagers' needs for what might be called 'social emotional learning' in the context of health education. Furthermore, young people experience a lack of empathy and understanding of their concerns on the part of adults. This is a serious gap, and requires more attention if we are to make a genuine attempt to improve the health of adolescents.

The Lifespan Developmental Model

Having looked at the views of both adults and young people, which is more correct in relation to health and healthy lifestyles in adolescence? We would suggest that both points of view have merit, and that health will always be a complex, multifaceted concept. We agree with Stone (1987), who suggested that health should be regarded not as a static ideal state, but as a dynamic concept involving movement in a positive (or negative) direction. According to this definition an individual can be more or less healthy at different points in the life course, and indeed at different times of the day, depending on different situations. To clarify this viewpoint, we will briefly introduce here the Lifespan Model of Developmental Challenge (Hendry and Kloep, 2002) and apply it to adolescent health.

We start by emphasizing that no event or behaviour is an isolated occurrence, but is embedded in a whole system of other events and behaviours, all of which influence each other. For that reason, no event has the same impact on different individuals, and not even on the same individual in different situations. This is why pursuits or activities that are healthy for one person can be unhealthy for another and without any health consequences for a third.

A teenager on a night out with his peers could be ostracized for refusing to drink alcohol, and this outcome might put his emotional health more at risk than if he were to drink. A young woman who is a talented tennis player and who spends all her leisure time training may be physically strong and fit, but may miss the chance to learn all the social skills her peers are acquiring during their adolescent years.

Within this theoretical framework we regard the individual's health as consisting of various elements, within a dynamic interactive system of resources. An individual has more or fewer resources at different times and in different circumstances. These resources, interacting with each other, can enhance or diminish other environmental and psychosocial resources. It is obvious that the more resources the individual has, the more likely it is that he or she will lead a healthy life. Some of the resources are ones we are born with, such as our genetic or constitutional characteristics. Thus an individual may be born with a genetic disposition to heart disease, or schizophrenia. Other resources, such as education, good nutrition and so on, are acquired during the life course.

Smoking, the misuse of alcohol or drugs, and lack of exercise potentially diminish health resources and so, according to this perspective the adult view of health is correct. However, social and interpersonal skills, such as coping mechanisms, can also enhance health resources, so the adolescent's view is equally correct. In some cases one has to make a choice between different priorities, since one may be able to strengthen one resource at the expense of another. Furthermore, resources interact together, enhancing or inhibiting each other. Mental well-being has an effect on physical health and vice versa. A happy person is more likely to engage in health-enhancing activities; one is more likely to catch a cold if one is stressed, and feelings of stress are more likely to occur if the body is not functioning well.

However, what exactly these resources can be used for is not really evident until we know what health challenges the individual encounters. Quite different resources may be needed to cope with a disease, to withstand peer pressure, to function satisfactorily in daily life, or to develop habits that have positive long-term health effects. Thus a young person managing peer pressure in relation to alcohol or smoking may require somewhat different resources from one dealing with a sports injury, or chronic illness.

In the context of these remarks, what is a healthy lifestyle for a young person? We suggest the following solution to this dilemma. A healthy lifestyle is anything that adds resources to the individual's dynamic resource pool. Since almost nothing we do or experience will only add resources, but will at the same time come at a cost, we regard a healthy lifestyle as anything that maximizes gains and minimizes costs, in both the short and long term.

As an example of this argument, we can recognize that young people often learn from what, on the surface, may appear to be unhappy or negative experiences. In resolving not to respond to a similar event in a similar manner again, they can develop a range of social skills which assist in the development of resilience and coping mechanisms for future use (Hendry and Kloep, 2002). Rutter and Smith (1995) have talked about 'steeling' experiences, small 'injections' of unlucky experiences that immunize young people against future risks in the same way as a vaccination works. From this viewpoint it is clear that even experiences that seem to be hazardous and risky from an objective perspective can add to the health resources of young people.

Writers on adolescent health (e.g. Eccles *et al.* 1996) have argued that there is a 'mismatch' between the needs of the developing adolescent and their experiences at school and in the home. This 'mismatch' may possibly have a negative effect on psychological and behavioural development. What do we mean? As we have seen, adult health concerns for young people centre on the *avoidance* of behaviours that could be a potential health risk. This approach is often experienced as attempting to constrain young people, to hold them back, to prevent them doing things they want to do. On the other hand, adolescents emphasize the need for *engagement* with some health risk activities, as without this they cannot learn skills and gain resources to develop a healthy lifestyle.

These two differing views are not necessarily mutually exclusive, especially if there is a recognition that both aims can contribute to better health. Lerner (2002) argues that we should concentrate not only on diminishing risks, but also on building the strengths and qualities of young people so that they have the capacity for positive development. As he puts it:

> *Preventing a problem from occurring does not, in turn, guarantee that we are providing youth with the assets they need for developing in a healthy manner. (Lerner, 2002 p. 528)*

In sum, we suggest that what is healthy or unhealthy is a trade-off between different choices in the face of health challenges. The more resources the individual has, the more choices are possible. In order to achieve the greatest degree of resources, the individual needs to be proactive and aware, and even take risks sometimes. By simply doing nothing, no new resources are gained, and existing ones might become depleted. In meeting and coping with challenges, developing skills to assess and deal with risk, and balancing benefits and costs, young people stand the greatest chance of developing a healthy lifestyle.

Influences on Adolescent Health

It will be clear that young people vary hugely in their health status. Imagine for a moment two 16-year-old boys. One lives in a deprived inner city area. He has not seen a doctor or dentist for the last three years, he has a poor diet, he smokes and drinks, has never played sport, suffers aches and pains in his joints, and has frequent toothache. The second boy is a keen sportsman. He lives in a middle-class area, and has seen both a doctor and a dentist within the last year. He has no symptoms of ill-health. He does not smoke, but does drink alcohol at parties. His parents are interested in healthy food, and he regularly eats fruit and vegetables. It does not take much to see that the two boys are likely to have very different health outcomes as adults.

There is a wide range of factors that impinge on, or affect young people's health. Such factors include the family, cultural background and the environment, with poverty and disadvantage having a particularly strong effect on young people's health. In addition to these factors, gender plays a key role, as do social and geographical variables. As an example we will be looking at some international comparisons of substance use and teenage conceptions, where we can see marked variations which are not always easy to explain.

We will first consider gender, as it may be that this is the variable that has the greatest degree of influence on health status. We can think of a multitude of health indicators that vary according to gender. Thus, for example, from the earliest years boys are physically more active, and show a different pattern of health and ill-health to girls. When we come to adolescence, we know that puberty itself differs markedly between the two genders. Girls reach puberty earlier, and the sequence of events during the pubertal period is not the same for males and females. It is at this point that the marked differences in body shape, in size and in musculature become so apparent, and in addition we know that psychological factors come into play, with girls showing more dissatisfaction with their bodies than boys during this stage.

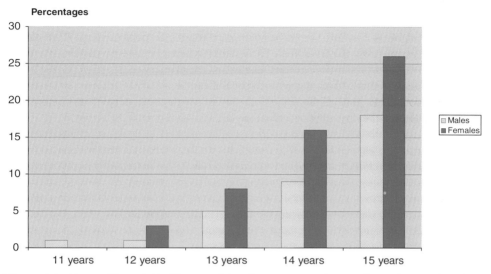

Figure 1.1   Proportion of 11–15 year-olds who were regular smokers, by gender, 2003 (Boreham and Blenkinsop, 2004).

As will be apparent, gender can be shown to have an impact on any number of health indicators and behaviours, and we do not have the space here to explore these in great detail. However, as one reflection of the importance of gender, we will consider the behaviours of smoking and drinking in this context. Evidence presented in Figures 1.1 and 1.2 shows that,

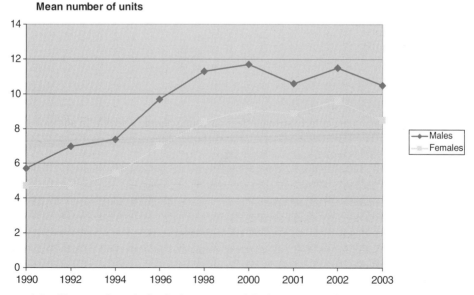

Figure 1.2   Mean units of alcohol consumed in last seven days among 11–15 year-olds, in England, by gender, 1990–2003 (Boreham and Blenkinsop, 2004).

while girls are very much more likely to be regular smokers in adolescence, it is the boys who are drinking more alcohol. Why should this be so? The argument set out in Lloyd and Lucas (1998) is that smoking can only be explained through notions of social identity. While factors such as family and stress may play their part, smoking behaviour is very much affected by identification with particular peer groups, and this is the primary explanation for the higher levels of smoking in girls. Much the same argument can be advanced for boys in relation to drinking alcohol. Thus gender impacts on the way in which social behaviour develops, and this in turn affects health.

As we noted, family factors play a key role as determinants of health in adolescence, and smoking reflects this as well as any other indicator. In the study by Lloyd and Lucas (1998) they looked closely at family factors, and were able to show that both family composition and the smoking behaviour of parents were influential in affecting adolescent smoking behaviour. Thus young people growing up in step-families or in lone parent households were significantly more likely to smoke than those growing up in two-parent households. This they explained in terms of higher stress levels among these young people. As far as the smoking behaviour of other family members is concerned, the evidence is clear.

> *We found a strong association between the smoking behaviour of most family members and adolescents' smoking behaviour....Half the adolescents who reported that a parent smoked had tried a cigarette. Two thirds of pupils who had an older sibling who currently smoked had tried a cigarette themselves....Parents influence their children's smoking both directly, and indirectly through their influence on older siblings....When a family member was reported never to have smoked, it was much more likely that the adolescent reported that they had never smoked either. (Lloyd and Lucas, 1998, p. 64)*

It is of interest now to look briefly at international comparisons, since we know that health behaviours vary widely from country to country. One example that is frequently in the news is the fact that Britain has a higher rate of teenage births than any other European country. The differences between countries are illustrated in Figure 1.3. Many different explanations have been advanced for this finding, including inhibited attitudes to sex among British families, inadequate sex and relationships education in school, and low levels of investment in good quality sexual health services specifically targeted at young people. This issue will be discussed in more detail in Chapter 5.

Rates of conception are of course not the only health indicators that vary across countries. A recent large-scale WHO study (Currie, 2004) shows, for example, that British youth are more likely than their counterparts in most other countries to drink alcohol, and to indulge in binge drinking. Other countries with high rates of adolescent drinking include the Netherlands and Denmark. The use of cannabis among young people also varies greatly across countries, with Switzerland currently heading the league table. The most recent findings show that 40% of adolescents have used cannabis during the past year in Switzerland, as compared with 35% in England and 25% in France (Currie, 2004).

Lastly in this section, we will consider the impact of poverty and disadvantage on the health of young people. In the report by the British Medical Association (Nathanson, 2003) on adolescent health it was noted that there appears to be more health equality among young people than among other age groups. This is largely due to the fact that health risk behaviours such as drinking, smoking and substance use are widespread. However, the report went on to

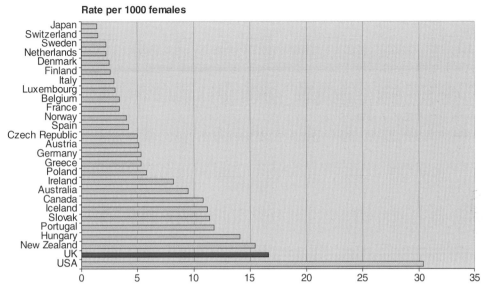

Figure 1.3   Birth rates for women aged 15–17 in OECD countries, 1998 (UNICEF, 2001).

accept that for a wide range of health concerns, those from less advantaged social backgrounds are likely to show higher rates of ill-health or health risk. Thus eating habits are related to social background, problematic drinking and drug use are more pronounced among disadvantaged groups, and mental health problems are closely associated with poverty and deprivation.

In Roker's (1998) study of young people growing up in family poverty, health was an issue which was frequently mentioned by those she interviewed. Many indicated that there was not enough money to buy food; "Sometimes it's that bad we rarely have enough meals to last us the week" and others complained of poor dental or physical health; "I smoke a lot and that makes my chest feel bad". The most striking descriptions related to the emotional health of the sample.

> "I get problems with my nerves when our mum and dad's having a row. I wake up in the morning and my legs and arms are all shaking and that … I was going to leave the house, but I can't leave my (alcoholic) dad in case he gets any problems, so I just had to come back here." (Roker, 1998, p. 58)

Since 1998 the Joseph Rowntree Foundation has been monitoring the changes in poverty and deprivation across the UK, and their publications have provided a valuable source of information on health, among other things. One of the indicators that the foundation has included each year has been suicide rates, and these have routinely shown the shocking disparity between different social backgrounds where severe mental health problems are concerned. As can be seen from Figure 1.4, young men who are from routine and manual backgrounds are three times as likely to commit suicide as those from professional and managerial backgrounds. Could there be a starker reflection than this of the impact of poverty and social background on health?

To conclude, we have explored here some of the factors that impact on the health of young people. As we have shown, a variety of factors play a part in determining health status,

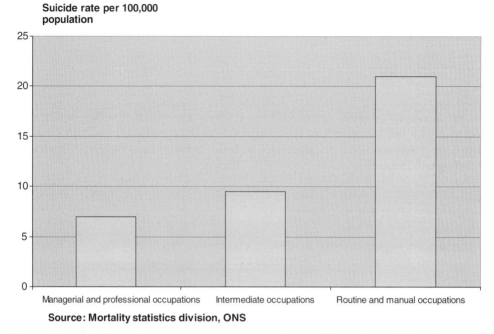

Suicide rate per 100,000 population

Source: Mortality statistics division, ONS

Figure 1.4 Suicide rates among young men from different social backgrounds: average rate for years 2001 to 2003.

although, of course, the factors we have selected are not the only ones that could be included in a discussion of variations in health outcomes. Particular populations are at particular risk, such as those in custody, or those who are looked after by local authorities. We have also paid little attention to the affect of culture on health, and this too could be a subject deserving more attention. For present purposes it is important to note that not all young people are the same where their health status is concerned. This conclusion, obvious as it sounds, is not always given sufficient attention in the planning of health services, or in the development of health promotion activities. It may be argued that there is more health equality among adolescents than among other age groups (Nathanson, 2003). Yet this is to miss the point. There is substantial inequality where adolescent health is concerned, and this should not be ignored or played down.

Conclusion

Understanding adolescent health is no simple matter. As we have seen in this chapter, there are many questions that arise when considering this subject, and few of them have easy or straightforward answers. Let us first look at the issue of how adolescents compare with other age groups in their health status. As we have noted, it is often argued that young people between the ages of 11 and 19 are the healthiest group in society. This assumption is based on two premises. One is that adolescents appear to use services less than other groups, and the second is that adolescents give the impression of being less worried about health than older people.

Both these premises are open to debate. As far as the use of services is concerned, many health professionals believe that young people would use services more if they were more easily accessible, and more adolescent-friendly. It is often the case that clinics are not always open at hours that are convenient for young people, and attendance may entail a journey on public transport that is costly for a teenager. Furthermore, the issue of confidentiality is high on the priority list for young people, and everyone knows the classic story of the young woman who goes to the GP (general practitioner) for contraceptive advice, only to find that the receptionist is one of her mother's friends. It is also important to note that, in fact, young people do visit the doctor. 75% of all teenagers under the age of 16 visit the doctor at least once a year, a figure which is comparable with the visiting rates of adults. Many people, including GPs themselves, are surprised at this finding.

Turning now to the possibility that young people worry less about their health than adults, one explanation for this is that adults and young people have different definitions of health. As we have pointed out earlier in this chapter, adolescents are not particularly concerned about long-term health risks. This is due to their having a relatively short-term time perspective, worrying about tomorrow, rather than about next month. Yet, in fact, teenagers are worried about health. They worry about their skin, their hair, their appearance, their weight, their body shape, nutrition, and about various aspects of sexual and emotional health which do not impinge on adults. Thus, young people may give the older generation the impression they are not worried about health, but this is misleading. It is just that health concerns for young people are different from the health concerns of adults. Indeed, as we pointed out, there are many possible definitions of health, and this fact is highlighted when we think about the way different generations understand their health.

A further dimension of the differences between adults and young people was exemplified when we discussed the idea of a 'mismatch' between different approaches to health education. As we saw, when approaching the notion of health risk, many adults take the view that avoidance is the most sensible option. The 'abstinence' movement in relation to sexual behaviour or the 'Don't do drugs' campaigns are good examples of this viewpoint. However, for many young people this is a counterproductive message. It makes the risk behaviour even more enticing, and creates the impression that sex, drugs and alcohol are associated with adult status, something that all young people want to attain.

Young people are more likely to take the view that some experience of risk is essential for healthy development. They wish to explore, to understand, and to learn what they can and cannot manage in order to develop the skills to cope with the risks inherent in their social settings. As we have said when talking about the notion of resources, if you do nothing (avoidance), you will not be able to develop any new resources. Unless health educators take these beliefs into account, it is unlikely that young people will engage with their programmes.

Our final thought in this introductory chapter has to do with the question of what is a healthy lifestyle for young people. There is much concern today about obesity, lack of exercise, poor mental health, unsafe sex, the use of drugs, and other behaviours that are anxiety-arousing for adults. We noted at the beginning of the chapter that the tone of many recent reports on adolescent health is gloomy to say the least. Is this pessimism justified? And if the health of young people is so much at risk, how would we define a healthy lifestyle for this generation? Firstly, it is important to note that there are some signs of progress. Services are improving, and there is more focus on the health of adolescents today than has been the case in the past. Good statistics and better research have helped to highlight the areas which need more attention. Various chapters in this book will draw attention to promising developments both in health care and in our understanding of adolescent health-related behaviours.

On the other hand, it is certainly true that there has been less improvement in the health of young people than in the health of children and of adults. Furthermore, some indices of risk behaviour, such as alcohol use, and sexually transmitted infections, have shown worrying rises in recent years. The picture is mixed, and more government resources undoubtedly need to be directed to both services and effective health promotion. In this context, what about a healthy lifestyle? The answer to this question has been outlined in some of what we have said earlier. A key lies in the opportunity for young people to develop resources for health without incurring too much cost. In this context we understand health to have the widest possible meaning, and to include emotional as well as physical health. The notion of a healthy lifestyle is obviously relative, and will depend on the circumstances and risks to which any individual is exposed. We have called these 'health challenges'. We argue that a healthy lifestyle for an adolescent must include the acquisition of knowledge and skills, access to health services when required, and the opportunity to engage in moderate risk behaviour in order to enhance learning. It is this we mean when we say that a healthy lifestyle is something that 'maximizes gains and minimizes costs, in both the short and the long term'.

CASE STUDY 1.1

Some years ago, when I was interviewing a relatively small number of adolescents for a pilot study on health, I had to carry out four individual interviews in a local comprehensive school in Scotland.

After a couple of interesting conversations with second year pupils, I was waiting in a small office – possibly the interview room for visiting health care staff – when I heard giggles and banging noises coming from the corridor outside. I went to the door, opened it, and stepped outside to be joyfully greeted by a slightly built, almost puny boy in a wheelchair, guided by two girls.

He began by saying: "Hello Sir, I'm your next victim. My name is Charlie. What are you called?" With introductions over, I began the interview, which was attempting in an open and unstructured way to find out what young people perceived as a healthy lifestyle. As the conversation continued, Charlie revealed that he played a bit of soccer and swam, and together with a careful diet, he considered that he was fit and healthy and had indeed a very healthy lifestyle.

Later in the interview Charlie mentioned in passing that he required regular, intensive medical treatment. Since this was a pilot interview and confidentiality had been stressed, I did not enquire further as Charlie did not seem to regard his medical treatment as a matter of any consequence and neither of us developed the topic further. Rather he moved on to "really important" issues in his life, such as whether Glasgow Rangers or Celtic would win the league that year.

As it came to an end, I realized that this had been one of the most enjoyable interviews I had ever carried out.

However, the denouement came when I was having a cup of tea in the staff room after all the interviews were over. I said how much I had liked visiting the school and thanked the Head Teacher for allowing the research team to carry out the interviews. I said that I would especially remember the little boy, Charlie, who was so cheerful despite his having to be in a wheelchair for extensive periods during the school year. "Yes" said the Head Teacher. "It's so very sad. The specialist estimates that Charlie will die of cancer in three to six months."

Source: Hendry *et al.*, 1998

CASE STUDY 1.1 QUESTIONS

1. Describe a person you know whom you regard as healthy. What were your criteria in choosing this person?
2. On which criteria does Charlie base his judgement of his health status?
3. Do you consider that Charlie's perceptions of his own state of health are correct? Why?

Further Reading

Bradshaw, J. and Mayhew, E. (eds) (2005) *The well-being of children in the UK*, The Save the Children Fund, London.

Coleman, J. and Hendry, L. (1999) *The nature of adolescence*, 3rd edn, Routledge, London.

Coleman, J. and Schofield, J. (2005) *Key data on adolescence*, 5th edn, The Trust for the Study of Adolescence, Brighton.

Heaven, P. (1996) *Adolescent health: the role of individual differences*, Routledge, London.

Roche, J., Tucker, S., Thomson, R. and Flynn, R. (2004) *Youth in society*, 2nd edn, Sage Publications, London.

Discussion Questions

1. Are adults right to be worried about adolescent health?
2. Do you consider some element of risk-taking essential for a healthy adolescent?
3. Many of the things that young people want from their health services are the same as those desired by adults. Should adolescents be given special treatment?
4. How does lifespan developmental theory help you to understand adolescent development?
5. What do you consider to be the major influences on adolescent health?

Chapter 2

Young People: Physical Health, Exercise and Recreation

Ruth Lowry

Department of Sport, Culture and the Arts, University of Strathclyde

John Kremer and Karen Trew

School of Psychology, Queen's University Belfast

- ■ Introduction
- ■ Young People and Exercise – History and Current Trends
- ■ Exercise – As Good for You Today As It's Ever Been?
- ■ Taking Up and Dropping Out – The Reasons Why
- ■ Encouraging Healthy Exercise
- ■ Conclusion

Learning Objectives

After reading this chapter you should:

1 Understand the level of activity and inactivity reported by young people.
2 Have considered the nature of the association between physical activity and physical health.
3 Be aware of the impact of exercise and physical activity on psychological dysfunctions such as depression, anxiety and stress responsivity.
4 Be able to assess the explanations linking physical exercise and well-being.
5 Be able to describe the personal, social and structural factors that interact to either encourage or discourage young people from involving themselves in physical activity.
6 Understand community-based interventions, school-based interventions and parental interventions that have been recommended to encourage young people to maintain an active lifestyle.

Introduction

We are constantly reminded (and often by our grandparents) that the world of our grandparents was a healthier place. While nostalgia may help blur our collective memories, it is undoubtedly true that bygone ages were more active times. For example, it is estimated that today's young people on average expend between 600 and 700 kcal per day less than their counterparts 50 years ago (Boreham and Riddoch, 2001). It is also true that the opportunities for sedentary alternatives to an active lifestyle are far greater now than they ever were (Currie *et al.*, 2004; Norman *et al.*, 2005) and the consequences for the future health of the nation should not be underestimated.

To many, the malaise can be traced to the experiences of childhood. During the 2004 Athens Olympics, when one pundit was asked why he thought North African athletes were so dominant in middle-distance running, his answer was simple and to the point – 'no school runs'! Indeed it was even suggested that Ethiopian Haile Gebrselassie's idiosyncratic but effective running action (with his right arm held awkwardly away from his body), owed more to running several miles to school each day with his books under one arm than the intervention of any biomechanist.

Without doubt, before the advent of computers, televisions, music centres and mobile (sic) phones, physical exercise tended to play a more integral and necessary part in most young people's lives. However, to follow the lead of our grandparents by overstating the case is tempting but dangerous; instead there is a need to reflect objectively on available evidence. With this in mind, the chapter will begin by summarizing current statistics on levels of activity and inactivity among young people by key demographic variables. The following section will identify associations between physical exercise and well-being before considering the reasons why young people take up and discontinue sport. The chapter will end by a consideration of intervention strategies and their effectiveness, looking at the role of significant others and including peers, parents and coaches, as well as the types of engagement that are more or less likely to encourage physical activity.

Young People and Exercise – History and Current Trends

For people who live in prosperous societies, physical exercise is no longer considered a necessity but may represent a lifestyle choice (Dishman, 2001). Although adolescents can now choose to engage in a wide range of individual and team sports which were not accessible to their parents, there is widespread concern that the well-being of increasing numbers of young people is at risk because these young people are generally less active than previous generations.

The British Medical Association (BMA 2003) sees the sedentary lifestyles and the unhealthy diets of many adolescents as contributing to 'a global epidemic' of obesity. The BMA report notes that the 1998 Health Survey in England showed an increase in the prevalence of those classified as overweight and obese with a 21% prevalence rate for adolescents aged 13 to 16. Changes in both exercise and diet are assumed to contribute to the growth in obesity but until relatively recently there was limited research into the actual level of physical activity of young people. However, according to Prentice and Jebb (1995) the growth in obesity in Britain is more closely related to changes in proxy measures of physical inactivity such as car ownership, computer use and television viewing than to measures of household food consumption. The importance of monitoring the physical activity of young people has been increasingly recognized and although considerable problems with definition remain, we now have some evidence on the activity levels of young people and the relative importance of sport in their lives.

Defining Sport and Physical Activity

The following definition of sport is now widely accepted:

> *Sport means all forms of physical activity which, through casual participation, aim at expressing or improving physical fitness and mental well-being, forming social relationships or obtaining results in competition at all levels. (Council of Europe, European Sports Charter, 1993)*
>
> *There is less agreement between experts on the definition of physical activity levels sufficient to achieve health benefits. Currently, it is recommended that all young people should participate in one hour of moderate physical activity every day and that those young people who were inactive should be encouraged to participate in 30 minutes of at least moderate activity per day. (UK Department of Health, 2004)*

Involvement in Sport and Exercise

Sport England employed national surveys of over 3000 young people (6–16 year-olds) and sport in 1994, 1999 and 2002, to document the changing patterns of sport participation (Sport England, 2003a). Over the eight years, there was a small increase in the numbers of young people (15% in 1994 to 18% in 2002) who were not taking part in at least one sport regularly in lessons. In contrast, the percentage of young people spending two or more hours a week in PE lessons increased from 46% in 1994 to 49% in 2002.

The time spent on sport out of lessons is fairly consistent across the surveys. Almost all the 11–16 year-olds surveyed over the eight years had taken part in some sort of sporting activity and the number of sports which had been tried at least once out of lessons increased from 10 in 1994 to 11 in 2002, and the number of sports participated in frequently had risen from four in 1994 to five in 2002. The most popular sports outside lessons in all three surveys were swimming, cycling and football. Football remained the favourite sport of boys, and swimming was the top sport for girls but regular participation by girls in football in school almost doubled from 7% in 1994 to 13% in 2002.

The Sport England surveys found that young people spent more time participating in sport in their leisure time in 2002 than they did in 1994. However, in 2002 (see Table 2.1), young people aged 11–16 spent more time each week watching television (11.4 hours) and in part-time work (8.8 hours) than taking part in sport (8.1 hours). The average figures derived from over 3000 students hide wide differences between individuals and groups. In common with nearly all other surveys of young people (Scully, Reilly and Clarke, 1998), on average boys appear to spend over three hours more per week taking part in sport than girls. Furthermore, girls show a decreasing involvement with sport with increasing age.

Large scale surveys concerned with the health of young people focus on activity levels in general rather than participation in specific sports. The World Health Organization (WHO, 2000) carried out an international study of health behaviour in school-aged children (HBSC)

involving over 120 000 11, 13 and 15 year-olds from 26 countries including England, Wales, Scotland and Northern Ireland. The time young people spent on vigorous physical activity varied widely between countries and by gender and age group. Table 2.2, which presents the percentage of students in the HBSC survey who reported exercising twice a week or more in the four countries within the United Kingdom, shows that generally levels of participation are quite high. Overall the percentage of boys who exercised regularly was maintained between the ages of 11 and 15 but girls' participation in exercise was consistently lower with only half the 15-year-old English girls reporting that they engaged in regular vigorous exercise. The survey found that regular exercise was strongly associated with feeling healthy but it was not possible to establish if those who felt healthy exercised more or vice versa.

Overall studies carried out over the last decade do not show that young people are inactive, but at the same time there is strong support for the belief that even though physical education is part of the curriculum there are children and young people who lead relatively sedentary lives.

Table 2.1   Mean time spent doing each activity out of school lessons (hours)

	Primary years 6–11 years old			Secondary years 12–16 years old			All years		
	Boys %	Girls %	Total %	Boys %	Girls %	Total %	Boys %	Girls %	Total %
Watched TV/videos/DVDs	11.6	11.7	11.6	11.8	10.4	11.1	11.7	11.1	11.4
Taken part in sport or exercise	9.5	7.2	8.3	10.3	5.6	7.9	9.8	6.5	8.1
Used a computer/Internet	3.6	2.9	3.3	5.4	4.3	4.8	4.5	3.6	4.0
Done school homework	2.1	2.4	2.3	3.6	4.8	4.3	2.8	3.6	3.2
Done a part-time job[a]				8.9	8.7	8.8	8.9	8.7	8.8

Base: All young people who have taken part in each activity (different for each activity).
[a] Only asked of young people aged 11–16.
Source: Sport England, 2003b.

Exercise – As Good for You Today as It's Ever Been?

As Ronald Reagan famously remarked, 'They say hard work never hurt anybody, but I figure – why take the chance?' Equally, when young people are repeatedly told that physical exercise is good for them, they could legitimately reply – is it really worth all that effort? This section will try to answer that question.

When reflecting on the pros and cons of exercise for adolescents, it is useful to distinguish between the effects on the mind and the body, the psychological and the somatic. In terms of

Table 2.2   Students who report exercising twice a week or more (percentages)

	11-year-olds		13-year-olds		15-year-olds	
	Females	Males	Females	Males	Females	Males
Northern Ireland	80	93	83	90	63	90
Scotland	82	89	75	90	61	85
England	73	78	63	82	50	79
Wales	82	87	71	89	56	82

Source: World Health Organization, 2000.

physiology, physical activity plays a positive role in the prevention and treatment of a range of physical conditions, and a physically active lifestyle does correspond to a healthy lifestyle. Research evidence confirms the long-term protection that regular exercise provides against many ailments including coronary heart disease, hypertension, various cancers, diabetes and osteoporosis (Biddle, Fox and Boutcher, 2000). What is more, there is growing evidence that an appropriate level of physical activity during childhood and adolescence will not only provide immediate improvements in health status and quality of life but it will also delay the onset of chronic diseases in adulthood (Boreham and Riddoch, 2001), at the same time hopefully establishing adherence to a healthy lifestyle that will last throughout life (Malina, 1996).

What is an appropriate level of physical activity? According to Biddle, Fox and Boutcher (2000), around 60 minutes of activity should be accumulated across the day, including a range of activities that help to promote strength, flexibility and bone health. There is also strong evidence to suggest that the benefits of exercise derive in large part from its effect on cardiovascular fitness and so the activity must be of at least moderate intensity to significantly elevate heart rate. Typically, and traditionally, a healthy level of exercise could be accumulated 'naturally' through general play and leisure activities but what once came naturally now may have to be actively managed.

Unfortunately, what comes 'naturally' for young children becomes less natural for adolescents, and especially in youth cultures that look upon 'breaking sweat' as 'uncool' (sic) (Bone and Gardiner, 2002). As the young person moves from a situation where physical activity is either mandatory (e.g. in school) or natural (e.g. spontaneous play) to one where it may become a lifestyle choice, so the challenge to ensure that exercise features in this brave new world is ever more pressing.

Young people themselves appear to acknowledge the need for change. A MORI survey (2001) found that while adolescents spent a great deal of their spare time either watching television or playing computer games, they wished they spent more time being physically active. Bone and Gardiner (2002) likewise found that young people aged over 16 years stated a preference for clubbing or going to the cinema over watching television, the former at least involving physical activity.

The converse of too little activity is too much – can too much be done, and too soon? There is increasing evidence pointing to the dangers (physical and psychological) of overtraining at a young age in many sports, including, for example, the long-term damage associated with inappropriate muscle development before the skeletal framework has had the opportunity to fully mature. Among elite sportspeople the pressure to succeed at a young age can be immense, and responsibility must rest with parents, coaches and teachers to ensure that the long-term well-being of the young person is centre stage irrespective of short-term aspirations. Certain sports have recognized these dangers and have placed age restrictions on participation, a proactive stance that is to be applauded. Among young athletes, overuse injuries, while still relatively infrequent, nevertheless occur and indeed often have more serious consequences than traumatic injuries.

Turning from the physical to the psychological effects of exercise, in general terms the literature indicates that healthy forms of exercise can play a role in the promotion of mental health (Biddle and Mutrie, 2001), and most significantly among those with a predisposition towards mental illness. While the relationship is well established, unfortunately our understanding of both the direction of causality and the relationship between psychosocial and physiological changes remains best defined as unfinished business (Morgan and Dishman, 2001). Equally, it is appropriate to proceed with caution as the good news story is not without qualifications, and most especially where the motives for engaging in exercise in the first place may be less than healthy, and where exercise moves beyond habit to signs of morbidity, abuse or even addiction, more commonly referred to as 'excessive exercise' (Loumidis and Roxborough, 1995). For example, in the same way as unhealthy practices such as smoking may be used as a form of weight control so inherently healthy means such as exercise may be used for unhealthy ends, again including pathological weight control.

Regarding the healthy effects of exercise, several thorough reviews (see Grant, 2000) have confirmed that various psychological dysfunctions can benefit from an involvement in physical activity, including the following.

Depression

Across the lifespan it is estimated that between 5% and 12% of males and 9% and 12% of females in the UK will suffer from clinical depression and this figure is rising. While the elderly are especially vulnerable, adolescents are not immune, as the recent increase in suicides among young men in the UK bears witness (a trend not reflected among young women), with the age range 15 to 34 years now seen as the most vulnerable.

Can exercise help deal with depression in young people? Yes, but its use is not without problems. Emotionally the symptoms of depression often include feelings of worthlessness, guilt and shame, thoughts of death, sadness, chronic pessimism, irritability and an inability to continue to derive pleasure from previously enjoyable activities (such as sport and leisure). In cognitive terms depression can interfere with the ability to concentrate and make decisions. What is more, people may report physical symptoms such as lethargy, insomnia and tardiness of movement, all of which may make it less likely that the depressed young person will exercise at all. Hence, exercise may help but an exercise regime may be difficult to put in place given the symptoms of depression – Catch 22. Furthermore, while physical exercise does have both an immediate and longer-term antidepressant effect, it is most effective among those who were most unhealthy to begin with and among older age groups in particular.

Notwithstanding all these caveats, clinical depression still shows the most consistent positive responses to physical exercise, with the most powerful effects among those with the most severe symptoms (Martinsen, 1994). Aerobic exercise appears to be most effective and also repetitive activities such as walking, jogging, cycling, light circuit training, and weight training, with regimes extending over several months apparently yielding the most positive effects.

Anxiety

Since 1980 there have been over 30 reviews of the effects of exercise on anxiety (Raglin, 1997). Despite this concerted effort, Scully *et al.* (1998) note that there is still uncertainty as to what level of exercise intensity is required for anxiolytic effects to occur. According to some research, even a single, five-minute exercise bout may be sufficient to induce a reduction in anxiety levels (Long and Stavel, 1995), although more powerful effects tend to be noted when programmes have run over an extended time period (from 10 to 15 weeks or even longer). The nature of the exercise does not appear to be crucial and hence affording individuals the freedom to exercise at a self-selected level of intensity may be most appropriate. For adolescents the associated feelings of control and self-determination may be especially valuable in encouraging adherence to any exercise regime.

Stress Responsivity

Related literature has considered how exercise may protect against the negative effects of stress. Increases in physical condition or improved fitness are likely to facilitate the individual's capacity for dealing with stress although some studies report negligible differences between the physically fit and the less fit. While it may be that aerobically fit individuals do show a reduced psychosocial stress response, the role that exercise can play is probably preventative rather than corrective, and the stress response itself remains only partially understood. For young people it is recommended that a regime of aerobic exercise (i.e. continuous exercise of sufficient intensity to elevate heart rate significantly above resting pulse rate for over 21 minutes duration) may significantly enhance stress responsivity, and in particular stress that is lifestyle or work-related.

Mood State

Numerous studies have investigated the mood-enhancing properties of exercise and have shown that exercise can indeed have a positive influence on mood state (e.g., Crabbe, Smith and Dishman, 1999). However, early optimism has been tempered by the discovery that the effects may not be as pervasive across non-clinical populations (Scully et al., 1998). Research suggests that the relationship may be far more complex than earlier research implied and that various forms of exercise, both aerobic and anaerobic, can be associated with an elevation of mood state in particular circumstances. Whether the effect is based on psychosocial, psychological, psychopharmacological or psychophysiological factors has yet to be determined.

Self-Esteem

As expected, research suggests a positive link between exercise and self-esteem and especially among those whose self-esteem is relatively low, including adolescents as they strive to develop a sense of self (Fox, 2000). While the idea that exercise enhances self-esteem makes intuitive sense, Johnsgard (1989), among others, has emphasized that exercise will do little to improve self-esteem if it is deficient primarily in other areas of life such as education, emotional or behavioural problems or a lack of social skills. However, if the young person's low self-esteem has its roots in poor body image or lack of fitness or weight control then exercise can have a positive effect and the effect appears to be most powerful when aerobic activities are used.

Recent work in this area has employed multifaceted measures of self-esteem including the Physical Self-Perception Profile (PSPP; Fox, 2000) a scale which distinguishes between global self-esteem and physical self-esteem and which in turn has been related to factors including body image and sports competence. Subsequent work indicates that physical activity is associated with higher levels of self-esteem in young men and women. In general, research indicates that exercise can bolster self-esteem in cases where it is fragile or underdeveloped, and adolescence may be a time of life where in particular it may play a useful role.

Body Image

When recommending physical activity, it is important to ensure that exercise does not create more problems than it resolves. There is now considerable evidence of the dangers associated with excessive exercise and of the type of individual who is more prone to use exercise inappropriately (Johnston, 2001). The gendered nature of physical activity should not be disregarded in this debate. Scully, Reilly and Clarke (1998) and Franzoi (1995) describe how women, and especially young women, focus on their body as an aesthetic statement whereas traditionally at least, males have been more likely to attend to the dynamic aspects of their bodies, such as coordination, strength and speed. This emphasis on the female form in exercise settings may foster feelings of social-physique anxiety (SPA), constrain enjoyment of the activity itself, and may even be exacerbated by the nature of the clothing required (Frederick and Shaw, 1995). McAuley *et al.* (1995) reported that SPA correlates with self-presentational motives for exercise such as weight control and attractiveness, and is higher among women (Frederick and Morrison, 1996). Women consistently score lower than men on measures of self-confidence regarding their bodies and physical competence and hence there is a need to think carefully about the design of sport and its venues (e.g. clothing, changing facilities) in order to make women feel more comfortable with their body image during exercise.

More generally, research shows that body image tends to be less positive among women (Koff and Bauman, 1997), and is more closely linked to women's overall self-esteem than men's, and may make young women more susceptible to disorders linked to exercise, including the

Female Athlete Triad (FAT). Referring to disordered eating, amenorrhœa and osteoporosis, FAT is the physical manifestation of a pathological adherence to exercise, often coupled with inappropriate diet (Arena, 1997). It is especially common in sports that emphasize low body weight for performance or appearance (e.g. gymnastics, ice skating and dance). Furthermore, not only may exercise be associated with body dissatisfaction, once undertaken it may sustain the cyclical, repetitious nature of eating disorders (Davis, 1999).

While traditional discussions of such issues tend to focus on young women, increasingly there is an acknowledgement that young men are also at risk of exercise-related disorders including not only anorexia but also muscle dysmorphia or the pursuit of greater bulk and, in particular, muscular definition (Olivardia and Pope, 2002).

To conclude this section, there is no shortage of research into the relationship between physical exercise and health and while the general picture is positive, there is a need to proceed with caution. This is especially true because the underlying mechanisms, whether biochemical, pharmacological, physiological or psychological, remain so poorly understood. For example, why should exercise influence self-esteem among adolescents, and why should exercise improve mood state and depression? Exercise psychology is now characterized by an array of increasingly sophisticated mechanisms and models used to explain a range of phenomena (Buckworth and Dishman, 2002) but a clear consensus has yet to emerge. The main contenders follow in the box below.

Which theories, models or hypotheses provide the best explanations? The best guess would be that all play some role but the significance of each will vary considerably depending on context.

Explanations of Physical Exercise and Well-Being

The catecholamine hypothesis

Catecholamines (i.e. adrenaline, noradrenaline and dopamine) act as transmitters in the central nervous system and are implicated in the control of movement, mood, attention, as well as endocrine, cardiovascular and stress responses. The catecholamine hypothesis suggests that exercise activates the release of catecholamines, which in turn are associated with euphoria and positive mood states.

The endorphin hypothesis

In the 1980s, the phrase 'endorphin high' or 'runner's high' came to describe the effect that endorphins (otherwise known as endogenous morphines or 'pleasure peptides') may have on feelings of well-being following exercise. Endorphins are naturally occurring opiate-like transmitters that appear to bind with specific receptor sites in discrete parts of the central nervous system associated with pain information and effect. Exercise has been shown to cause a significant phasic increase in the release of endorphins into the bloodstream from the pituitary gland.

The thermogenic hypothesis

This suggests that the increase in body temperature brought about by exercise reduces tonic muscle activity, in turn reducing somatic anxiety and thereby inducing a positive psychological effect. It has been suggested that the increase in temperature may alter the levels of brain monoamines (including neurotransmitters such as noradrenaline, adrenaline, serotonin and dopamine; see above), although research is not plentiful (Youngstedt *et al.*, 1993).

The distraction or time-out hypothesis

This hypothesis leans towards a psychosocial explanation of the positive effects of exercise, suggesting that through the act of engaging in exercise, a psychological release is provided from the primary source of worry or depression (Alfermann and Stoll, 2000).

The mastery hypothesis

Any exercise that involves the mastery of particular skills is likely to have a positive effect on self-efficacy which in turn will reflect in heightened self-esteem and a positive affective state (Casper, 1993). The critical variable here is likely to be perceived success or achievement associated with the physical activity rather than the activity per se.

Taking Up and Dropping Out – The Reasons Why

From the earlier sections in this chapter you should now be able to construct a picture of the health and physical activity levels of adolescents and how they compare with previous generations. In addition, you should have a clear understanding of the potential health benefits that an active lifestyle can bring, whether through organized sporting activities or by regular unstructured exercise. We now turn attention away from the 'what' of physical activity and towards the 'why' – to the underlying reasons why adolescents do or do not take exercise. Research within the area of participation motivation has focused on structured youth sports rather than adolescents involved in various activities involving exercise. However, many of the findings have resonance to those involved in less formalized activities. When asked why we take part in sport or exercise we could give many reasons but five main clusters of motives tend to be identifiable.

Participation Motives

1. **Skill:** to gain feelings of accomplishment or ability.
2. **Social:** to gain a sense of belonging or feeling affiliated to an organization or group.
3. **Fitness:** to improve strength, shape or stamina.
4. **Competition:** to achieve success either through competition or seeing progress.
5. **Enjoyment:** last (but certainly not least) for pleasure or fun.

(Buonamano *et al.*, 1995)

Often these reasons will change over the years and as we continue our involvement, or we may give a number of reasons at any one time. Similarly the reasons given for dropping out or disengaging from sport or exercise can be grouped into five themes:

Drop-Out Motives

1. **Limited improvement:** a lack of progress or noticeable improvement in the skills required for the activity.
2. **Conflicts of interest:** an increasing interest in other activities and resulting conflicts in time.
3. **Pressure from others:** feelings of excessive pressure from other people such as a coach, parent or other players.
4. **Lack of playing time or injury.**
5. **Boredom:** and finally, a lack of fun or excitement.

(Gould, 1987)

Again, if you were to ask someone why he or she withdrew or was dropping out of an activity the person may give a number of these reasons, or during long-term disengagement from an activity the reasons may change, perhaps reflecting an increasing disenchantment with their remaining involvement. It is also important to make the distinction between those who drop out of a specific sport (sport-specific) but remain active through other activities versus those who choose to withdraw from all types of sport or exercise (domain-general) (Gould and Petlichkoff, 1988).

From this list and drawing on your own experience you will be able to build a picture of a rather complex web of circumstances and people (influencing variables) that interact to either encourage or discourage young people from involving themselves in physical activity. We shall now look at these variables in three groups of facilitators or barriers: *personal* (motivation, goals and enjoyment), *social* (peers, parents and coaches) and *structural* (choice, access and alternative activities).

Personal

In general, when we use the term 'motivation' we tend to talk about those who are either highly motivated or those who have poor motivation, suggesting that motivation is a singular concept linked to personality. Researchers such as Deci and Ryan (1985, 1991) refer to motivation as falling on a continuum with *amotivation* (absence) at one extreme and *intrinsic motivation* (internal) at the other. In the middle of these extremities are various types of *extrinsic motives* such as recognition from others, avoidance of negative feelings and fulfilment of personal desires. Those participants who are more autonomous or who feel personally in control of their lives are more likely to be intrinsically motivated whereas those who feel as if they have little control over their situation are more likely to be extrinsically motivated or even amotivated (Vallerand and Losier, 1999). Researchers have found that exercise participants are more likely to cite extrinsic motives for the initiation of activity (e.g. fitness and appearance) while those involved in traditional sports reference more intrinsic motives such as enjoyment, competence and affiliation (Frederick and Ryan, 1993; Lowry and Kremer 2004).

As stated earlier, with sustained participation, motives may shift from those that originally determined the initiation of activity. Indeed intrinsic motives, and in particular competence and enjoyment, predict continuation whereas extrinsic motives, and specifically appearance, are better predictors of withdrawal from activity (Ryan *et al.*, 1997). It appears that motivation may also influence the frequency and duration of participation. Frederick and Ryan found a positive correlation for intrinsic motives and a negative correlation for extrinsic motives with hours per week of involvement. Thus, those exercisers who cited the intrinsic motives of enjoyment and competence participated more frequently and for a longer duration than those who cited extrinsic motives.

Achievement Goal Orientation Theory

Originally developed in relation to educational attainment (Nicholls, 1984), Goal Orientation Theory has been extensively explored within the context of sport participation motivation and in particular when relating to competitive youth sport (Roberts, 2001). White and Duda (1994) suggest that motives for participation are as a result of an individual's underlying goal orientation. Those who are identified as task oriented tend to participate for reasons of skill development or accomplishment, affiliation and fitness. By contrast those identified as ego oriented tend to cite participation motives of social status, competition and recognition. In reality an individual can possess both goal orientations to a greater or lesser extent; that is, they can be highly task and ego oriented, low in both task and ego orientation or high in one and low in the other orientation (Fox *et al.*, 1994). Papaioannou and Theodorakis (1996) found that task orientation predicted the intention to participate in physical activity but that ego orientation was poor at predicting intention to participate. At the same time it should be noted that with onset of adolescence there is also an increase in ego orientation toward involvement (Nicholls, 1978).

A common reason given for participation in a physical activity is enjoyment or fun, but despite its importance to the understanding of participation motivation the concept is poorly defined and often misinterpreted. Csikszentmihalyi (1990), who defined enjoyment in terms of flow or a process, proposed that enjoyment occurred when a person's ability or skill matched the demands of the activity whereas boredom resulted from a mismatch (either too easy or too difficult). An alternative perspective is offered by Scanlan and Lewthwaite (1986) who defined enjoyment as a positive response or product that arises from participation. Setting aside the process versus product debate, the findings of research reveal the significance of the variable to adolescent activity. Boyd and Yin (1996) have suggested that significant sources of sport enjoyment in physical activity of adolescents include greater task orientation, greater perceived competence and increased number of years involved in the activity. Similar sources of enjoyment in youth athletes were found by Scanlan *et al.* (1993), including factors such as effort, mastery, satisfaction with performance, as well as peer and coach support. As can be seen from these studies, enjoyment tends to be associated with intrinsic rather than extrinsic motivation factors.

Social

Adolescent and youth sport is generally a social activity performed in the company of or competing against fellow participants and under the instruction of coaches or teachers. In addition to peers and tutors, parents can become involved through the practical provision of transport and financial assistance and, on occasions, instruction.

Another reason that is cited for participation is to realize a sense of affiliation with others, and in particular the peer group. Peer influence is of great importance during early adolescence with peer comparison and evaluation particularly important sources of information about competence in sport (Horn and Amorose, 1998). Duncan (1993) suggested that peers will influence enjoyment, companionship and recognition; these in turn influence perceptions of competence and the affective (emotional) responses to participation. If the adolescent is accepted or rejected by his or her peer group this not only provides information about competence in the sporting arena but also provides an insight into social skills. Imagine for a minute the thoughts and feelings that accompany the player who is consistently picked last when teams are chosen. Not only is s/he left feeling rejected as the worst player in the group but that person may also begin to question his or her popularity within the group. These negative evaluations will subsequently influence self-concept and emotional reactions to the activity thus discouraging future participation.

Coaches and parents can be responsible for creating a *motivational climate*, emphasizing either mastery, or a *competitive climate* surrounding the physical activity. Consistently, researchers have found a significant correlation between differences in motivational climate and motivational effect, behaviour and cognition (Ntoumanis and Biddle, 1999). It appears that parents or coaches are perceived as showing preference for certain reasons for participation, and associated goals, and it is this perception of the climate (be it true or not) that contributes to the young person's enjoyment, satisfaction, beliefs about being involved and ultimately the quality of involvement (Seifriz *et al.*, 1992). Coaches and instructors provide not only the necessary tuition involved in acquiring a skill but also cues regarding ability, progress and acceptance, accomplished through encouragement, feedback and reinforcement. The influence of the coach is determined by how the participant perceives these cues and acts upon them. Allen and Howe (1998) suggest that young people in a team situation perceive those who receive praise as competent and those who receive *corrective feedback* as having less ability. A coach's influence will also vary by factors such as age, gender, physical maturity and sporting experience (Allen and Howe, 1998). Parents play a significant role for children, especially in early to middle childhood (Jambor, 1999). Parental characteristics (as perceived by the child) are associated with a child's enjoyment, intrinsic motivation, perceived competence and perception of pressure (Babkes and Weiss, 1999). This is supported by Kendall and Danish (1994) who suggested that rather than providing a physical role model for their children, parents are a key source of support and encouragement through their attitudes, opinions and behaviour.

Reciprocity of Family Influence

Weiss and Hayashi (1995) highlighted the reciprocal nature of social influence upon the activities of those involved. For example, if a child is involved in a sport, family life is adjusted to accommodate practice and competitions. Parents and other siblings may choose to support from the sidelines or become involved in a specific sport or in a more active lifestyle.

Parents, especially, reported attitudinal and behavioural changes as a consequence of their son's or daughter's intensive sport involvement, supporting the existence of reverse socialisation effects through sports participation. (p. 46)

Structural

Our understanding of the structural or environmental factors associated with the adoption and continuation of physical activity sadly lags behind that of either personal or social factors. However, perceptions of the immediate facilities as well as the surrounding environment undoubtedly influence the likelihood of that venue being used for exercise or sport. Perceived environmental factors such as a lack of pedestrian safety (volume of traffic, lighting, crossings, cycle lanes and pavements), increased levels of crime in the area, poor accessibility of facilities (parks, grounds and centres) and limited access to public transport are associated with decreased levels of physical activity (Kirtland et al., 2003; Timperio et al., 2004). Significantly, it is the perception of unsuitable environmental factors that relates to low levels of activity rather than the reality of these characteristics (Timperio et al., 2004). An analysis of these environmental factors could usefully extend to issues including the layout of changing and showering areas, and the effects these designs may have on, for example, young people's fear of embarrassment, but to date sadly such issues remain under-researched.

Another structural factor that has a bearing on physical activity levels is socio-economic status (SES). Lasheras et al. (2001) found that children from medium to high SES families are more active than those from a low SES family. This may be related to the financial investments required for equipment, coaching and transportation. They argued that an active lifestyle need not mean added expense, suggesting that by encouraging traditional games, walking, cycling, and making use of community grounds, an active lifestyle could then be adopted. However, the findings of Timperio et al. (2004) would suggest that those of lower SES are located in communities that are perceived as unsafe and thus unsuitable for allowing young people the freedom to play. Finally, consideration should be given to the geographical location of the young person's home. If located in a larger town, children are more likely to be involved in sport several times during the week and more likely to be involved in organized sport than those from a rural area (Lasheras et al., 2001).

As suggested earlier in the chapter, adolescents' participation in physical activity appears to be strongly influenced by experience of Physical Education (PE) while in school. A survey of 2400 young people carried out by the Sports Council for Northern Ireland found that 31% rated school as the most influential factor in their continuation with sport and 26% stated that school was influential in fostering interest in the sport they played most frequently (Kremer et al., 1997). Coakley and White (1992) found that adolescent participation in community-based sports programmes was also influenced by the experiences of school PE. Despite the strong influence of school, De Knop et al. (1999) suggest that there has been a move away from organized interactive activities by adolescents towards individual recreational activities that are less physically demanding. This departure from traditional sport is echoed both at the elite level of competitive sport and in government policy. The International Olympic Committee (IOC) continually reviews the sports that are included in the summer and winter events. Recent inclusions have been beach volleyball which debuted in 2000 and snowboarding and freestyle skiing in 1998. In 2004, the British government pledged additional money to increase the provision of PE in schools; when making his announcement, the Prime Minister cited the inclusion of activities such as yoga, Tai Chi and cheerleading as suitable activities.

Although adolescents appear to have a vast choice when it comes to physical activity, does the choice of activity influence the quality of participation? The relationship between group cohesion and performance is greater for those involved in team activities than those involved in more individual activities (Carron and Dennis, 1998). Team cohesion or a lack thereof has been found to differentiate between participants who remain in a team to those who drop-out

(Carron, 1982), and between those who regularly attend practice or exercise to those who are often absent (Spink and Carron, 1992, 1993).

In conclusion, as this section should illustrate, an understanding of the 'why' of adolescents' participation in physical exercise requires a consideration of a wide array of personal, social and structural factors, factors that combine to determine levels of activity and changes over time. The transition from formal organized activity as part of the school curriculum to voluntary engagement during adolescence is a bridge too far for many young people. However, only through a systematic consideration of how these complex variables interact can we ever hope to encourage lifestyles where physical activity plays an integral and important role, and it is towards effective interventions that we now turn.

Encouraging Healthy Exercise

Generally speaking, we have seen that as children enter into adolescence there is a decline in their engagement in physical activity, this trend being more pronounced for girls than for boys. What can be done by others to stem this decline and encourage adolescents to maintain an involvement in sport and exercise? To date, a number of physical activity interventions, based on theoretical concepts and models, have been designed to tackle individual behaviours, attitudes and knowledge (Wechsler *et al.*, 2000). Another approach has been to develop an intervention outwith the individual adolescent, by focusing on the contextual factors associated with physical activity. In the previous section we examined a number of contextual or structural factors that influence activity such as significant others, the environment and school-based experiences. In a recent Department of Health report, *At least five times a week* (2004), the Chief Medical Officer proposed a number of actions that could be taken at local authority, school and parental level in order to improve the health of the nation. Using this framework we shall examine the possible interventions that can be used as well as evidence of their effectiveness.

Exercise Recommendations

DHSS report, *At least five times a week* (2004), Recommendations (p. v –vi)

Local authority and community level

- Local transport plans to give particular consideration to walking and cycling as means of commuting and personal travel.
- Local authorities to take steps to make neighbourhoods and communities more 'activity-friendly' – pleasant and safe for walking, cycling and playing.
- Town planners, architects and engineers to ensure that physical activity is facilitated, and not discouraged, in new buildings, streets, housing developments and schools.

Schools

- Education professionals and play leaders to encourage children and young people of all abilities, shapes and sizes to take part in sports and activities that engage them throughout life.
- Walking to school and college to be supported and encouraged.

- Higher education to help train a high-quality, professional workforce as experts in promoting health-enhancing physical activity.

Parents

- Parents to encourage children to be active, and set active role models themselves.
- Sedentary, housebound activities to be reduced and more active, outdoor pursuits increased.

Community-Based Interventions

Perhaps surprisingly given the pivotal role played by the community, there is a lack of research on community interventions in encouraging a more active lifestyle (Kahn *et al.*, 2002). Even more apparent is the lack of evidence based on young people, with many of the studies using the adult worker, the elderly or younger children. There are a number of benefits to community-level intervention over and above those conducted in schools:

- Young people spend their free time in the evenings, weekends and holidays in the community.
- There is involvement of potential role models other than teachers.
- Involvement takes place in an informal setting.
- Provision of facilities at community level allows for easier implementation of an active lifestyle. (Pate *et al.*, 2000)

In terms of the first and second recommendations for community-based intervention offered by the Chief Medical Officer (Department of Health, 2004), local authorities should consider and implement walking and cycling as a means of travel and recreation. Within the UK, Sustrans, a charity for sustainable transport **(www.sustrans.org.uk)**, has been recently involved in organizing the 'Safe Route to School' campaign which aims to provide every child in the UK with a safe route that they can take to school. The charity is also responsible for the national cycle network and other campaigns including the 'Safe Routes to Stations' and 'Home Zones' projects where clusters of streets in communities give road use priority to pedestrians. Initiatives such as the latter should allow better, safer access to outside space for young people to participate in recreational activities.

As mentioned earlier, there is a gender gap in terms of the types of activities and the intensity to which these activities are engaged in by men and women, with young women falling behind their male peers. Community organizations should be encouraged to widen the opportunities for non-competitive activities that appeal to this group in particular, and to be imaginative in terms of available resources. For example, religious communities and voluntary organizations may be a useful resource to the wider community for the provision of physical activities, often having both the space and volunteers available. A further recent phenomenon in North America is the activity of 'mall walking' where people are encouraged to use the indoor, safe space of the shopping centre out of normal working hours to walk and exercise (Bland and Colby, 1999).

To help develop knowledge, national and community media campaigns can target behavioural change by giving people information on the benefits of choosing an active lifestyle. Recent UK media campaigns such as those funded by the Health Promotion Agency and other bodies have encouraged the public to become more active, to take regular exercise and to actively commute to work or school. In a review of the effectiveness of activity interventions, Kahn *et al.* (2002) were unable to find many research studies that had evaluated the effectiveness of mass media campaigns, but nevertheless concluded that they appeared to provide useful improvements in knowledge and awareness of the benefits of physical activity. In contrast, a number of studies have looked at the effectiveness of activity prompts (point-of-decision prompts). These prompts can be visual posters placed in strategic locations when the individual needs to make a decision as to whether to make an active or a sedentary response. Typically, posters will be placed near to the lifts or escalators of public buildings so as to encourage people to choose the staircase as an active alternative. Blamey, Mutrie and Aitchison (1995) found that male stair use increased from 12% to 21%, while female stair use increased from 5% to 12% when posters were placed between the stairs and escalators of an underground train station.

When considering the layout of many new multi-level public buildings such as shopping centres, a number appear to be designed with the sedentary in mind. Stairs can be inconveniently located and may be fewer in number whereas escalators and lifts are usually located at the points of entrance to these buildings. Indeed, Kahn *et al.* (2002) suggested that some have the appearance of being the unsafe choice with poor lighting and maintenance.

School-Based Interventions

Young people questioned as part of the Sports Council Northern Ireland (SCNI) survey (Kremer, Trew and Ogle, 1997) reported that the most common reason for participation was 'because of school' (31%). Therefore it would be logical that any intervention that encouraged greater physical activity among young people should do so within the school setting. School-based interventions can be at the individual level of the teacher or they can be at an organizational level. The following are two such illustrations.

The school teacher as a role model will have a significant impact on the individual pupil's participation or withdrawal from physical activity. The messages conveyed to pupils through the structure and climate of the PE class, and the cues given by the teacher need careful consideration. As seen earlier, the type of feedback given by a teacher or coach can significantly influence motivation and subsequently impact on levels of engagement in physical activity. Feedback will allow the individual to evaluate his or her progress over and above the outcome of competition against others. Sarrazin and Famose (1999) offer educators a useful framework to structure the feedback given to pupils to reflect task rather than ego orientation without expunging the competitive nature of many sports.

Sarrazin and Famose (1999) – Feedback Guidelines

1. Avoid situations where students are evaluated by a win or loss – emphasize improvement and mastery of the skills involved.
2. Avoid publicizing the results of class competitions.
3. Avoid situations where students perform individually in front of their class.
4. Avoid situations that highlight differences between levels of competence (first equates to best or last is punished).

By underselling the competitive references embedded in sport, Sarrazin and Famose (1999) are suggesting that sport competition will become an opportunity for young people to gain an insight into their own ability and progress rather than continually judging themselves against others.

Many schools offer a range of extracurricular sports and physical activities, both interscholastic (competing against teams from other schools) and intramural (competition and activity within the school). Interscholastic activities are a traditional feature of adolescent education where talented athletes are selected to compete at county, regional or national level whereas intramural activities are offered to the masses but less frequently and tend to carry less status in terms of recognition from the school (Wechsler *et al.*, 2000). The dilemma here is that intramural activities have better potential to encourage a greater number of pupils to adopt good health practices, associate physical activity with learning and enjoyment and to remain involved in physical activities during their time at school and beyond (Stone *et al.*, 1998). By their very nature, activities restricted to the school membership can be more fluid and interactive in nature. They are not constrained by external structures and standards and therefore can offer greater choice, be more inclusive to different ability levels and offer pupils the chance to be involved in its organization (Wechsler *et al.*, 2000).

Parental Interventions

Changing family structures in recent years will invariably influence the role that parents play in the socialization of their children towards physical activity. Divorce, single parent families, working parents and pressures of work or finance all may potentially impact on the emphasis and importance that adult role models place on physical activity (Greendorfer *et al.*, 2002). Elkins *et al.* (2004) suggested that the pressures of modern life can lead to additional responsibility being placed on burgeoning young adults with many working part-time, caring for younger siblings and/or infirm family members, all of which can inhibit engagement in extracurricular activity. These findings sadly suggest that parents have less free time available for their children and may indeed be inadvertently encouraging their adolescents into a sedentary lifestyle.

The recommendations of the Chief Medical Officer (Department of Health, 2004), to parents were to offer a positive *role model* to their children, personally demonstrating the benefits of an active lifestyle over more sedentary pursuits. Individuals primarily gain information about their own capabilities through personal experience but another source of information can be by vicarious experience or the experiences of others (Bandura, 1977). If the participant feels capable of performing or being involved in the activity they are more likely and willing to engage. A parent can act as a suitable role model especially at the early stages of adoption when their child is still uncertain about their own abilities. By seeing another involved in the new activity they will make a judgement about their own ability (Poag and McAuley, 1992). The concept of role modelling can also be applied to the subtleties of sports such as attitude towards competition and sportsmanship.

Parents can also encourage their children to be physically active by being involved in their child's participation. However, this process can be a careful balancing act. The parent needs to offer support and encouragement but not to the point where this involvement is perceived as a domineering or controlling pressure. In a retrospective look at the involvement of parents of professional baseball players, Hill (1993) found that the players cited the following supportive behaviours: financial assistance (for sport and a general allowance), transportation, attendance at games, willing to practice with players and encouragement to pursue a professional career in the sport. Researchers have suggested that girls require more parental support and encouragement than boys in order that they continue within sport (Anderson *et al.*, 2003). This may not be entirely the whole story as our culture still reinforces gender stereotyping which endorses male participation in sport whereas female participation in any other than the aesthetic sports (dance, skating, gymnastics) is discouraged and labelled as unfeminine (Scully and Clarke, 1997). Parental pressure in sport can be characterized by such behaviours as criticism, responses to losing, concern about winning and pressure to succeed (Leff and Hoyle, 1995). Curiously Anderson *et al.* (2003) found that children reported greater parental pressure towards their involvement in sporting activities rather than artistic activities or involvement in group or club activities; this perhaps reflects the high esteem and financial security athletes enjoy within society.

Pushy Parents or ABPD

An increasing literature is developing around the phenomenon of 'pushy parents' in sport – those who are willing to go to extreme lengths to ensure that their progeny achieve and often at any cost (otherwise known as achievement by proxy distortion (ABPD), Tolfer, Knapp and Drell, 1998). For some insight into ABPD, have a look at the following web site, describing the relationship between the young tennis player Jelena Dokic and her father Damir, among others.
http://news.bbc.co.uk/1/hi/uk/812924.stm

Conclusion

In this chapter we have examined research and theory relating health to exercise and sport. The survey evidence indicated that in general young people's participation in sport had risen slightly over the last decade but there are wide individual and group differences. Adolescent

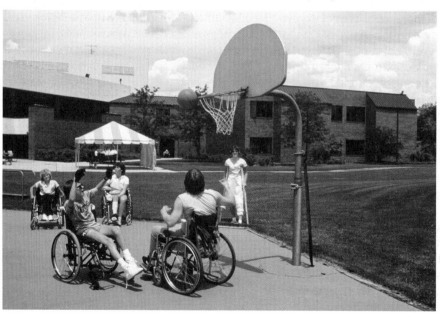

girls are less involved in sport than adolescent boys and this gap increases with increasing age. We noted the large body of research which demonstrates the importance of appropriate levels of physical exercise for maintaining both physical and mental health as well as evidence that there can be detrimental effects of overtraining at a young age.

Under the right conditions, appropriate exercise has been found to improve self-esteem and mood, impact on depression and anxiety and help prevent stress, whereas excessive and inappropriate exercise has been associated with various exercise-related disorders. There is no clear consensus as to exactly what factors account for the observed effects but it is probable that pharmacological, physiological and psychological mechanisms are all involved to some extent in linking physical exercise to psychological well-being.

Research is also beginning to unravel the complex web of circumstances and people that interact to either encourage or discourage young people from involving themselves in physical activity. In terms of personal factors, both intrinsic and extrinsic motivation have a part to play in promoting involvement in exercise. Extrinsic motivation is seen as important for the initiation of activity while adolescents' continuing enjoyment of sporting activities tends to be associated with intrinsic motivational factors. Studies of participation motivation have also demonstrated the importance of social factors, such as the influence of peers, parents and coaches. There has been less research on the structural factors that are associated with the young person's engagement with physical activity, but poor accessibility of facilities and low socio-economic status do provide barriers to participation.

The chapter concludes by describing a number of specific interventions by communities, local authorities, schools and parents that encourage young people to maintain their involvement in sport and exercise.

CASE STUDY 2.1

Jack was brought up in a family with a strong sporting history. His mother had been a county netball player and his father had captained his local rugby team and was now president of the town's rugby club. His older brother was a good swimmer who was close to the national squad. At primary school Jack was an automatic choice for every school team. He played soccer for the district team and ran in the county cross-country championships which he won easily. His sport came easily to him and he enjoyed being active, trying out new sports and meeting friends along the way. Both his parents were very supportive but often his father's presence would inhibit his performance. At his secondary school Jack played soccer and he was clearly very talented – attracting the attention of several local scouts. His father was involved with mini-rugby at his club and Jack would play rugby in the morning before playing soccer in the afternoon. On occasions when there was a school soccer game he had to miss mini-rugby which his father accepted begrudgingly. His PE teacher was a keen athletics coach and Jack would still compete although he did not have time for specific training. At the age of 15 Jack's enthusiasm for his sport seemed to wane. During this period he picked up a leg injury that kept him out of sport for six weeks, and his parents noticed he became very quiet and withdrawn. After recovery, Jack seemed to have lost his flair and found it hard to lose weight. His father tried to put pressure on him to play but to no avail, and Jack found himself spending more and more of his time playing on his computer.

CASE STUDY 2.1 QUESTIONS

1. With reference to relevant theories and models, how would you interpret what is happening in this case study?
2. What interventions could be used to help deal with this situation?

Further Reading

Berger, B. G., Pargman, D. and Weinberg, R. S. (2002) *Foundations of exercise psychology*, Fitness Information Technology Inc., Morgantown, WV. This is an introductory text to the area of exercise psychology and is aimed at students. The book covers the key information on how physical activity and exercise influence quality of life and motivation. Topics addressed include self-esteem, mood, stress, injury, eating disorders, flow and motivational strategies. There are also separate chapters on working with children and youth populations and gender-related issues in exercise.

Cale, L. and Harris, J. (eds) (2005) *Exercise and young people. Issues, implications and initiatives*, Palgrave Macmillan, Basingstoke, Hampshire. Written from a predominately UK perspective, this book examines adolescent physical activity. The chapters explore issues such as the current status of physical activity in young people, current recommendations and the determinants of activity. Various examples of activity promotion and intervention at an individual, school and community level are discussed. The book is aimed at students and practitioners working with young people.

Gard, M. and Wright, J. (2005) *The obesity epidemic: science, morality and ideology*, Routledge, London. Written by Australian authors, this book explores the validity of scientific contributions to the obesity debate. The scientific and social construction of what we commonly refer to as obesity are explored. It is not designed to provide the definitive answer to health-related issues but rather to stimulate debate and question our naïve acceptance of the 'facts'.

Murphy, S. (1999) *The cheers and the tears: a healthy alternative to the dark side of youth sports today*, Jossey-Bass Publishers, San Francisco. Written by an American sport psychologist as an aid to parents and coaches of youth athletes, the book offers an insight into the possible sources of stress children experience as a result of parental and coach interaction, whilst offering adults a number of practical solutions to these issues.

Weiss, M. (2004) *Developmental sport and exercise psychology: a lifespan perspective*, Fitness Information Technology Inc., Morgantown, WV. This edited book provides a synthesis of relevant theories which influence various developmental age groups. Part 2 explores the age group of youth and adolescents, looking at issues including the influence of parents and peers as well as the wider issues of self-perception and motivation. The book is aimed at students but provides a balance between the relevant theories and practical interventions that can be employed.

Discussion Questions

1. With reference to the theories and models of participation motivation outlined in the chapter, critically evaluate the extent to which we fully understand the reasons why young people take up and discontinue sport and physical activity.

2. Do you accept the argument that the population is heading towards an obesity epidemic? If so, what forms of intervention are likely to be most effective in encouraging more active and healthy lifestyles among young people?

3. Under what circumstances will physical exercise have either a positive or a negative effect on psychological well-being?

4. Pushy parents – who are they and what can be done to help deal with them?

Chapter 3

Emotional Health and Well-Being

John Coleman

Department of Educational Studies, University of Oxford

- Introduction
- What is Emotional Health and Well-Being?
- Why has there been Increasing Interest in this Topic?
- Mental Disorders in Children and Young People
- Risk and Resilience – Fostering Protective Factors
- Programmes to Enhance Emotional Health and Well-Being
- Mental Health Promotion Programmes – Do they Work?
- Conclusion

Learning Objectives

After reading this chapter you should:

1 Understand the problems of definition relating to emotional health and well-being.
2 Appreciate why this is a topic of growing importance.
3 Know something about mental ill-health in young people.
4 Understand risk and resilience, and the role of protective factors.
5 Know about mental health promotion programmes for adolescents.
6 Be able to say whether these programmes work or not.

Introduction

Everyone wants to be happy, and yet there is little agreement about how to achieve happiness. Since early thinkers first started to discuss the human condition there have been debates about this topic. Over the centuries it is probably the case that more has been written about happiness than about almost any other aspect of philosophy. In the social sciences considerable attention has been paid in recent years to what is called positive psychology, involving a consideration of what constitutes a balanced and fulfilling life.

Questions of this type are of course closely related to the topic of emotional health and well-being. Can we say that someone who is emotionally healthy is likely to be happy? Is well-being the same as happiness? How does emotional health relate to positive psychology? Are concepts of well-being and emotional health in adults the same as those which apply to adolescents?

There are no simple answers to these questions, and they take us closer to philosophy than to education or to psychology. However, they are of intrinsic interest to us all, and they underlie the growing concern with emotional health and well-being which will be explored in this chapter. Why should this topic have received so much attention in recent years?

One reason for the growing interest has been a focus on what has been called emotional intelligence. Many have argued that the emotions have for too long been on the periphery when it comes to understanding human functioning, and that much can be gained through a better grasp of this aspect of our lives. There has been much concern about poor mental health and its consequences for children and young people. The notion of the healthy school, and the need for criteria and standards against which to assess this concept, has raised a number of interesting questions about the role of emotion in schools.

In addition to all this, the debate over public health, and the impetus within government during the last few years to address key concerns such as obesity and alcohol use, has had the added benefit of drawing attention to public health issues relating to emotional health and well-being. In this chapter I will consider some of the problems surrounding definitions of this concept, and I will explore in greater detail some of the reasons behind the growing interest in the topic. I will look at mental disorder and at protective factors, and go on to review the evidence available so far on the value of mental health promotion programmes for children and young people.

What is Emotional Health and Well-Being?

The topic of emotional health and well-being is fraught with problems of definition. Everyone has a slightly different perspective on the subject. Firstly there are a number of overlapping terms in use, such as, for example, emotional literacy, well-being, emotional health and so on. In addition, there is the problem of distinguishing between health and ill-health. Different professional groups prefer to use different terms, and there is no one phrase or word that has become accepted usage for the concept of emotional health and well-being.

For writers such as Katherine Weare (2004) the term 'emotional literacy' is seen as the most helpful. Weare defines emotional literacy as:

> *The ability to understand ourselves and other people, and in particular to be aware of, understand, and use information about the emotional states of ourselves and others with competence.*

It includes the ability to understand, express and manage our own emotions, and respond to the emotions of others, in ways that are helpful to ourselves and others. (2004, p. 2)

For Weare the importance of this definition is that it allows her to go on to define a range of competencies relating to emotional literacy, thus putting the underlying concept into operational terms. The competencies she outlines include self-understanding, the understanding and managing of emotions, and the understanding of social situations and making relationships.

Many others working in the field of mental health promotion take a similar view. There are clearly advantages in having a definition which refers to something measurable, yet it has to be recognized that emotional literacy as defined by Weare is not the same as well-being, if by that we mean some sense of feeling good about ourselves. It is possible to envisage someone who is skilled in the understanding of emotions, and yet not necessarily at ease with themselves.

Those who wish to use a concept that implies a continuum ranging from healthy to unhealthy also face a problem here. Part of the difficulty is that the term mental health is almost always a synonym for mental ill-health. However much writers or professionals claim that when using the term mental health they want to include both good and poor health, the fact is that this term is almost always used in the context of disorder. This issue is further compounded by the fact that different professional groups use different terms when they refer to mental disorder. Thus teachers may refer to emotional and behavioural difficulties, whilst those working in psychiatric services might use terms such as 'psychological disorder'.

We have to acknowledge that there is no commonly accepted term that can be used in the context of good mental health. As we have said, well-being is a more general term than emotional literacy, having the disadvantage of being slightly woolly, and being associated with happiness, calm, tranquility, and so on. On the other hand it is probably better than mental health, as it does not carry with it the overtones of disorder or mental ill-health. We have used emotional health and well-being for the title of this chapter primarily because it is the term currently in use in policy circles, and because of all the terms it is the one most widely favoured by writers on this subject.

Why has there been Increasing Interest in this Topic?

A number of reasons can be identified to explain the increased attention being given to emotional health and well-being. Daniel Goleman's book *Emotional intelligence* (1996) is a good place to start. While there has been little consensus over the validity of his arguments, nonetheless the attention given to his work, and the debates that followed the publication of his book, served to raise awareness of the whole idea that emotions and emotional health were subjects fit for discussion. Mental health promotion in various guises had been in existence well before the mid-1990s, yet Goleman represented a landmark in the development of thinking to do with emotional health and well-being. From his work flowed ideas about emotional literacy, and much of the work relating to mental health promotion received a boost from Goleman's ideas. As Weare says:

The idea of emotional intelligence triggered an explosion of interest in scientific work on how the brain works, and in particular on the central role that the emotional side of the brain plays in the process. It focused attention on the links between social and emotional intelligence and educational outcomes such as learning, cognitive development, school attendance and job success. (2004, p. 5)

Another strand of thinking has concerned the levels of mental health problems currently seen in children and young people, and the costs associated with mental ill-health. In 1999 the Office for National Statistics (ONS) carried out a survey of psychiatric disorders in those between the ages of 5 and 16, showing that approximately 10% can be considered to have a mental health problem (Meltzer *et al.*, 2000). A comparable survey was carried out in 2004, indicating a very similar level of mental ill-health (Green *et al.*, 2005). Boys were more likely than girls to have a mental disorder. Among 5–10 year-olds, 10% of boys and 5% of girls had a disorder. Among the 11–16 year-olds, the proportions were 13% for boys and 10% for girls. Further discussion of these statistics will be found in the next section.

The concern with mental ill-health is also closely linked to anxiety about stigma. Many professionals have focused attention on this aspect of mental health in the past few years. Indeed Helen Cowie and colleagues (2004), in their book on emotional health and well-being, argue that defeating stigma is one of the primary reasons for introducing mental health promotion in the school setting. As they say:

> *While today's young people seem to face severe stresses that were unknown a generation ago, society still has negative and stereotyped views of mental illness and mental health problems. The sense of shame and embarrassment that surrounds the concept of a mental health disorder contributes to the fact that young people's mental health difficulties are often unrecognized or even denied. (Cowie* et al., *2004, p. 4)*

A further prompt for the growing interest in emotional health and well-being in the United Kingdom has come from the international movement relating to mental health promotion. Major programmes in Australia, New Zealand and Canada have been shown to have a significant impact on the functioning of the school, and in particular work such as that carried out by Pauline Dickinson (Dickinson, Neilson and Agee, 2004) has had a major impact on thinking in this country. Dickinson showed that it was possible to work with all the stakeholders in one school district in New Zealand, and to raise awareness of emotional health to the point that all teachers and pupils subscribed to a programme which had clearly identified benefits for attainment as well as for school ethos.

Finally it is important to note that a number of other initiatives in Britain, both within and outside government, have had a cumulative effect on the levels of awareness and interest in this topic. At least three major literature reviews have been carried out, one by the EPPI Centre at the University of London (Harden *et al.*, 2001), one by the SCRE Centre at the University of Glasgow (Edwards, 2003), and the third by Wells, Barlow and Stewart-Brown (2003). In addition, work by Stewart-Brown (2005), commissioned by the Department of Health, and work by Katherine Weare for the DfES on Social and Emotional Aspects of Learning (SEAL), have all been influential in different ways.

In addition to all this, there is no doubt that the introduction of the National Healthy Schools Programme encouraged the asking of questions about emotional health in schools. In spite of the fact that notions of emotional health in school are still far from being fully worked out, nonetheless the impetus of the programme focused attention on the subject. Ofsted have also been taking an interest in the topic, and their report *Healthy minds: promoting emotional health and well-being in schools* (2005) draws attention to the distance we still have to go in promoting emotional health and well-being in schools.

Mental Disorders in Children and Young People

As has already been indicated, the links between emotional well-being and mental disorder are complicated. The two concepts are often confused in the literature as well as in practice, and this leads to considerable ambiguity in much of the debate about this topic. As has been noted above, a major impetus for mental health promotion, and for the interest in emotional well-being, has to do with the costs of mental ill-health. It is well recognized that mental disorder carries with it a significant degree of disadvantage extending to almost all aspects of human development. In discussing the most recent survey of mental health problems in Britain (Green *et al.*, 2005), the authors pointed out that those with such disorders were likely to miss more school, have fewer friends and a more limited social network, and that their problems would be likely to impact on their families as well.

Mental ill-health has other costs too. As many writers have pointed out, mental health problems are often associated with physical health problems, thus causing additional distress as well as increased interruption of normal functioning. Mental health problems are economically costly for society, disrupting school attainment, increasing the need for services, and placing demands on a range of institutions within communities. For all these reasons there is a pressing need, as well as a genuine incentive to develop effective mental health promotion initiatives.

In view of the fact that a major impetus for the development of work on emotional health and well-being has to do with the reduction of mental disorder, it is important in this chapter to spend a short time outlining what is currently known about mental disorders in children and young people. The headline for the press release associated with the most recent survey (Green *et al.*, 2005) was as follows: 'One in ten children has a mental disorder'. In fact this figure is an average taken from a number of different statistics. Fewer girls than boys have mental disorders, and the numbers for both genders increase with age. Boys are more likely to have conduct disorders, whilst girls have higher levels of emotional disorders, including depression and anxiety.

Mental health problems are not equally distributed across society. One of the strongest findings of the survey relates to the fact that mental ill-health is closely associated with poverty and disadvantage. Rates of mental disorder are twice as high among children being brought up in lone parent families as they are among children living in couple families, as well as being very much higher among families where neither parent is working. Parents of children and young people with a mental disorder were also more likely than other parents to have no educational qualifications. Factors such as these link with other indices of deprivation, so that there is lower family income, poorer housing, and greater ill-health generally among families whose children have a mental disorder. The combined weight of disadvantage seen here as being associated with poor mental health is a critical factor in the overall picture, and cannot be ignored when considering prevention or intervention (see Figure 3.1).

One of the important findings of the 2005 survey is that there has been no change in the rates of disorder if these are compared with the rates reported in a similar survey carried out in 1999 (Meltzer *et al.*, 2000). This is pertinent, because of the fact that much attention has been paid recently to the possibility that mental ill-health is deteriorating among children and young people.

Two studies in particular have contributed to this view. Both studies used exactly the same measures with different cohorts, one study going back to 1974, and the other to 1987. In the first of these studies (West and Sweeting, 2003) the researchers have used Scottish data on

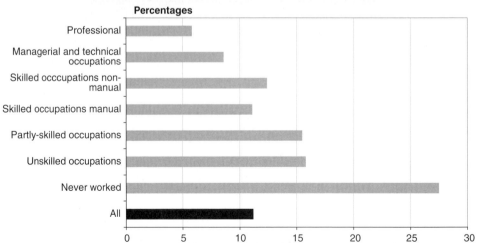

Figure 3.1   Prevalence of mental disorder among 11–15 year-olds by social class of family (Meltzer *et al.*, 2000).

15 year-olds, and have looked at changes in anxiety and depression over a 12-year span. Results show marked increases among girls in psychological distress, but no significant changes among boys. A study by Collishaw *et al.* (2004) investigated a variety of disorders over 25 years. The results of this study showed that between the years 1974 and 1999, among both boys and girls, there were increases in both conduct disorders and emotional problems, although, as might be expected, there were higher levels of conduct disorder among boys and a higher level of emotional problems among girls (see Figure 3.2).

It has been suggested that changes such as those reported in these studies could be due to increased exam stress, the changing job market, and the difficulty in finding stable employment,

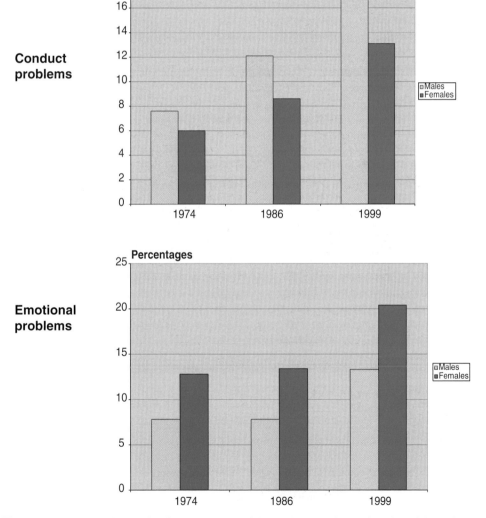

Figure 3.2   Proportions of 15/16 year-olds with conduct and emotional problems in the UK, by gender and cohort (Collishaw *et al.*, 2004). *Time trends in adolescent well-being. Journal of Child Psychology and Psychiatry. 45. 1350–1362, Blackwell Publishing.*

particularly for less able young people. However, the fact that the ONS surveys appear to show no change over a recent five-year period is also important, and may indicate that the deterioration in mental health which appeared to take place during the 1980s and 1990s has slowed down or halted altogether.

In considering the mental health of children and young people, it seems important to make some reference to suicide and self-harm. Suicide rates have been seen by government as important indicators of the nation's mental health, and since Virginia Bottomley's 'Health of the Nation' policy initiative in the early 1990s the reduction of suicide rates has been a key government target. In 'Choosing Health' (Department of Health, 2004) the target is to reduce the rates of death by suicide or undetermined injury by 20% by the year 2010.

As far as the statistics on suicide are concerned, few young people below the age of 15 take their own lives, although there are always exceptions to this rule. If we look at those in the 15 to 24 year-old age range, rates among young men peaked in the early 1990s, and have gradually fallen since then. The rate in 2003 for young men in England and Wales was 12 per 100000, compared with a rate of 17 per 100000 in 1992. The rate for young women is much lower, at 3 per 100000, and has not varied over the last decade. However, there is considerable regional variation, illustrated by the fact that in Scotland the suicide rate for young men in 2003 was 30 per 100000, almost three times the rate for England and Wales (Coleman and Schofield, 2005).

In relation to self-harm it will be evident that statistics are very much harder to come by. Voluntary sector agencies such as Childline and the Samaritans have produced figures suggesting that self-harm in the form of cutting and self-injury has increased dramatically over the last few years, but such claims are hard to validate due to the nature of the evidence being collected, most of which is through telephone calls. More systematic studies have been carried out by people such as Keith Hawton at Oxford. In his study of those admitted to the Radcliffe Hospital as a result of self-poisoning during the years 1990 to 2000, he showed an increase among girls and young women of roughly 20%, with no change in the rates for boys and young men (Hawton et al., 2003).

Hawton also carried out a community survey of self-harm among nearly 6000 adolescents, and the results indicated that 3% of males and 11% of females had been involved in some form of self-harm during the past 12 months (Hawton et al., 2002). Such figures show this to be a significant area of concern for professionals as well as for parents, although the figures are perhaps less alarmist than media speculation would have us believe.

There is a very considerable literature on mental disorders in children and young people, and this is not the place to carry out a comprehensive review. However, before closing this section it may be worth noting some results from the most recent report of the Exeter Schools Health Education Unit (Balding, 2004). This study is an annual survey of a large population of secondary school pupils, and the worries of young people is one of the topics studied. Results of the most recent survey find that girls worry more than boys, and that the extent of worries increases with age. Many adolescents worry about their families (19% of boys and 35% of girls), with about the same numbers worrying about careers and school work. The factor creating most worry is appearance, with 21% of boys and 49% of girls expressing anxiety about this aspect of their lives. Such findings should give us pause for thought (see Table 3.1).

This short review of mental disorders is helpful in our consideration of emotional health and well-being. An awareness of some of the variables associated with mental ill-health can guide our discussion about intervention as well as prevention. Thus, factors such as gender, family, and social background may impact on the approaches which are most effective in mental health promotion. We will be able to make use of this information in later sections of the chapter.

Table 3.1   Proportions of 10–15 year-olds responding 'A lot'/'Quite a lot' to the question: 'How much do you worry about these problems?' (percentages)

	Boys			Girls		
	10–11	12–13	14–15	10–11	12–13	14–15
School-work problems	17	14	24	17	14	31
Health problems	20	14	13	22	18	22
Career problems	*	14	24	*	13	30
Problems with friends	14	13	13	26	24	27
Family problems	25	17	19	32	23	35
The way you look	15	18	21	25	39	49
HIV/AIDS	*	5	6	*	7	8
Puberty and growing up	12	10	8	24	16	12
Bullying	*	8	6	*	11	8
Being gay, lesbian or bisexual	*	3	3	*	2	3
None of these	53	54	46	41	40	25

Source: Balding, 2004. *Reproduced by Permission of Schools Health Education Unit*

Risk and Resilience – Fostering Protective Factors

In our discussion so far we have referred to a variety of factors that might be perceived as risk factors for mental disorder. Thus, for example, certain family factors might heighten the risk of a mental disorder, and as we have seen there is a strong association between deprivation and mental ill-health. We have noted that gender is a variable that cannot be ignored when considering mental health, with the clearest example being the fact that four times more young men than young women take their own lives through suicide. On the other hand, the gender ratio for self-harm is almost exactly the opposite, with at least three times more young women than young men being involved in self-harming behaviour.

There are also particular groups of young people who show much higher rates of mental disorder than others. Research by Meltzer *et al.*, (2003) indicates that 49% of young people looked after by local authorities have some form of mental disorder, compared with 10% of the general population (see Table 3.2). Among those in custody rates are probably even higher, although the use of diagnostic categories varies across different studies. Hagell (2002) reports rates of mental disorder among adolescents in prison varying between 41% and 80%, depending on the population studied and the measures used.

Finally there is the question as to whether ethnicity has any part to play where mental disorder is concerned. Not all studies agree on this point, but if we consider the findings of the survey reported by Meltzer *et al.* in 2000, this showed that young people from Black backgrounds had substantially higher levels of mental disorder than other ethnic groups (16% as compared to 10%). By contrast, those from Indian backgrounds reportedly had significantly lower levels of disorder (3.5%).

It will be self-evident that an understanding of risk factors is important for any consideration of mental health promotion. If prevention is one of the key goals of mental health promotion,

Table 3.2   Prevalence of mental disorders amongst 11–15 year-olds looked after by local authorities in England, by gender, 2002 (percentages)

	Boys	Girls	All
Emotional disorders	8.4	16.1	11.9
Conduct disorders	45.4	34.5	40.5
Hyperkinetic disorders	10.9	2.4	7.1
Less common disorders	8.2	1.5	5.2
Any disorder	54.7	42.8	49.3
Base	265	216	480

Source: Meltzer et al., 2003

then any interventions aimed at prevention will need to be clear about both the morbidity and the risk factors associated with these disorders. However, mental health promotion is concerned not only with the prevention of mental illness. It also has the goal of promoting emotional health and well-being, and for this we need to be able to identify protective factors as well as risk factors.

Many writers have argued that, in order to achieve both prevention and the enhancement of well-being, we must strive for 'public mental health', which includes a focus on the mental health of the whole population. This 'universal' approach puts the spotlight on schools, neighbourhoods and communities as having a protective role. The physical and social environment must be targeted if the goals associated with mental health promotion are to be achieved. Of course this is not an easy task. As Stewart-Brown neatly expresses it:

> Health improvement across the entire population can be difficult to imagine and to aspire to. It is easier to focus on changing the health of the least healthy than that of the majority of the population. (2005, p. 5)

Nonetheless many have argued that the promotion of emotional health and well-being is a worthwhile and achievable goal, and we will be looking at some programmes that espouse this goal in the next section of this chapter. But first we need to consider the question: what exactly is it that we are trying to achieve?

Tilford and colleagues (1997) have put forward the view that there are three key protective factors which may be said to underlie good mental health. These are:

• coping skills
• self-esteem
• social support.

If we imagine an individual who is adapting to the stresses and challenges of everyday life, then this adaptation may be facilitated or inhibited by individual factors such as coping skills and self-esteem, as well as by social factors such as family and community support.

The Health Education Authority (Friedli, 1997) sets out a complementary framework for mental health promotion, outlining both promoting and demoting factors. These factors are classified in terms of 'emotional resilience', 'citizenship', and 'healthy structures'.

'Emotional resilience' is defined as 'how people feel about themselves, the interpretation of events, and people's ability to cope with stressful or adverse circumstances', and includes 'self-esteem, coping and life skills and opportunities to make choices and exercise control over one's life'. (Friedli, 1997, p. 8).

'Citizenship' is defined as 'a positive sense of belonging and participating in society', and includes 'social support, strong social networks, a sense of integration and social inclusion' (ibid., p. 7).

'Healthy structures' including social, economic and cultural factors, relate to the fabric of society, and refer to the institutions and organizations impacting on the lives of the individuals concerned (ibid., p. 8).

As we have noted in the earlier part of this chapter, Weare (2004) and others who focus on emotional intelligence outline goals which are more closely related to the notion of competence than to protective factors. Thus Weare defines three key competencies, including self-understanding, understanding and managing emotions, and understanding social situations and managing relationships. Because these three competencies are so central to concepts of emotional health and well-being, I believe it is worth looking at these in a little more detail here. This is how the three competencies are elaborated in Weare (2004, pp. 3–4).

Self-Understanding

- Having an accurate and positive view of ourselves.
- Having a sense of optimism about the world and ourselves.
- Having a coherent and continuous life story.

Understanding and Managing Emotions

- Experiencing the whole range of emotions.
- Understanding the causes of our emotions.
- Expressing our emotions appropriately.
- Managing our responses to our emotions effectively, for example, managing our anger, controlling our impulses.
- Knowing how to feel good more often and for longer.
- Using information about the emotions to plan and solve problems.
- Resilience – processing and bouncing back from difficult experiences.

Understanding Social Situations and Managing Relationships

- Forming attachments to other people.
- Experiencing empathy for others.
- Communicating and responding effectively to others.
- Managing our relationships effectively.
- Being autonomous, independent and self-reliant.

A closer look at these competencies will show that there is considerable overlap with the approach of someone like Tilford *et al.* mentioned above. Both coping and self-esteem are integral to many of the competencies suggested by Weare. When we turn to look at the programmes designed for mental health promotion we will see how all the issues raised here are addressed in one way or another within interventions. Thus, some writers approach the task from a risk perspective, others identify protective factors that can be enhanced, others focus on competencies, while others again seek to provide essential information about mental health issues. Just as with the problem of definitions, we will see that different approaches to mental health promotion may lead to different outcomes for young people, and to significant difficulties in ensuring high quality evaluation.

Programmes to Enhance Emotional Health and Well-Being

It is generally recognized that there are many different types of programme designed to enhance emotional health and well-being, and a huge number of interventions of one type or another to be found in the literature. Harden *et al.* (2001) mentioned finding over 800 examples of intervention programmes relating to young people and mental health, and this search was not exhaustive. As part of the exercise reported in the Harden review, an attempt was made to classify interventions, according to whether their aim was primary or secondary prevention. Primary prevention was described as follows:

> *Primary prevention of mental ill-health or promotion of emotional well-being is defined as any initiative that is directed at young people who do not have an established diagnosis of a mental health problem. (Harden, 2001, p. 18)*

Primary prevention can also be further divided into 'universal' interventions, that target all individuals, 'selective' interventions, that target those individuals at increased risk of developing mental health problems, and finally 'indicated' interventions, targeting those showing early signs of mental ill-health. All these primary intervention programmes are distinguished from secondary programmes, which focus specifically on individuals who have an identifiable mental health problem.

What is clear from all three major reviews (Harden *et al.*, 2001; Edwards, 2003; and Wells, Barlow and Stewart-Brown, 2003) is that there is an enormous range of activity in this field, and the difficulty arises in trying to decide what to include in any review. A variety of systems of classification have been used, but the most comprehensive is that developed by Harden *et al.* (2001), and I shall use this as a model for the present chapter.

In the first place interventions can be divided according to their mental health focus. Thus, Harden *et al.* (2001) found that out of a total of 345 interventions that had been evaluated, 148 were designed to prevent specific disorders, whilst 197 were designed to promote positive mental health. Of those that could be called either selective or indicated programmes, there were some addressing self-harm and suicide, some concerned with depression and anxiety, and others addressing eating disorders, behaviour problems and stress. In the other group, those that could be called universal programmes, the focus was usually on general mental health, but some included a focus on coping, the self-concept or self-esteem.

Interventions can also be classified according to the age of the population concerned, for example under 11, 11–15, 11–19 or some combination of these ages. The target groups involved can also be used as a classification. Thus, some studies looked at socially excluded young people, while others were designed for young parents, refugees, those with a disability and so on. Another important classification has to do with the site or location of the intervention. Thus, out of the 345 programmes studied by Harden *et al.*, over 70% of them were designed to take place within an educational setting. However, not all were set in schools, and some took place in community settings, others in the home, whilst a few were channelled through the mass media.

Perhaps most important of all for our purposes is a classification that breaks down the type of intervention that is based in the school setting. Wells, Barlow and Stewart-Brown (2003) divided the interventions they studied into those that could be described as taking a whole school approach, those that were classroom-based, and those that extended beyond the classroom to all or part of the school.

As will be apparent, there is no simple classification that will sweep up all the programmes and interventions relating to the promotion of emotional health and well-being in children and young people. Even within primary prevention activities there are a range of aims and objectives, not to mention the diversity of methods and locations chosen for this type of work. For the present purposes it is important to note that the great majority of evaluated programmes are to be found in the United States, with a small number being found in Australia and Canada. As Edwards says: 'Research in the UK as a whole has been very limited, and most of the studies reported come from the USA' (2003, p. 22).

This leads on to another crucial distinction. The three major reviews referred to here have selected only those interventions which have been subject to rigorous evaluation. It is not surprising therefore that the great majority are to be found in the United States, given the well-known limitations associated with evaluation here in the United Kingdom. In spite of the lack of what might be called rigorous evaluation, there is still a range of activities taking place in the United Kingdom covering all aspects of mental health promotion.

To take some examples, Alexander (2002) reports case studies in five English schools designed to promote good mental health, and the Mental Health Foundation (MHF, 2002) found seven projects in London aiming to develop systems of peer support with young people of secondary school age as a way of promoting positive mental health. Cowie *et al.* (2004) report on the development of a mental health module for use in secondary schools, and note that this was subject to a process of evaluation, with positive results. Other programmes in use in the United Kingdom include circle time, the use of ENABLE, the PATHS programme currently in use in Scotland, and many others. There is no shortage of activity in this field, and it is now time to turn to the question: Do these programmes work?

Mental Health Promotion Programmes – Do They Work?

It will come as no surprise to find that there is no simple answer to the question as to whether programmes designed to enhance emotional health and well-being actually work. There are many obstacles and challenges that get in the way. In the first instance, there is no agreement about what should be the focus of an intervention programme. Some believe it should be designed to enhance skills, such as coping skills, whilst others take the view that good information about mental health is all that is needed. Wells, Barlow and Stewart-Brown (2003) argued that interventions that were entirely skills-based should be excluded from their review, on the grounds that these were not measures of mental health, although they agreed that the relation between the two things was complex. They make a nice point when they say:

It is also important to note from the included studies that many of the components of
positive mental health have not been the subject of interventions in schools. ... None of
the programmes reviewed included amongst its goals improving pupils' ability to enjoy
life, to laugh at themselves and the world, or to develop emotionally or spiritually, all of
which have been suggested as important components of mental health. (Wells, Barlow and
Stewart-Brown, 2003, p. 216)

This point, however, illustrates well the problem of definition. What exactly is mental health, and if we want to promote well-being, what aspects should we focus on? Programmes, as well as evaluation research, can hardly be compared if different definitions and approaches are being used.

Another problem is that even if there is agreement about what positive mental health is, there is still such a wide range of intervention programmes in operation. As we have seen, some are based in the classroom, while others take a whole-school approach. Some argue that programmes should be based in the family, involving the parents, if they are to have any hope of success. No two evaluations really compare like with like, and thus any answers about effectiveness have to be hedged with caution. We must also face the difficulty raised by the fact that much of the research originates from the United States.

Not surprisingly, reviewers have asked the question as to whether findings stemming from research in a very different culture can be considered to be relevant here in the United Kingdom. Furthermore, the type of evaluation may not be the same, with more rigorous methods of evaluation being in use in North America, while 'softer', process evaluation approaches are more likely to be used in the United Kingdom.

Finally, the most difficult problem of all is that the reviews themselves do not necessarily come to similar conclusions. Harden *et al.* (2001) provide the best summary when they say:

Although the evidence base is currently limited, this systematic review has found that
interventions to promote mental health and prevent mental ill-health have been, under a
variety of different circumstances, demonstrated to be effective for a variety of outcomes.
However, many other tested interventions show no or unclear effects, and some even show
harmful effects. Other interventions have yet to be tested in a rigorous way. A clear pic-
ture of what relates to success or failure is therefore currently lacking. (Harden et al.,
2001, p. 125)

They then go on to quote two reviews that come to opposite conclusions. Durlack and Wells (1997) argue that the majority of participants who receive primary prevention programmes will experience positive changes in mental health outcomes, whilst Nicholas and Broadstock (1999) believe that few interventions apart from those aimed at substance abuse and conduct disorders have any measurable effect at all.

One of the key points here has to do with the type of outcome being measured. Interventions can be assessed according to a variety of criteria. On the one hand, it may be considered appropriate to study whether an intervention has an effect on behaviour over a long time period, yet in another study it may simply be a case of finding out whether people feel better after involvement in the programme. Inevitably it is much harder to show the former than the latter effect. This difference explains many of the confusing findings from the large reviews. The more rigorous the criterion, the less likely it will be that positive outcomes can be demonstrated. The great majority of evaluations which look at whether people feel better or not show positive outcomes. In that sense they can be said to work. However, this may not be a sufficient criterion for those promoting or funding the intervention.

In spite of this somewhat disappointing answer, there are some broad conclusions that can be drawn from the reviews. Firstly, it is clear that there is a scarcity of good quality research evaluating the effectiveness of mental health promotion programmes, especially in the United Kingdom. As Harden *et al.* conclude:

> *Despite the lack of good research, this review did identify a small number of rigorous evaluations which have shown that a range of different types of mental health promotion can be effective in changing some outcomes for some groups of young people. What is not yet clear is what the key components of effective interventions are, whether there are any long-term benefits, and to what extent conclusions about effectiveness are generalisable to other populations of young people. (Harden* et al., *2001, p. 144)*

A second critical conclusion is that young people themselves have clear views on the barriers to good mental health. Relatively few programmes take these views into account. Thus, a major finding of the reviews is that the more programme planners are able to involve young people at the earliest stages of designing and implementing mental health promotion, the more likely it is that activity will prove effective.

A third conclusion from the reviews is that the more focus the intervention has, the more likely it is to be effective. Thus, if the intention is to enhance self-esteem, then the programme should be designed with that specific goal in mind. There is no point in designing a general mental health module, and then expecting that self-esteem will be enhanced as a result of the programme.

Finally, the reviewers found that few programmes had developed effective ways to involve socially excluded groups in mental health promotion. While clearly groups of young people such as those looked after by local authorities, refugees and asylum seekers, those in custody and so on should be key target groups for mental health promotion work, there appears to be little evidence available to guide those wishing to work with these groups.

Conclusion

- There are major problems of definition where emotional health and well-being are concerned.
- In relation to mental health promotion, the involvement of young people is critical.
- In mental health promotion there is too often an adult-centric view of emotional health.
- Programmes that provide information only are less effective than those which provide both skills development and information about mental health.
- Mental health promotion programmes are popular with young people, but we do not yet know that they have long-term effects on behaviour.

In this chapter we have considered a range of topics concerning the emotional health and well-being of children and young people. We have seen that, over the last decade or so, there has been a considerable amount of interest shown in this subject, with educationalists, mental health practitioners, and academic researchers debating the issues associated with mental health promotion. In spite of a major research exercise involving dozens and dozens of studies, together with the combined wisdom of at least three meta-analyses in Britain since 2001, there are still no clear-cut answers to many of the questions surrounding mental health promotion for children and young people.

We cannot be sure which are the most effective ways to promote positive mental health, and while there are many different programmes available, we do not know which work best. Nonetheless, there are some very important conclusions that can be drawn from the research and the reviews, all of which have implications for future policy initiatives.

The first point to make, and this will come as no surprise, is that more research is needed. This may sound an odd conclusion, given the number of studies already in the literature. However, many key questions do not appear to have been addressed, particularly in the context of the United Kingdom. The main reviews, such as Harden *et al.* (2001), point out a number of gaps in the research. Most striking of all is that there has been no systematic and rigorous evaluation of any mental health promotion programme in any of the UK countries.

We particularly need research that goes beyond first-level process evaluation (studying the 'feel-good' factor), and looks at longer-term outcomes. There seems little doubt that we could benefit enormously from a planned research initiative, tackling some of the issues we have raised as part of this review. Some questions that would be particularly helpful to investigate include a study on the long-term impact of mental health promotion on school functioning, a comparison between teachers and other professionals as mental health promotion leaders, a study of the effectiveness of peer mentors in the field of mental health, and some properly evaluated work which involves the development of materials suitable for socially excluded groups of young people.

A second major conclusion from all the reviews is that the involvement of young people is a critical factor in the effectiveness of programmes. Where young people have been involved from the beginning in the planning and design of mental health promotion interventions, these are more likely to score well on process evaluation measures, and more likely to have enthusiastic take-up by staff and pupils alike. This can be linked to the point powerfully made by Edwards (2003), when she says that we need to be asking young people what they think are the barriers to their mental health. Studies that have done this find that children, as well as teenagers, are articulate about the things they believe either assist or detract from their mental health, and they often point to material and physical resources just as much as social capital. Programmes designed for mental health promotion need to incorporate ideas such as these into their framework.

This point can also be linked to the finding that there is too often an adult-centric view of what coping consists of for young people. Again a number of reviewers pointed out that not all young people see talking to others as an effective coping strategy. Some, especially young men, may feel that physical activity, or creative activities, may be just as important as a way of expressing emotion. It may be that music, or drama, can offer a medium for the development of self-esteem, for example, or even a means of exploring painful memories or anxieties. Too often, it is argued, adults simply assume that talking is the best way to promote better mental health.

In terms of the programmes themselves, there is an important conclusion to be drawn from the reviews of effectiveness. While we cannot be confident that we understand everything about effectiveness, we do know that programmes which provide information only are less effective than those which combine both skill development and information. It appears from the evaluations that young people are less likely to experience enhanced mental health if the intervention is one whose focus is on information-giving. By the same token, those that focus only on skills also appear to be less effective. Those that combine the two approaches are to be preferred. In addition, we have learnt from the research that the tighter and more directed the programme, the more likely it is that it will show an effect on the designated outcome. The more general the aims and materials of the programme, the more difficult it is to show an effect on an outcome measure.

As has been noted, these conclusions have implications for policy. We need to be realistic and accept that we are not yet at the point where we can say that mental health programmes have long-term effects on behaviour. Neither are we clear about how mental health promotion programmes impact on the whole school, and on its ethos and development. However, we can say that programmes are popular with young people, and that in the great majority of cases there is an impact on knowledge and attitudes. We know a considerable amount about what makes programmes more effective, and we need to build on that knowledge to ensure that these lessons are incorporated into practice. Thus, involving young people, having programmes that include both information and skills development, and ensuring that the goals of any intervention are tightly defined and structured, should all be key components of any future developments.

We know that mental disorder has high costs not only for the individual young person, but also for the school and for the wider community. For this reason our priority has to be to design high quality mental health promotion programmes. It is to be hoped that some of the lessons identified in this chapter could be helpful in moving us closer to this goal.

CASE STUDY 3.1

A Healthy School

In 2005 the UK Government launched the National Healthy Schools Programme. In order to qualify as a healthy school four key themes have to be addressed: physical activity, healthy eating, Personal, Social and Health Education (PSHE), and the emotional health and well-being of pupils.

A secondary school that aspires to healthy school status might, for example, plan for and pay attention to the following:

- leadership and management;
- teaching and learning;
- school culture and environment;
- giving pupils a voice;
- provision of pupil support services;
- staff professional development;
- curriculum planning and resourcing.

Each of these elements contributes to the overall ethos of the school. Thus leadership and management may involve having a clear vision for the school, making sure that this is articulated and known by all, and having senior staff committed to and involved with all the activities necessary to meet the goals of a healthy school.

Teaching and learning will involve support for all pupils, irrespective of their ability level, and may include having innovative approaches to the development of learning skills. The school culture and environment will consider the way pupils are organized into groups, movement around the school, the safety of pupils at all times, codes of conduct and behaviour management, and discipline systems.

Giving pupils a voice requires a genuine commitment to hearing the views of young people, and allowing them to contribute to the development of the school.

The provision of pupil support services should ensure that support is available, and that young people know the routes to finding help when they need it. Staff professional development should ensure that teachers and other staff are provided with training where issues of mental health are concerned, and finally curriculum planning should involve high quality provision for PSHE.

The healthy schools programme can create a value-added dimension to any school. Some of the benefits of a healthy schools programme might include:

- the engagement of the pupils and parents in the process;

- the development of complementary developments in healthy eating and physical exercise;

- schools being more inclusive;

- the raising of awareness of emotional health and well-being, and the provision of a focus for this as a legitimate goal within the school;

- more effective use of specialist services in the curriculum;

- the development of clearer pathways to specialist intervention;

- evidence for Ofsted of the school's contribution to the five outcomes in the Every Child Matters agenda, namely being healthy, staying safe, making a positive contribution, enjoying and achieving, and achieving economic well-being.

Source: Particular thanks to the Highfield School, Letchworth, Hertfordshire, United Kingdom, for providing a model on which this description is based.

CASE STUDY 3.1 QUESTIONS

1. Do you agree with this as a description of a healthy school?
2. Are there other dimensions you would add?
3. Are there other ways you would address the needs of pupils in respect of their emotional health and well-being?
4. What do you think are the barriers to any secondary school becoming a healthy school?
5. There is considerable stigma associated with mental health problems in most school settings. If you were a head teacher, what steps would you take to address this?

Further Reading

Cowie, H., Boardman, C., Dawkins, J. and Jennifer, D. (2004) *Emotional health and well-being: a practical guide for schools*, Paul Chapman Publishing, London.

Dwivedi, K. and Harper, P. (eds) (2004) *Promoting the emotional health and well-being of children and adolescents and preventing their mental ill-health*, Jessica Kingsley Publishers, London.

Goleman, D. (1996) *Emotional intelligence*, Bloomsbury, London.

Weare, K. (2004) *Developing the emotionally literate school*, Paul Chapman Publishing, London.

Discussion Questions

1. Of the terms emotional intelligence, emotional health and well-being, or mental health, which do you prefer, and why?

2. Which do you think is most influential as far as the emotional health of adolescents is concerned: the family, the school or the peer group?

3. Some say that mental ill-health among adolescents is on the increase. From your own observations do you think this is the case?

4. Do you believe that there is a place for the teaching of emotional literacy in school? What are the obstacles and challenges in doing this effectively?

Chapter 4

Eating Disorders, Dieting and Body Image

Susan Faulkner

University of Glamorgan

- Introduction
- What are Eating Disorders?
- Anorexia Nervosa
- Bulimia Nervosa
- Theories of the Aetiology of Eating Disorders
- Obesity
- Treatment of Eating Disorders
- Conclusion

Learning Objectives

After reading this chapter you should:

1 Be aware of the controversies and issues surrounding attempts to define eating disorders.
2 Be able to understand and recognize the main symptoms of anorexia and bulimia.
3 Have some knowledge of the major theoretical approaches to the aetiology of eating disorders.
4 Understand social and cultural approaches to eating disorders.
5 Have learnt about obesity and binge eating.
6 Know that there are different approaches to the treatment of eating disorders.

Introduction

Eating can be both an enjoyable and social activity. Nevertheless, society is becoming increasingly anxious about body weight, exercise and nutrition. Dieting, healthy eating and body image are issues which occupy the thoughts of many adolescent girls, and increasingly, adolescent boys. This is hardly surprising given the media's obsession with the weight and body shape of celebrity role models. Whilst this increase in awareness has probably led to healthier eating habits in many young people, it is also likely to be associated with a high increase in eating disorders, which, for many, are significant causes of physical and psychological suffering.

This chapter focuses on the major eating disorders – anorexia nervosa (AN), bulimia nervosa (BN) and obesity. The aims are to provide an overview of these disorders and the factors that contribute towards their development and progression in young people. In so doing, the main symptoms will be described and discussed, highlighting the major issues and controversies regarding their precise nature and the difficulties associated with identifying and treating them. Case studies will be used to illustrate topics of importance and to demonstrate the true nature of the experience of these types of disorders for adolescent sufferers.

Whilst it is fair to say that the actual causes of eating disorders are extremely complex and not well understood, the major explanations will be reviewed and a range of perspectives, including biological, psychological, psychodynamic, cognitive, family systems and social approaches will be evaluated. Finally, how these approaches relate to different methods of treatment will be reviewed.

What are Eating Disorders?

Anorexia Nervosa

The term anorexia nervosa was first coined in 1873 by William Gull, an English physician who referred to a strange disease involving severe weight loss, refusal to eat, loss of appetite, alertness, amenorrhoea (loss of menstruation) and lethargy. He stated that the condition usually occurred in young women between the ages of 16 and 23. The word anorexia means 'loss of appetite' and Gull suggested that this loss of appetite was due to a psychological condition. Around this time Ernest Lasegue, a French physician, also reported a condition which he referred to as 'anorexie hysterica'. It was really the work of these two physicians that marked the starting point for our understanding of this disorder.

Explanations of eating disorders have changed over time to incorporate many differing views. The influence of a medical model where illness is perceived as a consequence of some underlying physical disease had a significant influence on the way we understand AN. As a consequence of this model we have a set of diagnostic criteria outlining the symptoms of the disease which are used in its assessment and treatment.

An alternative approach to understanding eating disorders is a sociocultural approach which highlights the importance of social and cultural influences. Many people believe that the increase in the numbers of young people suffering from eating disorders is a consequence of media and social pressures on young people to be very slender. Young people are particularly vulnerable to this constant, high level of exposure to extremely thin models portrayed as being beautiful and successful. Magazines and advertisements targeted at adolescents are full of advice on dieting and how to achieve a particular body shape. Pencil thin celebrities cover the pages of magazines and celebrities who gain a few pounds are vilified and often portrayed in unattractive images. For the majority of young people the only way to achieve the desired body image would be to adopt a starvation diet and an unsustainable exercise programme. This may lead to feelings of inadequacy, body image shame and 'yoyo' dieting or restrained eating followed by binge eating and general unhappiness.

Whilst, as stated earlier, the term anorexia implies 'loss of appetite', in most cases the anorexic is in fact very hungry indeed and very interested in food. Frequently sufferers will read cookery books, cook meals for the family and be proud of the fact that, despite their hunger, they do not allow themselves to eat.

The main features of anorexia nervosa are said to be:

- a morbid fear of becoming fat
- significant weight loss
- distorted body image
- cessation of menstruation.

Morbid Fear of becoming Fat

A fundamental feature of this disorder is an 'abnormal' sensitivity about becoming fat; hence it has been referred to as a 'weight phobia'. Sufferers are morbidly fearful of gaining weight or losing control over their eating. This is believed to be the reason for their dramatic reduction in calorie intake. They strictly limit their eating and in particular restrict carbohydrates as in bread, cakes and sweets, as well as fatty foods. Most sufferers are very knowledgeable about the calorific content of foods. It is not uncommon for anorexics to use strategies such as eating small meals very slowly and cutting food up into tiny pieces. Other strategies for weight loss may include excessive exercising; they may spend large amounts of their time jogging, taking strenuous daily workouts or excessively swimming in an almost frenzied effort to 'burn off' calories. Another strategy used by some is self-induced vomiting (the binge/purge subtype) and some resort to laxative abuse which can result in electrolyte imbalances and mineral deficiencies. Although anorexia is less common in boys, its incidence is said to be increasing, while shape appears to be more of an issue than weight. Boys fear being flabby and unfit, or being the wrong build (e.g. Lask and Bryant-Waugh, 2000).

Significant Weight Loss

Diagnosis is based largely upon significant weight loss. Other physical or psychological illnesses as reasons for weight loss need to be eliminated. Body mass index (BMI) is used to measure the degree of emaciation. This is a measure which considers weight to height ratio and there are standard tables for normal, below normal and above normal BMI for males and females of different ages. BMI is calculated by dividing weight (in kilograms) by height squared (BMI = weight (kg)/height^2). A BMI of less than 18 is regarded as a symptom of anorexia.

Distorted Body Image

Many argue that a disturbance in the way in which body weight or shape is experienced is a specific feature of the disorder. There is commonly a denial of their low body weight by young people who perceive their body as being larger, wider or fatter than it actually is.

Although sufferers report this distorted evaluation of their body size and shape, it is not unusual for young people who are not anorexic to overestimate their body size and to express dissatisfaction with their body shape and weight.

Anorexics also sometimes have distorted internal perceptions reporting severe bloating and/or distension after eating small amounts of food. Whether this reported distortion reflects their actual perceptions or whether it is self denial to justify 'not eating' is a further issue.

Cessation of Menstruation

Amenorrhœa is another key feature of this disorder. This symptom can also be problematic as it is not uncommon for anorexia to start during puberty and delay the onset of menses.

CASE STUDY 4.1

A Young Anorexic Woman

I started down the path to anorexia nervosa eight years ago. My mother had a stroke and my father, who is obese, had developed diabetes and was about to have triple bypass surgery. I saw this as my own future and it scared me. I decided to exercise and eat healthily. Although I wasn't dieting, I lost 12 pounds. I thought I was eating plenty, but I now know it wasn't so. Over the next six years, I would periodically lose my appetite and drop a few pounds. Once the weight was gone, I didn't want it back. I felt powerful for being able to lose weight – something most people want but never achieve.

It wasn't until three summers ago, at a particularly low point in my life when I was feeling miserable and out of control, that I made an active decision to see how much weight I could lose. My body was the only area of my life where I felt completely in control. In the midst of enormous fear combined with a desperate attempt to feel good about myself, I turned to food restricting and exercise.

I appeared normal on the outside, but I retreated into my own world. Every thought during every minute of every day revolved around food. Despite nagging hunger, I hardly allowed anything to pass my lips. Instead, I planned around food, dreamed about food and prepared food for others. Eating alone became a necessity so that I could eat exactly what I wanted – how I wanted. I was so debilitated that just standing up or walking up stairs took all my energy. When I sat in chairs, it felt like my bones were being crushed.

If I ever ate a few extra bites, I worried incessantly, only calming down when the scale confirmed that I hadn't gained weight or I had power walked a second time that day. I was so weak that I sprained my ankles easily, but I would rather have poked out my eyeballs than miss a day of exercise. I remember a single moment of regret – I had tried to pick up my new beautiful baby nephew, but I couldn't because I didn't have the arm strength.

CASE STUDY 4.1 QUESTIONS

1. What key features of anorexia can you recognize in this case study?
2. How could you recognize an eating disorder in a young person you know?
3. There is a huge market in advertising, weight loss, diet food, and fitness products. Should any of the blame for increases in eating disorders be placed on these industries?

Bulimia Nervosa

Bulimics have a compulsion to eat large quantities of food over relatively short periods of time. Whilst there are similarities between AN and BN (in fact up to about 40% of anorexics engage in binge eating), many binge eaters do not develop anorexia. Most of those who suffer from bulimia are usually normal to above average weight, and approximately 10% of those who may be classified as being obese engage in bouts of binge eating. Although earlier references to a binge/purge cycle can be found, it was not until 1979 that BN was officially recognized, and since then the incidence of this disorder has increased significantly, exceeding that of anorexia(Fairburn *et al.,* 1999, Fairburn and Brownell 2002). Many people have been found to engage in binge eating. Pyle *et al.* (1986) state that significant numbers of college students reported periodic binges and many had tried vomiting. Those suffering from BN binge frequently, often more than twice a week, and feel that they have lost control over their eating. Bulimics usually acknowledge that they have an eating disorder and, unlike anorexics, are not commonly in denial. This is a feature that distinguishes BN from AN, whilst a feature they frequently have in common is their fascination with food – reading about and preparing food for others.

Binge eating in bulimics is preceded by intense feelings of anxiety and tension. They may have palpitations and begin to perspire. During the binge itself the tension starts to dissipate and they may experience a sense of freedom from the anxieties and worries they have been experiencing. Following a binge, feelings of anxiety and guilt start to build and purging (usually done by vomiting) has the function of 'getting rid' of the food and preventing weight gain and also of removing the feelings of anxiety, panic and guilt.

Frequent Episodes of Binge Eating

Binge eating is a central core of this disorder and involves eating very large amounts of food in a limited period of time. What constitutes a binge can, of course, vary significantly, but some may consume 30 times the amount of food normally eaten in one day. Most will gulp down large amounts of food, sometimes stuffing food frantically into their mouths. Some select food that will be easy to swallow (and easy to regurgitate afterwards). Sometimes they will eat foods that they do not allow themselves at other times such as cream cakes and biscuits.

The main features of bulimia nervosa are:

- frequent episodes of binge eating
- lack of control over eating
- regular purges
- concern about body shape and weight.

Lack of Control Over Eating

The core feature is the loss of control over eating. The binge is described by some as 'a re-lease' or 'abandonment', often following days of strict control and restricted eating. Following a binge, sufferers will feel disgusted with themselves and often vow not to repeat the cycle. However, the lack of control is demonstrated not only in the frenzied binge episode but also in the frequent and ongoing repetitions of the binge/purge cycle.

Regular Purges/Concern about Body Shape and Weight

The purpose of these is to prevent weight gain. As with anorexics, bulimics place great emphasis on body weight and shape, such that it becomes overvalued and drives their desperate efforts to prevent weight gain.

CASE STUDY 4.2

The Experience of Bulimia

"You've ruined everything. You gave in. You're weak", I whispered fiercely. The eyes in the mirror filled with tears. I looked away from her, allowing her the space to cry. My eyes fell on the red door to the handicapped stall of the stark bathroom. I walked slowly toward it, wiping my eyes on my sleeve. I took a fateful step into that stall, and tumbled down the rabbit hole. I shut the door and slid the lock into place, oblivious to the metamorphosis that had just occurred. I looked cautiously at the white porcelain toilet with its silver handle and pushed the sleeves of my brown and cream striped shirt up to my elbows. Lifting the seat, I took a deep breath. I opened my mouth as wide as I could and slid my right index finger down my throat.

I gagged and choked, watching the yet undigested pizza and breadsticks splash into the water. Listening to the echo of my retching, I gasped for breath. The mixture of bile and pizza sauce stung my tongue, and my eyes began to water. The acrid smell of vomit pervaded my nostrils, but I pushed my finger back down my throat as if in a dream.

The door creaked. I froze, terrified that I would be caught. Spinning around so my feet faced the right way, I carefully suspended my right hand above the toilet in order to allow the saliva and food particles to drip into the disgusting pool instead of on the floor. My heart pounded as I listened to the intruder enter the stall next to mine. I listened, petrified, as she flushed the toilet and unlocked the door. I heard the water in the sink begin to run, the hand dryer start, and finally the creak of the door signalling her exit. I turned around and thrust my finger back into my epiglottis. My fingernails scratched my throat as I forced the gagging, and the stomach acid was bitter in the back of my mouth. I watched as the last of my gluttonous dinner joined the revolting mixture already present.

When I could no longer expel anything, I decided I'd done all I could do. I looked at the undigested food that filled the bowl and was struck by an intense feeling of pleasure. Wiping the grotesque remains of mucus and saliva off my right hand and forearm, I felt clean. Empty. I had regained control.

Worse than the physical pain, however, was the emotional and mental anguish. I could not concentrate since I thought incessantly of food. During class, instead of listening to lectures or taking notes, I thought about what I had eaten that day, when I would eat again, what I would eat, and whether I would have the opportunity to throw up. I baked nightly and brought the treats to school the next day, distributing them among my friends. I watched others eat, vicariously savouring each bite. I read cookbooks and hoarded recipes. I never looked in the mirror without thinking, "fat". I saw so much lard on my 5'2" frame that I was genuinely *shocked when people said I was getting too thin. At the beginning of the disease, I weighed myself each morning, then each morning and each night, then several times in between, until I literally weighed myself a half dozen to a dozen times a day. I thought of nothing but how I needed to be thinner. Eating unsafe foods sent me flying to the nearest bathroom, slamming the door and shoving all the fingers of my right hand down my scratched and aching throat.*

CASE STUDY 4.2 QUESTIONS

1. What features of BN do you recognize in this case study?
2. There is much evidence of the pressures on young women to be thin or have a particular body shape. What do you think may be the pressures on young men?
3. How would you explain the fact that all young women in western society are exposed to cultural images of thinness but only a minority develop an eating disorder?

Comparisons between Anorexics and Bulimics

The underlying psychopathology common to anorexia and bulimia nervosa is the overwhelming fear of weight gain. To prevent weight gain they engage in a range of behaviours including extremes of dieting, food avoidance, fasting, excessive exercise, laxative abuse, binge eating and/or vomiting.

Bulimics are more likely to engage in antisocial behaviour which may include substance abuse or promiscuity. Anorexics tend to be more conformist and obsessional than bulimics who are generally more impulsive and emotionally unstable.

Bulimics are more trusting of people who may help them and are more open about the abnormality of their behaviour whereas anorexics are more likely to be in denial and mistrusting of others, particularly therapists and family. Anorexics have greater self control and are emotionally over-controlled with difficulty expressing emotions and feelings.

For details regarding the way AN and BN are classified and diagnosed you can refer to either *the Diagnostic and statistical manual of mental disorders*, volume IV (DSM-IV) from the American Psychiatric Association (APA) or *The (ICD-10) classification of mental and behavioural disorders* from the World Health Organization (WHO). Diagnostic criteria are constantly being revised.

The disorders identified include anorexia nervosa (restricting type and purging type), bulimia nervosa (purging and non-purging type) and other types of eating disorder less well specified.

Who Suffers from these Eating Disorders?

The Eating Disorders Association states that 60000 people in the United Kingdom are diagnosed with an eating disorder but that the real figure for those suffering from an eating disorder is in the region of 1.1 million. The underestimation may be because those with eating disorders are reluctant to acknowledge the fact and also because of delays in recognition of the disorder and diagnosis. Howlett *et al.* (1995) state that about 1 in 250 females and

1 in 2000 males experience anorexia, usually in adolescence and about five times this number suffer from bulimia.

Eating disorders are responsible for a higher number of deaths than any other psychiatric disorder (Palmer, 1996), yet, whilst more common than anorexia, BN is not generally as physically dangerous. Bulimia, however, is associated with the excessive use of laxatives and self-induced vomiting which can have serious health consequences such as rupture of the oesophagus, mineral deficiency and dehydration. Bulimia is also associated with major depression and suicide in adolescents. Complications of anorexia include heart, kidney, gastrointestinal and fertility problems.

Theories of the Aetiology of Eating Disorders

Causes of eating disorders are still disputed and many controversies surround the identification of ætiological factors. Lask and Bryant-Waugh suggest that 'searching for a single cause for eating disorders is a fruitless task' (2000, p. 63). They are more likely to be multi-determined involving the interaction of a range of factors including genetic, physiological, neurochemical, personality, familial, psychological and sociocultural. Garner and Garfinkel (1980) state that a range of factors is associated with the development of eating disorders, and distinguish between those which predispose an individual to develop an eating disorder (preconditions); other factors which precipitate the onset of the disorder (triggers); and a further set of factors which perpetuate the disorder (maintenance). This model provides a bio-psychosocial perspective on how eating disorders may be influenced by the interaction of biological, psychological and sociocultural factors, and research from these perspectives is reviewed below.

Biological Perspectives

These can be further subdivided into research on genetic predisposition, structural damage and neurochemical theories.

There is evidence that eating disorders 'run in families' (there is a greater incidence of eating disorders in first degree relatives of those with these disorders than in the general population, Strober, 2000). Studies of twins have found that the concordance rate (i.e. where both twins develop the disorder) for monozygotic twins is in the region of 55% while for dizygotic twins it was nearer 5%, and for bulimia 35% and 30% respectively (Treasure and Holland, 1995). This suggests a genetic component, in particular for anorexia and to a lesser degree bulimia. Care in interpreting these figures should be taken, however, because:

- there seems to be a wide variation in studies regarding the estimates for a genetic contribution;
- usually the twins in these studies have a shared or common environment as well as shared genes;
- usually these studies are conducted on those attending clinics for treatment and do not therefore include those who suffer from the disorder but have not had a formal diagnosis. Furthermore, the actual numbers in many of the studies are relatively small.

Despite these reservations, Lask and Bryant-Waugh (2000) suggest that genes may be an important predisposing factor and whilst there is no clear agreement regarding the ways in which eating disorders may be inherited, there is agreement that genetic factors do play a role. One argument is that people inherit personality traits such as emotional instability, obsessionality or perfectionism (Klump and Gobrogge, 2005).

Other biological research focuses on systems regulating appetite, hunger, satiety and the initiation and cessation of eating. A disorder of the endocrine system affecting the hypothalamic-pituitary-gonadal axis has been suggested, although exactly what the disorder is remains unclear. Disregulation in any of the neurochemicals involved in this system, including noradrenaline, serotonin and dopamine have also been suggested. So, for example, low levels of serotonin activity have been associated with impulsivity and this could be related to symptoms of bulimia, whereas high levels may lead to a cluster of symptoms including rigidity, anxiety, obsessiveness, all of which are characteristic personality traits associated with anorexia. The problem with most of the findings in relation to endocrine changes is that these may be a consequence, rather than a cause, of weight loss and return to normal when weight is regained.

Psychodynamic Approaches

Early psychodynamic perspectives were based around the theme of 'oral conflict' and the view that children are unable to separate themselves from their mothers and become especially frightened as adolescence approaches, because they have to confront independence, separation from parents and sexual maturity. Anorexia is seen as a way of avoiding this. Crisp (1980) defines anorexia as 'a phobic avoidance of puberty or growing up'. Other psychodynamic theorists such as Bruch, (1985), Lawrence (1989) and Orbach (1986) offer a slightly different perspective.

Bruch (1985) suggests that mothers of anorexics are overanxious and try to anticipate their child's every need. Her response may be inappropriate: feeding the child at times of anxiety rather than hunger, and comforting when they are tired rather than when they are anxious. This leads to confusion regarding their need for food and their emotional needs as the mother constantly defines what the child's needs should be. This produces problems in the child's autonomy and emotional well-being and a failure to develop a sense of independence. Furthermore, this results in compliance, feelings of helplessness, being controlled from outside and unable to challenge others. In order to overcome these feelings they achieve extreme self-control over their eating and body size. Some are 'successful' and become anorexic whereas others are less 'successful' and develop the binge/purge eating pattern. Binging symbolizes the desire to be close to the mother and purging reflects the desire to reject her. This may explain why bulimics binge when they have feelings of anger, guilt and anxiety; the experience of these emotions becomes confused with the need to eat. Further support for Bruch's perspective comes from the common findings that anorexics tend to seek the approval of others, are high on conformity and have an external locus of control. (e.g. Lask and Bryant-Waugh, 2000; Tchanturia et al., 2004).

Lawrence (1989) suggests that symptoms of eating disorders develop as a way of expressing distress and unhappiness. Young people express their distress, which cannot be put into words, through their bodies, which become both a focus of anxiety as well as a source of possible control. Only treating the symptoms of the eating disorder without understanding the emotions behind it will not be effective. Orbach (1986) states that food symbolizes caring, nurturing and meeting basic needs: physical and emotional needs are not entirely separate. We cuddle and feed babies providing nourishment, love and security. Later we distinguish between the physical need for food and our emotional needs although we still sometimes use food for emotional purposes.

Orbach emphasizes the conflict inherent in Western culture whereby women (in their role as mothers and wives) are expected to provide food for the family and yet deny their own needs in order to maintain a particular body size which conforms to Western standards of attractiveness.

Psychodynamic perspectives can provide some important insights into eating disorders. However, it is an approach which is difficult to test or verify. The focus on unconscious desires requires interpretation and is therefore based on the subjective view of the specific therapist. The next case study highlights some of the underlying feelings and emotions of a young bulimic person.

CASE STUDY 4.3

How It Feels

Eating disorders are diseases of silence. We are all silently screaming for something: attention, love, help, escape or forgiveness. Although we might be looking to fill different voids, we never ask for the things we need. We feel unworthy, that for some reason we don't deserve them. So, we play the game of guess what I need from you. Your inability to guess just feeds our feelings of worthlessness. When you finally realize there is a problem, it is much too late. We will now fight, lie, and cheat to hold on to the one thing that has given us support. You see the symptoms, weight loss, weight gain, or depression. You watch us starve, eat, purge, and isolate. You tell us to eat or not eat, to sleep or to get up and do something, you can't understand why we can't just get better.

We will push you away. We will make you angry with us. We will tell you we don't need you and to leave us alone. We will throw temper tantrums and even throw food. We will close up and lock you out. We will blow off important appointments. We will do the things we've been told we can't, exercise, chew gum, drink Diet Coke…we will push every limit. We do not do these things to hurt you; we are just scared and feel threatened. You want us to give up something we can't imagine living without.

CASE STUDY 4.3 QUESTIONS

1. Should we consider a preoccupation with losing weight and body shape an indication of a psychological problem (i.e. a cognitive distortion or an obsession) or should it be considered normal, given its very high incidence?
2. How do we make the distinction between normality and abnormality?

Family Systems Approaches

As well as research focusing on the child's development and relationship to their mother there is research including the child's role within the family and other family members. This view suggests that there are particular features of certain families which predispose young people to the development of anorexia. Researchers from this perspective include Palazolli (1974) and Minuchin *et al.* (1978) who argue that the family can be viewed as a 'system' where each member of the family may influence others and in return be influenced by others. This view does not necessarily see the family as the cause of the disorder but emphasizes the family as the context within which eating disorders can develop. The characteristics of families with a person suffering from an eating disorder are listed below and it is suggested that the family context creates and maintains the symptoms of the illness. More recent findings by Bryant-Waugh and Lask (1995), however, suggest that the possible conflict within the family may be a consequence of the anorexia rather than a cause of it, and that these features are not unique to families with an anorexic member but to any family in which someone has some form of psychosomatic problem.

Palazolli emphasizes the following characteristics:

- lack of conflict resolution
- marital disillusionment
- self-sacrifice
- covert coalitions.

Minuchin emphasizes the following characteristics:

- enmeshment
- over-protectiveness
- rigidity
- avoidance of conflict.

Cognitive Approaches

Cognitive approaches suggest that 'distorted thoughts' about body shape and weight underpin the clinical features of eating disorders in young people. Garner and Bemis (1982, 1985) proposed a 'Cognitive Behavioural Model,' based on Beck's cognitive model of depression, which describes a set of dysfunctional cognitions motivating their behaviour. Thoughts such as 'If I eat one piece of chocolate I will feel bloated and distended' or 'If I am thin I will be happy and popular' characterize and dominate their thinking. These thought patterns become entrenched as their behaviour is reinforced through their success in exercising control over their weight. There is often initial social reinforcement for losing weight, and as the weight loss progresses more attention is received from family and friends who are concerned about the weight loss – which is additionally reinforcing.

A modification of this cognitive approach was developed by Fairburn, Shafran and Cooper (1999) who suggest that the central feature of eating disorders is the extreme need to control eating. This develops out of a more general need for self-control which is related to the characteristics of perfectionism, lack of control and low self-esteem. Controlling food intake is experienced as reinforcing in three ways:

- Control over eating enhances the sense of being in control and feelings of self-worth.
- Success leads to starvation and the physiological and psychological changes may themselves promote further dietary restriction. This goes along with a preoccupation with food and even more importance is centred on the control of eating.

- In a society where thinness is admired and fatness stigmatized, judging one's self-worth in terms of shape and weight is reinforced. Weight gain or even the absence of weight loss is seen as evidence of poor control which intensifies efforts to restrict eating.

As weight starts to drop, it is necessary to eat less and less to achieve further weight loss, and this can be enhanced by using additional methods of weight control such as excessive exercising, self-induced vomiting and laxative misuse which may also become self-perpetuating. In bulimia, vomiting and laxative abuse may lead to loss of control which sets up the vicious cycle of eating and purging.

The major practical advantage of this model is that it can inform programmes of treatment. Furthermore, there is evidence which supports the notion of disordered thinking patterns in those with eating disorders (e.g. Fairburn, Cooper and Shafran, 2003). The main drawback is the fact that the model is better at explaining the maintenance of eating disorders than finding actual causes. Questions regarding the causal nature of faulty thinking have been raised: did the cognitive distortions develop after the onset of eating disorders or was the eating disorder caused by the faulty attitudes?

Social and Cultural Approaches

Socio-cultural models of eating disorders emphasize the social context in which these eating disorders develop and focus largely on the various conflicts which young women find themselves having to negotiate. These conflicts may be associated with gender roles, issues of control and vulnerability, as well as identity issues, and they are expressed via the young person's control over their eating and body size.

Although the incidence of eating disorders is rising in young men, as they are increasingly concerned with body image, these disorders are still much more prevalent in young women. This may be associated with the role of young women in Western society. During puberty – when eating disorders are most likely to develop – boys produce testosterone which promotes muscular development. Boys' growth spurt involves eating more and developing muscle mass – the proportion of fat in their body composition is largely unchanged. In girls however, there is no similar increase in muscle mass. After puberty, young girls usually eat about the same as before but the proportion of body fat naturally increases. Young women might be expected to develop a more rounded body with a higher proportion of body fat. In previous generations and in other societies this rounded feminine form was appreciated as symbolic of beauty. In modern, Western society the biology of young women is in conflict with what society deems appropriate and attractive. Extremely slender young women are portrayed as more beautiful and more successful.

The ideal female body as portrayed in the media has become progressively thinner since the 1960s, which culminated in the 1980s and 1990s where the emaciated look of catwalk models such as Kate Moss were being promoted. Along with this there has been a massive increase in advertisements and articles on weight and dieting in women's magazines. Direct exposure to images of thin and attractive women has been found to increase the incidence of body dissatisfaction in adolescent girls (Shucksmith and Hendry, 1998; Durkin and Paxton 2002). Heinberg, Thompson and Stormer (1995) found that the internalization of societal pressures to be thin were an important aspect of body dissatisfaction and eating disturbance.

Culture of Thinness

By the 1980s, thinness, in Western societies, had come to represent success and beauty and being 'fat' or overweight was stigmatized. This could be observed even in children as young as 6 –9 years of age (Hill, Oliver and Rogers (1992). The pursuit of thinness has become almost a moral imperative and young women experience huge pressure to conform to a particular body shape. In a study by Nichter and Nichter (1991), adolescent girls stated that the ideal girl would be 5 ft 7 in., 100 lb in weight, with long blonde hair and blue eyes – a totally unrealistic image!

In order to achieve such an impossible shape, women are not only resorting to unhealthy diets but also to cosmetic surgery. In fact, cosmetic surgery has become one of the fastest growing medical specialities with more young women resorting to 'the knife' as a means of controlling their body shape. What was unattainable by way of extreme food restriction is now becoming attainable by means of surgical procedures such as breast implants and liposuction. Unfortunately, young women who undergo these procedures often continue to be dissatisfied with aspects of their body shape or size and return for further surgical interventions in an endless, and impossible, quest for a particular body shape which they think will make them happy and successful (Wolf, 1991). Although body image dissatisfaction is a widespread phenomenon amongst young women, it has been found that women with anorexia and bulimia are significantly more dissatisfied with their body size and shape than others (Cash and Deagle, 1997).

Feminist perspectives suggest that the association between eating disorders and cultural pressures and conflicts is important for identity development in young girls who cope with an insecure sense of self by adhering to the 'feminine ideal'. Young women may be encouraged to assess themselves, not for who they are or what they do, how clever or creative they are, but rather by how they look. Conflict exists between their desire for success and beauty and between desire for achievement and society's barriers to achievement for young women. The social context reinforces submissiveness and concerns about physical attractiveness, and mitigates against the development of independence and assertiveness.

Obesity

As well as its association with bulimia, binge eating is also frequently associated with obesity and unstable weight (Fairburn *et al.*, 1998). Furthermore, longitudinal studies investigating factors associated with the onset of obesity in adolescence have found strong evidence of an association between dieting and the subsequent onset of obesity and other eating disorders (e.g. Patton *et al.*, 1999). A study by Neumark-Sztainer *et al.* (2006) followed a diverse population of male and female adolescents over a five-year period and found that young people are concerned with their weight and body image, and yet, despite (or as a consequence of) their attempts at dieting and weight control increasing numbers became overweight and obese.

Like other eating disorders, rates of obesity are said to be increasing hugely. According to the Economic and Social Research Council (ESRC), rates of obesity in the United Kingdom have quadrupled in the last 25 years. In 2002, 22% of men and 24% of women were classified as clinically obese (43% of men and 34% of women were overweight). The World Health Organization (WHO) report that obesity rates have increased in many European countries since the 1980s and they predict that at these rates an estimated 150 million adults will be obese by 2010. Figures for children and adolescents given by the Office for National Statistics in 2000 were that 27% of girls and 20% of boys aged 2 to 19 years were overweight. In the same year, 7% of girls and 5% of boys were obese. They suggest that there is not much evidence for there being a significant increase in the quantity of food eaten during the last 10 years, but there is evidence of a decrease in the amount of physical activity taken.

Why do People become Overweight and Obese?

Like other eating disorders discussed earlier there is no simple explanation for why young people become obese but rather a complex interaction of a number of different factors. We have already considered the role of dieting and weight control in adolescence and how that increases the likelihood of later weight and eating problems. Other theories are based on physiological factors including genetic influences on vulnerability to weight gain, psychological and social factors, as well as nutritional issues and energy expenditure.

Genetic Factors

Like anorexia, obesity and being overweight runs in families and the likelihood of being overweight increases significantly if you have an obese parent. It is estimated that having two obese parents results in a 70–80% chance of being obese whereas the chances that children of thin parents will become overweight are much smaller – about 10% (Garn et al., 1981). To untangle environmental from genetic influences we may consider the weight of identical twins reared apart (i.e. identical genes but different environments) or compare the weight of adopted children with both their biological and adoptive parents. This research suggests that genetic factors do play an important role (a detailed review can be found in Kopelman, 1999). As with all genetic factors, however, there is never 100% concordance between genetically identical twins, suggesting that environmental factors need to be considered as well. Furthermore, how the genetic predisposition works is still unclear, though the influence of genetic predisposition on metabolic rate, the number of fat cells and hunger drive has been considered.

Metabolic Rate

Low metabolic rate is commonly cited as a reason for being overweight. However, evidence suggests that overweight people tend to have higher metabolic rates than thinner people, that is, they expend more energy for a given activity due to their increased size (Prentice et al., 1989). Environmental factors can influence metabolic rate; physical exercise increases metabolic rate both during the activity and for a period following the activity.

Fat Cell Theory

Fat cells allow us to store fat in periods of energy surplus and to mobilize energy when it is required. Overweight young people may have larger and sometimes more fat cells than those of average weight. It was believed that the number of fat cells was determined by genetic factors and early infancy. However, we now understand that the more we eat the larger our fat cells become and when they reach a certain size more fat cells develop. This happens over the lifespan and the greater the number of fat cells, the easier it becomes to store more energy in the form of fat.

> As the Association for the Study of Obesity (2006) points out, 'genes can only exert their effect by increasing energy intake or decreasing energy expenditure, for example through a genetically determined preference for high fat foods or a sedentary lifestyle. The rapid increase in the prevalence of obesity over the last 50 years (a very short period of evolution), suggests that obesity is more strongly determined by environmental influences since the gene pool has remained essentially constant.' (www.aso.org.uk)

Energy Input vs. Energy Expenditure

Clearly, the reason why people gain weight is the difference between energy intake and energy output. We gain weight when the amount we eat (calorie intake) exceeds the amount of exercise we take (energy output). A loss of 0.5 kg of body fat needs an energy output of 3500 calories, and a reduction in output of 3500 calories results in a weight gain of 0.5 kg. It is important, therefore, to consider not only what we eat but also how much exercise we take.

Physical Activity

The question of whether increases in obesity are a consequence of an increase in calorie consumption or a decrease in energy expenditure has been hotly debated. It seems that there has been a reduction in average energy expenditure over the last 50 years. The estimated reduction of 300–600 kcals/day per capita could have a significant impact on weight gain (www.dh.gov.uk/publications). A study by Prentice and Jebb (1995) considered increases in car use and television viewing from 1950 to 1990, concluding that the resulting lower levels of activity are making an important contribution to increased obesity. However, they do not address the 'chicken and egg' question – does low activity lead to obesity, or does obesity reduce the likelihood of physical activity? A number of prospective studies have shown that increases in physical activity reduce the probability of substantial weight gain and vice versa (Williamson *et al.*, 1993).

CASE STUDY 4.4

Compulsive Eating

I have been struggling with my overeating habits for the past five years. I have just recently entered counselling to discuss this disorder. Even now as I try to remember how it all started, I cannot. It was like it had happened overnight. Before I knew it, I was eating non-stop, numb to the fact that I would usually consume enough calories and fat for three or four people just in one day. I sit blankly, cramming food in my mouth when I am bored, sad, angry, or when I want to celebrate. It's like every emotion that I have has to do with eating. My weight has only gone up. Sometimes when I think about how much I've eaten, I vow to eat healthier. That doesn't last long; before I know it, I am overeating 'healthy' foods as well. Calories are calories and if you eat too many of them, you get fat. I have a very poor body image, and very low self-esteem.

CASE STUDY 4.4 QUESTIONS

1. Can you identify any similarities between those who develop bulimia and those who develop obesity?
2. Are teenagers' efforts to lose weight associated with gaining weight? How might you explain this?

Psychological Approaches

Psychological factors may also contribute to our understanding of why young people overeat. It has been suggested that overweight people eat for different reasons and that they are more susceptible to environmental cues such as the availability of food or appetizing smells. It is argued that average weight people are more in tune with internal cues of hunger, that is, they eat when they are hungry and they stop eating when they are full, whereas those who are overweight are less responsive to (or less governed by) these internal cues (Schachter and Rodin, 1974; Ogden and Wardle, 1990).

Another psychological explanation is similar to that described earlier in relation to anorexia and bulimia nervosa: overweight people are more inclined to overeat when bored or depressed or alternatively may substitute food and eating for emotional emptiness (Bruch, 1974). A longitudinal study by Richardson et al. (2003) found that depression in adolescent females significantly increased the chances of obesity in young adulthood.

Treatment of Eating Disorders

- Early recognition and help gives a much better chance for a full recovery.
- Treatment needs to address the psychological issues as well as food and eating.

(Eating Disorders Association, 2006)

Most of the different methods of treatment have evolved from the perspectives outlined above such as psychodynamic therapy, biological therapies (usually drugs), cognitive therapy and family therapy. There is much controversy regarding the effectiveness of treatment and, indeed, there is insufficient evidence regarding long-term efficacy. Different approaches may be more suitable for different people. For example, family therapy is reported as having a high degree of success where all family members meet with the therapist on a regular basis for a period of many months. This commitment is difficult to achieve. Furthermore, it usually means that the sufferer is still living with the family and is therefore likely to be under the age of 18 years. Therapy is more likely to be successful the earlier it starts, that is, the less time the person has suffered from the disorder. Is family therapy successful due to its distinctive method or is it due to the fact that this method is used mainly on younger patients, who have had the illness for a short period of time?

Psychotherapy

In psychotherapy, the therapist attempts to resolve the unconscious conflicts which give rise to the symptoms of the eating disorder. The therapy adopts a long-term approach and depends upon a trusting relationship between therapist and client. There is a large element of subjective interpretation, and the question is whether it works simply as a form of counselling, whereby the client has time to talk about personal difficulties on a one-to-one basis, or whether it is actually the identification of unresolved conflict which is at the root of the treatment's success.

Cognitive Behaviour Therapy

Cognitive behaviour therapy represents a more structured approach, focusing mainly on the thought processes and behaviour of the sufferer. The therapy is targeted at changing the distorted thought patterns of sufferers and involves regular sessions over a set period of about 12 to 15 weeks. A level of trust between the patient and practitioner is crucial, and its effect is dependent upon the patient's ability to articulate attitudes and anxieties. Cognitive therapy is probably one of the best documented approaches to treatment.

Conclusion

There is now a greater knowledge of the benefits of healthy diet and exercise and a greater awareness of eating disorders than ever before. A number of different theories have been developed to help explain the onset and progression of eating disorders. However, their precise cause(s) has yet to be established, and while different practitioners favour one approach over another, we may need to cross the boundaries of biological, cognitive, psychodynamic, social, cultural and family systems approaches to gain a better understanding. Other researchers stress a multi-factorial, systemic approach and focus on the distinction between predisposing, precipitating and perpetuating factors and processes.

Finally, in spite of all the issues we have discussed above, we should emphasize that the majority of young people do *not* develop eating disorders. Furthermore, as a society we are becoming increasingly aware of the dangers of nutritional problems, which can result in individuals becoming unhealthily over- or underweight, and awareness is the first step to intervention and prevention. Furthermore, as practitioners, we should focus on teaching young people the joys of *healthy* eating, of its social functions, and of acquiring an appreciation for the smell and sight of well-prepared meals. In other words, developing an eating culture where food is associated with fun, not guilt, and where young people truly understand the parameters of healthy eating for enjoyable living.

Assess Your Body Image Esteem

This 12-item scale assesses a person's self-evaluative thoughts and feelings in relation to their physical appearance. The range of scores is 1 to 96 – high scores indicate high levels of body image esteem.

1. I think I have a physically attractive body.

Definitely false	False	Mostly false	More false than true	More true than false	Mostly true	True	Definitely true
1	2	3	4	5	6	7	8

2. I don't think I am as attractive as many other people.

Definitely false	False	Mostly false	More false than true	More true than false	Mostly true	True	Definitely true
1	2	3	4	5	6	7	8

3. I think I have a good body build.

Definitely false	False	Mostly false	More false than true	More true than false	Mostly true	True	Definitely true
1	2	3	4	5	6	7	8

4. I am happy with my body.

Definitely false	False	Mostly false	More false than true	More true than false	Mostly true	True	Definitely true
1	2	3	4	5	6	7	8

5. There are lots of things about my body I would like to change.

Definitely false	False	Mostly false	More false than true	More true than false	Mostly true	True	Definitely true
1	2	3	4	5	6	7	8

6. I am not at all happy about my body build.

Definitely false	False	Mostly false	More false than true	More true than false	Mostly true	True	Definitely true
1	2	3	4	5	6	7	8

7. Lots of other people are more attractive than I am.

Definitely false	False	Mostly false	More false than true	More true than false	Mostly true	True	Definitely true
1	2	3	4	5	6	7	8

8. I wish I was more physically attractive.

Definitely false	False	Mostly false	More false than true	More true than false	Mostly true	True	Definitely true
1	2	3	4	5	6	7	8

9. I don't like my body build.

Definitely false	False	Mostly false	More false than true	More true than false	Mostly true	True	Definitely true
1	2	3	4	5	6	7	8

10. I am satisfied with my body shape.

Definitely false	False	Mostly false	More false than true	More true than false	Mostly true	True	Definitely true
1	2	3	4	5	6	7	8

11. I am very accepting of my body shape.

Definitely false	False	Mostly false	More false than true	More true than false	Mostly true	True	Definitely true
1	2	3	4	5	6	7	8

12. I'm not at all happy about my physical appearance.

Definitely false	False	Mostly false	More false than true	More true than false	Mostly true	True	Definitely true
1	2	3	4	5	6	7	8

Reprinted from Personality and Individual Differences, 7/38, Markham, A. Thompson, T., Bowling, A. (2005), "Determinants of Body Shame", with permission from Elsevier

Further Reading

Fairburn, C. G. and Brownell, K. D. (eds) (2002) *Eating disorders and obesity: a comprehensive handbook*, 2nd edn, The Guilford Press, New York.

Lask, B. and Bryant-Waugh, R. (eds) (2000) *Anorexia Nervosa and related eating disorders in childhood and adolescence*, Psychology Press, Hove.

Ogden, J. (2003) *The psychology of eating from healthy to disordered behaviour*, Blackwell Publishing, Oxford.

Web Sites

www.edauk.com – Eating Disorders Association, UK

http://www.kidzworld.com/site/p979.htm

http://www.teenoutreach.com/Online_Help/health/eating_disorders/anorexia.htm

http://www.something-fishy.org/ – see link to helping loved ones, what you can do.

http://www.anorexiabulimiacare.co.uk/road_to_recovery.html – for help.

www.statistics.gov.uk for a range of UK statistics on obesity and eating disorders.

http://europa.eu.int/comm/health/ph_determinants/life_style/nutrition/documents/iotf_en.pdf for European figures on obesity and overweight status.

http://www.bbc.co.uk/health/healthy_living/your_weight/bmiimperial_index.shtml
– helps to calculate BMI.

http://www.statistics.gov.uk/CCI/nugget.asp?ID5718&Pos5&ColRank52&Rank5448
– provides figures for obesity and overweight status in children and adolescents.

Discussion Questions

1. Research shows that body image esteem deteriorates around puberty, especially for girls. What are the reasons for this, and what can be done about it?

2. What are the strengths and weaknesses of the medical model in helping us to understand eating disorders?

3. Adolescence appears to be a time when eating disorders are most common. Why should this be so?

4. In your view, what role does the family play in determining attitudes and behaviour relating to food?

5. How close do you think the link is in Western societies between wealth and a consumer culture with eating disorders?

Chapter 5

Sexual Health

Lester Coleman

Trust for the Study of Adolescence, Brighton

- ■ Introduction
- ■ Defining Sexual Health and Establishing the Level of Sexual Health among Adolescents
- ■ What Sexual Behaviours Determine an Adolescent's Sexual Health, and How are these Changing?
- ■ How can we Explain Adolescent Sexual Behaviours?
- ■ Current Policy and Practice in Promoting Adolescent Sexual Health
- ■ Conclusion

Learning Objectives

After reading this chapter you should:

1 Be able to define the term 'sexual health'.

2 Have the knowledge to describe the level of sexual health among adolescents by looking at sexual health indicators (such as rates of sexually transmitted infections).

3 Understand why sexual health is an important feature of adolescent health.

4 Be aware of what behaviours are significant in determining an adolescent's sexual health (e.g. condom use).

5 Appreciate the array of factors which underpin these behaviours, with a view to understanding how best to intervene and promote better sexual health.

6 Appreciate current policy and practice efforts in promoting levels of sexual health among adolescents.

7 Understand where the current evidence base is now, and what gaps there are in our understanding of adolescent sexual health.

Introduction

The sexual health of adolescents has been attracting much attention in recent years. To illustrate, recent headlines plastered on the front page of *The Sun* (13 September 2004) read 'TEEN SEX TIMEBOMB'. Although such headlines may be somewhat alarmist, this chapter will reveal how adolescent sexual health is indeed an area of extreme public concern, interest and ongoing debate.

It is fair to state that the topic of sexual health, in particular that of young people, has become one of the major public health issues dominating the political agenda. From the early 1990s up to the present day, huge investments have been ploughed into curtailing rising teenage pregnancy rates and sexually transmitted infections, alongside providing National Health Service (NHS) and state-funded support for those in need. Before this chapter embarks on detailing the issues connected to adolescent sexual health, it is recommended that the reader contemplates how they feel sexuality and sexual health of young people may have changed in their own lifetimes. In doing this myself, a number of issues spring to mind about the nature of adolescent sexual health for today's young people. The issues at the forefront of my thinking include: (a) The sexual culture of the United Kingdom – explicit portrayals of sex and sexuality in the media although traditionally a lack of discussion and openness within the family setting; (b) how, within half a century, the traditions and expectations of sexual attitudes and behaviours among young people have changed; and (c) the contrasting sexual cultures of some of our European neighbours (e.g. the Netherlands) where some of the issues that will be discussed in the forthcoming chapter are of less relevance.

There will be two main themes running concurrently throughout this chapter. Firstly, the chapter will present information drawn from recent research, practice and policy. Secondly, this information will be complemented by points worthy of further debate. These 'discussion points' are designed to enable the reader to think more innovatively and broadly around the subject area. They may also be used as prompts for group work, either with practitioners, parents/carers or young people.

Defining Sexual Health and Establishing the Level of Sexual Health among Adolescents

An appropriate starting point is to define 'sexual health'. Following its prioritization as a public health issue in the Health of the Nation White Paper (in 1992), the term sexual health has become increasingly used. Asking people what they understand as sexual health is likely to conjure a range of responses. For example, 'teenage pregnancy', 'sexually transmitted diseases', 'AIDS', and *'sex under coercion'*. Indeed, there is no universal or single definition of sexual health. Perhaps at the broadest of levels, the fpa (formerly the Family Planning Association) defines sexual health as:

> *...enjoying the sexual activity you want without causing yourself or anyone else suffering, or physical or mental harm.*

In more detail, the World Health Organization (WHO) defines sexual health as:

> ...*a state of physical, emotional, mental and social well-being related to sexuality; it is not merely the absence of disease, dysfunction or infirmity. Sexual health requires a positive and respectful approach to sexuality and sexual relationships, as well as the possibility of having pleasurable and safe sexual experiences, free of coercion, discrimination and violence.*

It is clear that both definitions acknowledge that sexual health is more than the occurrence or prevention of negative outcomes. Although teenage pregnancy and sexually transmitted infections (STIs) may be the first things that come to mind, both definitions illustrate that sexual health is also about the enjoyment and pleasures associated with sex. These positive aspects of sexual health are clearly reflected in Jo Adams and Carol Painter's (2004) holistic model of sexual health and sexuality. Their seven components of sexual health and sexuality, depicted as individual petals in a 'sexuality flower' symbol, are as follows:

- sex/sexual practice – with oneself, partner (same or other gender), and celibacy;
- sensuality – e.g. food, music, and massage;
- emotions – e.g. love, pleasure, joy, and intimacy;
- spirituality – e.g. feelings of oneness, sense of deeper self, and deep bonding;
- self-image – e.g. body image, self-esteem, size, and physical disability;
- social relationships – e.g. monogamy, non-monogamy, and marriages;
- political identity – e.g. gay men, gay women, people with disabilities, and people with HIV.

Having presented some varied definitions of sexual health, the level of sexual health of adolescents in the United Kingdom will now be outlined. The first point to make, in the context of the above definitions, is that information on *all* the varied components of sexual health is difficult to obtain. For example, how can we understand or depict the levels of emotions, pleasures and enjoyments associated with adolescents' sexual health? By contrast, information on conception rates (or teenage pregnancy) and STIs are probably the most readily available data. Although much of the remaining chapter will focus upon these two indicators of adolescent sexual health, and that these may arguably be the more serious health issues, it must be reinforced that there is more to sexual health than conceptions and infections.

Routine surveillance data on both conception rates and sexually transmitted infection rates are readily available from the Office for National Statistics (ONS) and the Health Protection Agency (HPA) respectively. These data are readily updated and readers are advised to contact the appropriate web sites to obtain the most up-to-date figures if required (**www.statistics.gov.uk and www.hpa.org.uk**).

The reduction of teenage conception rates has been prioritized by the government, with the Teenage Pregnancy Unit (established in 1999) leading on this 10-year strategy. In 2001, for every 1000 young women aged 15–19 in England and Wales, 60 became pregnant. Over the last 10 years, rates peaked at 65 per 1000 in 1998 and have since declined. Rates of teenage *births* (number of births per 1000 women aged 15–19) in the United Kingdom are the highest in Western Europe. The teenage birth rates are around five times those in the Netherlands, three times those in France and twice those in Germany (UNICEF, 2001).[1] As revealed in the following table (Table 5.1), national data from England and Wales also show that over one third of all conceptions for under 20 year-olds results in a termination of pregnancy (this approaches one half for conceptions among 15–17 year-olds). This represents what could be considered as the minimum level of unintended conception, since an unknown proportion of conceptions leading to births may have been initially unintended. Given these European comparisons, and this indication of regret, it is easy to appreciate why the reduction of teenage pregnancy has been prioritized (see Discussion point 3).

Table 5.1   Conception, birth and termination rates for under-20 year-olds in England and Wales, 1993–2003

Year	Conception rate per 1000 women aged 15–19 years	Conceptions leading to maternities – rate and (% of conceptions)	Conceptions terminated by abortion – rate and (% of conceptions)
1993	59.7	39.3(65.8)	20.5(34.3)
1994	58.7	38.3(65.2)	20.4(34.7)
1995	58.7	38.4(65.4)	20.3(34.6)
1996	63.2	40.3(63.7)	22.9(36.2)
1997	62.6	39.6(63.3)	23.0(36.7)
1998	65.1	40.5(62.2)	24.6(37.8)
1999	63.1	38.7(61.3)	24.3(38.5)
2000	62.5	37.9(60.6)	24.6(39.4)
2001	60.8	36.3(59.7)	24.5(40.3)
2002	60.3	36.3(60.2)	24.1(39.9)
2003	59.8	35.7(59.7)	24.1(40.3)

Source: ONS, 2005.

In tandem with the concern surrounding teenage pregnancy rates, there has been a dramatic and recent increase in sexually transmitted infection rates among young people (see Table 5.2).

This table illustrates that increases in infection are particularly evident among young men, although young women tend to report a greater number of cases.

Aside to these national figures, it is important to note that there exists a wide variation in adolescent sexual health. For example, young women from unskilled manual backgrounds (social class V) are more than ten times as likely to become teenage mothers as those from professional backgrounds (social class I) (Botting, Rosato and Wood, 1998). Increased risk of becoming teenage parents is apparent among young offenders, minority ethnic groups and those reporting low educational attainment. In relation to the likelihood of STI, young people (particularly teenage girls), gay men and Black ethnic minorities also bear a disproportionate burden of

[1]Equivalent data comparisons for *conception* rates are not available.

Table 5.2   Trends in new infections of chlamydia and genital warts among young people aged 16–19 in the United Kingdom

Year	Chlamydia			Genital warts		
	Males	Females	Total	Males	Females	Total
1996	1448	5876	7324	2116	7793	9909
1997	1886	7560	9446	2609	8487	11096
1998	2444	8659	11103	2695	8875	11570
1999	3015	10350	13365	3262	8781	12043
2000	4009	12813	16822	3564	9343	12907
2001	4553	14307	18860	3629	9500	13129
2002	5661	16562	22223	3674	9530	13204
2003	6549	18475	25024	3986	10018	14004
2004	7618	19969	27587	4441	10711	15152

Source: HPA, 2005 © *Health Protection Agency 2005*

disease (Testa and Coleman, 2006). In addition, and in some way connected to these population subgroups, there is tremendous geographical variation in teenage conception rates in particular. This geographical variation has resulted in the teenage pregnancy strategy defining pockets of high conception rates as teenage pregnancy 'hot spots'. Equally, there is clearly much to be learnt from those areas where the reduction in teenage pregnancy has been most striking. To illustrate, the conception rate among 15–17 year-olds in England and Wales is currently 42.3 per 1000 women (ONS, 2005). However, this ranges from 30.3 in Dorset and Somerset to 67.3 in South-East London. Comparable variations in the proportion of conceptions terminated by abortion can also be seen across England and Wales. Therefore, when interpreting these indicators of sexual health, it is clearly important to understand that young people from particular backgrounds and geographical locations are more at risk than others.

Having outlined some trends in adolescent sexual health, it is now important to put these into context. In other words, why are these trends significant? The negative impact of STIs upon the health of adolescents is unequivocal. The medical complications associated with STIs are numerous, and may include pelvic inflammatory disease, ectopic pregnancy, miscarriage, infertility and recurrent episodes of infection. Furthermore, STIs and pelvic inflammatory disease also present serious medical complications for newborns, including premature delivery, low birthweight, stillbirth and neonatal complications. Aside to these medical complications, the effects upon a person's emotional well-being may also be significant. Although there is very little research in this area, the limited evidence suggests that STIs are associated with stigmatization, embarrassment and negative attitudes, and have implications concerning promiscuity or unfaithfulness (France *et al.*, 2001). Also, in terms of more societal issues, the rising incidence of STIs has placed extra burden upon GUM (genito-urinary medicine) clinics. Poor GUM clinic access is now widespread in England, and delays of up to two weeks have been reported for first appointments.

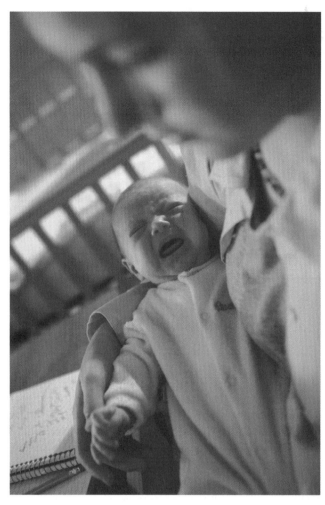

The impact of youthful pregnancy and childbirth is frequently viewed negatively. Certain medical conditions are clearly more prevalent among the pregnancies of young women such as anaemia, hypertension, prolonged labour and difficult or premature delivery. The risks to the child born to a teenage or young mother hinge upon the greater likelihood of low birth-weight and the medical complications associated with such a condition (such as congenital abnormalities and neurological and respiratory difficulties). Aside to these more *physical health* issues, there is also a link between teenage pregnancy and poverty and disadvantage alluded to earlier. An extract from an overview of teenage pregnancy research evidence illustrates the negative portrayal of teenage motherhood as follows:

> *Those who had been teenage mothers had experienced more socio-economic deprivation, more mental health difficulties and drug problems, had lower levels of educational attainment, and were more likely to be living in deprived neighbourhoods. Their partners were more antisocial and abusive. Their children showed reduced educational attainment, had more emotional and behavioural problems, were at increased risk of maltreatment or harm, and showed higher rates of illness, accidents and injuries. (Dennison, 2004, p. 7).*

Discussion point 1 – How should we define teenage pregnancy?

It is arguable that the government's stance is heavily weighted to the reduction of *unintended* pregnancies. For example, those originating from events which are subsequently regretted, or by failures or improper use of contraception. This is reflected in current policy which appears to be focused towards the increased provision of services, sex education, and the promotion of contraceptive use. By contrast, the issue of *intended* pregnancy among teenagers appears to be an area relatively overlooked. Although the boundary between intended and unintended pregnancy is admittedly difficult to define (for example, what about young people who are ambivalent towards being or not being pregnant?), research informs very little about those teenage pregnancies which are more deliberate or planned. It may be reasonable to assume that people with low expectations have less incentive to avoid pregnancy and thus may become pregnant intentionally. In conclusion, it is important to challenge the stereotypical view that teenage parents are a homogeneous group and acknowledge that, in reality, parenthood is a preferred option for some. Aside to service provision, raising expectations through education and job opportunities could act as a deterrent towards intended teenage pregnancy.

Discussion point 2 – How should we interpret the data on sexually transmitted infections (STIs)?

The data presented in this section shows a dramatic and alarming increase in STI cases over the last five or so years. It is important to contextualize how these data should be interpreted. There are two points that the reader should be aware of when assessing this information. Firstly, STIs may often show no obvious symptoms and, thus, many more people may be carrying an STI without knowing. It is for this reason that the new episodes of STI are *'only the tip of the iceberg'* (Fenton and Hughes, 2003, p. 199) and possibly an underestimate of the true number of infections. In this manner, the actual number of people infected with an STI may be far higher than the data suggest. Secondly, it is important to recognize the increased sophistication of the diagnostic tests that have been used during the time in which the data have been presented. With an increased awareness surrounding STIs many more people may also be volunteering for tests, and routine tests are being carried out more frequently. With this point in mind, the extent to which the increase in STIs indicates changing sexual practices is debatable.

Discussion point 3 – Is teenage pregnancy 'bad for your health'?

We have already outlined the health effects of STIs. The seriousness of these complications are unequivocal. However, the negative health effects of teenage pregnancy are more questionable. To examine whether teenage pregnancy is 'bad for your health', it is necessary to separate out the biological/physiological issues from the societal issues. I think all would agree that even if a young person is capable of becoming pregnant, perhaps at 12, 13 or 14 years of age, their probable lack of full physiological maturity may well have negative medical complications. Within the teenage age range, the difference in physiological maturity between a 13 year-old and a 19 year-old may be quite distinct. From this perspective, it could be reasonably argued that the negative health effects of 'teenage' pregnancy (as a whole for all teenagers) are unwarranted.

In terms of societal issues, we must consider the extent to which the 'disadvantage' associated with teenage pregnancy is a product of the society that we live in. The fact that teenage pregnancy rates are higher in more disadvantaged areas may be a reflection of the lack of opportunities, support or services in these areas. Similarly, is society at fault for not enabling young parents from these areas to escape this poverty and disadvantage? Furthermore, if we consider the quotation presented at the end of this section (Dennison, 2004), how accurate are we in saying that teenage pregnancy actually *caused* this evident disadvantage? Alternatively, if a teenager chooses to become pregnant to give them satisfaction and direction in life, perhaps to reintegrate them into the family, should this be argued as a negative impact upon their emotional health? To illustrate, innovative research exploring young teenagers' motivations for becoming pregnant highlights some of the strong perceptions and beliefs held by some young women (Cater and Coleman, 2006, p. 43). In looking back over the time since she became pregnant intentionally, this 18 year-old states:

> *I'm so glad she's here, she's like totally changed my life, and she's given me more confidence as well. I was like – before, I was very shy – I wouldn't even probably go into a shop and ask for something – with here – she's like a barrier there, she's like, gives me the confidence. I'm saying this is me – this is my baby and I'm gonna go in there and do that, and it's like really, it's much better.*

The key point to make is that assuming that *all* teenage pregnancy involves negative health implications may be overly presumptuous. Perhaps the distinction between 'intentional' and 'unintentional' pregnancy may be more indicative of health implications, rather than teenage pregnancy per se?

Summary of Section

- Sexual health is defined in a number of ways. Importantly, it should be acknowledged that sexual health refers to more than problem issues (such as unintended conception and STI), but also encapsulates the enjoyment and pleasures associated with sex.
- Research data on all the varied aspects of sexual health are unavailable (for example, the reported enjoyment of sex). The data most commonly available are the data on teenage conceptions and STIs.
- The reduction of teenage conception rates and STI rates has been recognized as a government priority.
- All teenage pregnancies should not be assumed to be 'unintentional' or 'unwanted'.

- The data on STI rates should be interpreted carefully. The reported increases must acknowledge the asymptomatic nature of some infections (that is, may be an underestimate) and also the wider and more routine testing for infections (that is, may not necessarily be indicative of more promiscuous sexual behaviour).
- The negative health effects of STIs are serious and unequivocal.
- The negative health effects of teenage pregnancy can be considered to be more debatable. Separating out the physiological and societal issues is necessary to assess the extent to which teenage pregnancy can be considered 'bad for your health'.

What Sexual Behaviours Determine an Adolescent's Sexual Health, and How are these Changing?

In consideration of the relatively high level of teenage conceptions and rising incidence of STIs, a deeper understanding of these trends will be provided by examining the sexual behaviours that are at work. Examining how these behaviours have changed over recent years will help to explain the levels of sexual health outlined previously. There are three key sexual behaviours of note:

Age at First Intercourse

Today's adolescents are reporting their first ever sexual intercourse at a younger age. This has been shown by asking survey participants when they first had sexual intercourse, and then comparing this with data gathered by earlier surveys. A comparison of surveys conducted by Schofield (1965), Farrell (1978) and Johnson et al. (1994, 2001) shows that there has been a progressive reduction in the age at first intercourse. The NATSAL surveys (Johnson et al., 1994, 2001) have been particularly useful in providing these data.[2] Of those aged 16–19 at interview, 30% of men and 26% of women reported first intercourse under the age of 16, compared to 27% and 14% of men and women respectively, aged 40–44 at interview (Johnson et al., 2001). The authors note the convergence of this behaviour among young men and women in the mid- to late 1980s, and the apparent stabilization of age at first intercourse among women in the 1990s. From a sexual health point of view, the NATSAL surveys also show that this progressively earlier intercourse has been associated with an earlier age at first conception, increased likelihood of STI, experience of termination of pregnancy, lack of contraceptive and/or condom use and subsequent feelings of regret.

Contraception and Condom Use

To prevent pregnancy, effective contraception must be used correctly. To prevent STI, condoms must be used, even if other forms of contraception are being employed. However, contraceptive and condom use among young people is inconsistent and, thus, does not fully eliminate the risk of pregnancy or STI. This inconsistent use has been documented by a number of sexual behaviour surveys and reviews. Lester Coleman (1999) reviewed eleven UK-based surveys of young

---

[2]NATSAL refers to the British National Survey of Sexual Attitudes and Lifestyles conducted among nationally representative samples (16–44 year-olds) of 18 876 (Johnson et al., 1994) and 11 161 (Johnson et al., 2001).

people's sexual behaviour and concluded the following. He identified, as *'broad estimates'* (p. 297), that non-use of contraception *at last intercourse* ranges from around 20% to 30%, and that non-use of condoms ranges from around 40% to 50%. Although adolescents report recent increases in their use of condoms, the use of contraception and condoms is still inconsistent.

Number of Sexual Partners

The likelihood of conception and STI has been increased by young people reporting more sexual partners. A comparison of the NATSAL surveys shows a notable increase in lifetime partners reported, with these increases being highest among young people. The number of sexual partners reported also shows marked variation. For example, the most recent NAT-SAL survey showed that of those aged 16–24 at interview, approximately one fifth of all men reported no sexual partners, and a further fifth reported 10 or more partners. Similar divergence was reported among women. Concurrent sexual partnerships (having more than one partner at the same time) are particularly important for STI transmission as they increase the probability of an infection being passed to more than one person. The NATSAL surveys also report increases in concurrent partnerships, with over 20% and 15% of men and women respectively aged 16–24 having such a partnership in the previous year.

   Collectively, the increasing proportion of young people reporting an earlier age at first intercourse, the inconsistent use of contraception and condoms, and increasing frequency of partner change account for the levels of adolescent sexual health reported previously. The emerging pattern is one of increased homogeneity between the genders at age of first intercourse, encouraging shifts to more condom use, but unfortunately offset by an increased number of sexual partners, including concurrent partners.

Discussion point 4 – What are the issues of interpretation where surveys of sexual behaviour are concerned?

The following discussion point provides two issues which need to be appreciated when interpreting surveys of sexual behaviour.

How 'adolescent' are these surveys? Much of the reported data has been derived from the NATSAL studies, the most recent surveys of nationally representative samples. The age range covered in these surveys was 16 to 44, so the information on adolescent sexual health is usually confined to 16–19 year-olds or 16–24 year-olds. Clearly this is not the most accurate information on *adolescent* sexual health. Surveys of younger people have rarely been undertaken, with a recent study by Daniel Wight and colleagues (2002), undertaken in Scotland, being a notable exception. From their survey of 15–16 year-olds, following a sexual health intervention (see later in this chapter), 41% of young women and 31% of young men report having experienced sexual intercourse. Other key findings were that 14% of young men aged 15–16, and 23% of young women aged 15–16 (from the whole sample rather than just those sexually experienced) reported evidence of sex unprotected from STIs. Of interest, this study was one of the few that have measured the positive aspects of sexual health. In relation to their last sexual intercourse, there was an overall enjoyment of this experience. From a mean score of enjoyment (from 1 to 5 depending on how strongly a person agreed with a statement reporting enjoyment), young men reported 4.6 and young women reported 4.3.

How do we measure condom use/risk? This point has been alluded to in the main section of the chapter. A wide range of measures of condom use have been used depending on the specific event of intercourse in question. For example, these events range from 'in last year', 'at last intercourse', 'at first ever intercourse', and 'at first intercourse with most recent partner'. Each measure has its own pros and cons. For example, a person having sex without using a condom 'at their last intercourse' may not necessarily be indicative of a risky or un-safe sexual experience. A partner may be on the pill and both may have been tested negative for any STI. Similarly, a person who failed to use a condom at their 'first ever intercourse' may have since used them consistently, thus hiding their predominantly safe sexual experiences. Ways around this have been by asking for a general assessment of condom use, such as 'how often have you used condoms?', but once more have been criticized over people's different interpretations of 'how often'. Similarly, in relation to number of sexual partners, a person reporting many different partners should not be assumed to be at greater risk from pregnancy or STI if condoms are used consistently. Perhaps a more accurate measure of risk from STI and pregnancy is to combine measures of contraceptive and condom use with number of partners, such as 'with how many different partners in the last year have you not used condoms?' Other advances could be to focus contraceptive or condom use upon 'higher risk' partners, although this in itself raises issues over interpretation.

Discussion point 5 – How does the age of puberty affect changing patterns of sexual behaviour?

This chapter has outlined how adolescents are reporting a progressively younger age at first ever sexual intercourse. It has been suggested that an earlier onset of puberty may partly explain these trends. The age at onset of puberty has implications upon service provision and the delivery of appropriate medical advice, timing of sex education, and legislation regarding age of consent. The current debate surrounding the age at which young people start puberty is clearly typified in recent competing press reports, such as: 'Straight from tot to teen…children nowadays simply reach puberty earlier' (*The Times*, 21 October 2000), and 'Pre-teen puberty is a myth, claim doctors' (*The Observer*, 4 March 2001). From a review of research dating back to the late 1960s, Lester and John Coleman (2002) assessed whether the age at menarche and onset of puberty has decreased in recent years. In summary, given the wide variation in methods used to assess puberty, it was only possible to draw inferences about whether the age at onset was changing. Methods of assessment, either by health professionals, parents or self, and the range in sampling techniques (e.g. general population versus those attending health centres, who in turn may be attending due to an earlier onset of puberty) were the main difficulties reported in this review. In summary, the authors of this paper note that the only firm conclusion is the need for an extensive piece of research in this area,

Bearing these [methodological] limitations in mind, however, some tentative conclusions can be advanced. With regard to the onset of puberty among girls, it appears possible that this may well have decreased in age in recent years.... As far as the onset of menstruation

is concerned, the evidence for a decrease in age of occurrence is less compelling.... It should also be noted that too little research on boys has been reported to come to any conclusions on whether there has been a decrease in the age of male pubertal development.... It is to be hoped that this review has demonstrated the need for further research, as well as providing encouragement to those seeking answers to critical methodological questions regarding the study of puberty. (Coleman and Coleman, 2002, p. 548)

Summary of Section

- Young people are reporting their first ever sexual intercourse at an earlier age compared to older age groups.
- Although encouraging recent increases in condom use, contraception as well as condoms are still used inconsistently by some young people.
- There have been recent increases in the number of sexual partners reported by young people, including concurrent partners.
- Most sexual behaviour data is oriented towards *young people* (from age 16) relative to *adolescents* (from age 12/13).
- The accurate assessment of sexual risk behaviour is problematic. A combined measure of condom use and numbers of sexual partners offers the greatest insight, although this is rarely used.
- The evidence for a decreasing age at onset of puberty is inconclusive, mainly due to methodological difficulties and wide variations in study design and sampling. Most research has been conducted in the United States and a nationally representative study of adolescents is required in the United Kingdom.

How can we Explain Adolescent Sexual Behaviours?

Given the levels of sexual health reported among today's adolescents, the promotion of better sexual health is of clear importance. Indeed, it is likely that many readers of this book are interested in improving the sexual health status of adolescents. It is clearly important to understand what makes some adolescents place themselves at risk from poor sexual health. Only by understanding this can we start to intervene and promote better sexual health in the most appropriate way. The first and overriding point to make here is that there are many factors at work which cannot be encapsulated in a single chapter; they are worthy of a whole book at the very least! Nonetheless, an attempt will be made to highlight some of the most significant factors which are more relevant for health promotion purposes. To achieve this, the following set of influences will be outlined: *individual influences, contextual influences, social influences,* and *cultural influences.*

Individual Influences

The theories of social cognition, such as the Theory of Planned Behaviour (Ajzen, 1988) and the Health Action Process Approach (Schwarzer, 1992), have long been used by social researchers in helping to predict health behaviour. By predicting and understanding health behaviour, we are in a better position to modify or, in this case, promote better sexual health.

Using these models as a framework, a person is more likely to protect themselves from any negative health effects according to particular individual attributes. Adopting condom use as a pertinent example, a person is more likely to use a condom if they:

- know about the protective effects of condoms;
- believe that they are at risk of pregnancy and/or STIs if condoms are not used;
- have positive attitudes to condoms;
- perceive that others (including their partners) share the importance attached to condom use;
- perceive they are capable of using condoms correctly, by negotiating and asserting their use where required (linked to self-efficacy, locus of control and self-esteem).

As can be shown, providing knowledge and facts about pregnancy, STI transmission and condom use is essential, but not enough to ensure consistent use. At the other extreme, helping people negotiate condom use, perhaps when a partner is less keen to, is a far more challenging but an equally important aspect.

Additional *individual influences* include the propensity for risk-taking in general. It is argued that some people are more likely to take risks than others. For example, it may be more likely that certain people, or 'risk takers', are more likely to engage in a multitude of different risky activities, such as fast driving, drug use, high risk sports, as well as risky sex. Large representative samples, especially from the United States, have shown that some adolescents have a greater propensity towards risk behaviour in a range of different domains. Having made this point, the question remains as to what increases the likelihood of a person being a so-called 'risk taker'? Professor Marvin Zuckerman's work (1994) in the United States highlights a personality profile of high sensation seeking and impulsivity which is predisposed towards a risk-taking nature.

In terms of health promotion, altering or changing the personality of an individual is an extremely arduous task. With this in mind, interventions focusing upon the constructs outlined in the social cognition models (such as knowledge, negotiation skills building, etc.) have been the main focus of such efforts in contrast to personality change.

Contextual Influences

These include those features present at a time when sexual interaction is occurring. For example, alcohol may be a powerful contextual influence in terms of sexual behaviour. Although the link between alcohol and sexual behaviour is complex, a number of studies have identified an association. Although not exclusively so, most studies highlight the negative effects of alcohol upon sexual health. For example, the first NATSAL survey found that two thirds of people who said alcohol was the main reason they first had intercourse used no contraception. Similarly, of 15–19 year-olds who had sex with someone they had known for less than one day (arguably, but not necessarily indicative of a more risky sexual experience), 61% of females and 48% of males reported alcohol or drugs as a reason (Ingham, 2001).

An additional *contextual influence* is that of the sexual partner. A sexual partner may not only affect whether sexual intercourse occurs, but also whether contraception or condoms are used. Previous research by Janet Holland and colleagues (1998) found that this partner influence, or 'gender power relation', is dominated by young men's influence over young women. Moreover, in terms of specific barriers to condom use, Lester Coleman and Roger Ingham

(1999), from qualitative research among 56 young men and women aged 16–19, found that the fear of a partner's negative reaction to using condoms was paramount in their likelihood of use. These barriers are summed up by the following 19 year-old from this study:

> *"I don't know 'cause it's quite hard to you know to just actually say something, but like you'd have to like, I don't know it would just probably be like trying to push him away a bit and like, sort of like, you know but, oh I don't know. I really don't know. I would just come out and say it really, I don't know, it is quite hard...you can't just stop and say, oh, can you put a condom on please."(Female, 19)*

Their qualitative investigation also showed that these barriers were most striking when condoms were objected to by young men, when the partner was older, when the partner had a higher social reputation, and when there was a desire for a long-term relationship with the partner.

Social Influences

These influences relate to the society that we live in, a point alluded to under an earlier discussion point. The detailed report into teenage pregnancy by the Social Exclusion Unit (1999) highlights the importance of 'low expectations' leading to teenage pregnancy. That is, given the perception faced by some young people about a lack of education or job prospects, they see no reason *not* to get pregnant. In addition, access to sexual health services has been shown to impact upon sexual health. In relation to termination of pregnancy, a recent study undertaken by Ellie Lee and colleagues (2004) found that access to abortion services was related to the proportion of conceptions that lead to abortions. Similar questions have been raised in relation to access to GUM clinics.

An additional key social influence is the delivery and quality of sex education provided through mainstream settings such as schools and pupil referral units. At present, the delivery and quality of Sex and Relationships Education (SRE) in schools is left to the individual school's judgement. The Social Exclusion Unit (1999) report into teenage pregnancy notes, in amongst the evidence of good and innovative practice, that:

> ...in some schools, SRE is an under resourced subject, squeezed for time, not supported by training, and not attached to wider local strategies to combat teenage pregnancy and improve sexual health. (p. 36)

Importantly, comprehensive SRE has been shown to increase the likelihood of contraceptive use and thus promote positive sexual health.

Cultural Influences

International comparisons in levels of sexual health show the importance of cultural influences. Although our European neighbours have also reported recent rises in chlamydia (rather than other STIs), the actual rates of infection are notably greater in the United Kingdom (WHO, 1999). Similarly, teenage birth rates in England are higher than any other Western European country, and are around five times those in the Netherlands (see earlier in this chapter).

Using the Netherlands as a suitable contrast, these differences in sexual health may be explained partly by the differences in how sex is portrayed between the cultures. In the Netherlands, the portrayal of sex is arguably more explicit and open. Sex is more openly discussed within schools and between young people, particularly when making choices over contraception prior to sex. By contrast, 'mixed messages' about sex have been documented as contributing to young people's poor state of sexual health in the United Kingdom. The following extract from the Social Exclusion Unit report illustrates the cultural influences relevant to the United Kingdom:

> One part of the adult world bombards teenagers with sexually explicit messages and an implicit message that sexual activity is the norm. Another part, including many parents and most public institutions, is at best embarrassed and at worst silent, hoping that if sex isn't talked about, it won't happen. The net result is not less sex, but less protected sex. (1999, p. 7)

These cultural differences may be reflected in the reasons teenagers give for their first sexual intercourse. In the Netherlands, 'love and commitment' is more commonly reported as the main factor, compared to 'opportunity', 'physical attraction' and 'peer pressure', all three of which were reported more by UK teenagers (Ingham and van Zessen, 1998). In addition, the contrast between these cultures is illustrated in the proportion of young people who talk with their parents about sex. In the Netherlands, it is more common for parents (both fathers and mothers) to talk with their children about sex. Although young people express a desire and a preference to talk to their parents about sex, parents in the United Kingdom tend to find this more of a problem compared to those in the Netherlands. There is growing evidence that improving family communication about sex is likely to lead to improved levels of sexual health among adolescents.

Discussion point 6 – Which of the influences that impact upon sexual behaviour are easiest to alter, and which are the hardest?

This section of the chapter has highlighted some key individual, contextual, social, and cultural influences upon sexual behaviour. By acknowledging these influences, we are now in a better position to consider how to promote safer sexual behaviour, and more positive sexual health outcomes. However, it should also be apparent that in understanding these influences, some are clearly easier to alter than others. In considering the *individual influences*, providing young people with the 'facts' and improving their knowledge is arguably the easiest of ways to intervene. Schools provide an excellent means to convey this information to groups of young people, at an appropriate age and in a cost-effective manner. In contrast, providing them with the necessary skills, for example, to insist on condom use or have effective ripostes to condom use objections, is likely to be more challenging. Nonetheless, with the exception of altering a person's risk-taking personality, it can be argued that of all influences, those at the individual level are the easiest to change in the short term. This is more obvious when comparing the *contextual influences* where, for example, it may be more difficult to prevent a sexual partner influencing the outcome. At the extreme, it is arguably most challenging of all to affect the *societal* and *cultural influences*, at least in the short term. Although these influences may be the most powerful in affecting sexual health, they are also the most difficult to change. Efforts, for example, to help parents talk to their children about sex would have beneficial outcomes, but changing the sexual culture of the United Kingdom to be more open and 'easy' for talking about sex is likely to be many years away.

Discussion point 7 – What is the relationship between alcohol and sexual health?

The relationship between alcohol and sexual health is complex. As shown in the main part of the chapter, alcohol has been shown to affect the likelihood of sexual intercourse, contraception and condom use, and ultimately, therefore, sexual health. A recent study of 64 adolescents, by Suzanne Cater and Lester Coleman (2006), provides a deeper insight into this relationship. Just under two thirds of their sample of 14–17 year-olds, who had been deliberately selected as having experiences of being drunk, recalled instances of regrettable or risky sex which had followed a drinking session. There were two key points to make from this study. Firstly, although risky sexual experiences were recalled, a sizeable proportion of the sample also noted how alcohol had enabled them to have more enjoyable sexual experiences. This included a greater ability to chat to people, to 'pull', and to have sexual intercourse. Also, there was some, albeit limited evidence, that the 'Dutch courage' enabled some young people to insist on condom use.

The second key point to make is that the qualitative analysis provided great insight into *how* alcohol impacted upon sexual behaviour, and ultimately sexual health. It was clear that alcohol operated in a number of different ways. For example, some young people spoke how, once drunk, people seemed more sexually attractive. Others also spoke of how they used alcohol as an excuse to explain socially unacceptable behaviour, to their friends or sexual partner, which they had 'secretly' intended and enjoyed. For example:

> *"If you do anything wrong... then you can just blame it on the drink... I planned to [have sex with someone] and then got drunk and did it and blamed it on the drinking... I say 'Oh, it was only cause I was drunk.' But 90 per cent of the time people were saying what they really feel.... Cause they can blame it on the drink." (Male, 17)*

Associated with more serious consequences, some adolescents recalled experiences where alcohol had clearly impaired their judgement, which was more likely to lead to negative sexual health consequences. In the following example, this impaired judgement was manifested through 'forgetting' the consequences:

> *"Yeah, because if like you're really nervous about having sex you'd have to drink more wouldn't you? And you'd be so out of it that you'd totally forget about using contraception." (Male, 17)*

Finally, some adolescents reported instances of being completely 'out of control' which was indicated by intoxication and collapse. In these situations, the potential for a risky sexual encounter was at its greatest, and where the choice of condom use would be left to the sexual partner. These situations following excessive alcohol consumption also had more potential to lead to sex which was not consensual. The following quotation illustrates this loss of control:

> *"I've had previous problems with alcohol where I've been so drunk that I can't actually remember things that have happened and the next morning, or the next couple of weeks, I get told about things and then it [having sex with someone] suddenly comes back and I think, oh my god, what have I done." (Female, 16)*

Suzanne Cater and Lester Coleman's research illustrates not only the complex nature of the alcohol and sexual health relationship, but also how alcohol operates in a number of different ways. On the one hand, using alcohol as an 'excuse' suggests that alcohol, per se, does not affect sexual health. However, the opposite may be true when excessive drunkenness leads to judgement being impaired or a loss of control over whether, for example, condoms are used.

Summary of Section

- Understanding the factors that underpin adolescent sexual behaviours can indicate how to intervene and promote sexual health.
- Key influences upon sexual behaviour can be categorized into individual, contextual, social and cultural influences.
- Individual influences include beliefs, knowledge, attitudes, perceptions of normality and perceived capabilities including negotiation and assertiveness skills. A risk-taking personality, fuelled by sensation seeking and impulsivity, is also included as an individual influence.
- Contextual influences include alcohol, drug use and the influence of the sexual partner.
- Social influences include education and job opportunities, poverty, access to sexual health services and sex education.

- Cultural influences are reflected in the 'mixed messages' about sex in the United Kingdom, the openness and ease about discussing sex, and communication about sex within the family.
- With the exception of altering a person's risk-taking personality, it can be argued that of all influences, those at the individual level are the easiest to change in the short term.
- The relationship between alcohol and sexual behaviour is complex. On the one hand alcohol can be used to encourage positive sexual experiences. However, alcohol can also lead to impaired judgement and complete loss of control which can lead to unsafe sexual practices.

Current Policy and Practice in Promoting Adolescent Sexual Health

Promoting improvements in young people's sexual health can be considered at government policy level and also through effective practice. In recent years, two significant policy documents have set out the strategy to promote sexual health. The Teenage Pregnancy Unit was established in 1999 to push forward the government's teenage pregnancy strategy. Around £60 million had been invested into this strategy by 2002. One of the specific aims (from a total of 30 action points) is to halve the rate of conceptions among the under 18s, and to set a firmly established downward trend in the rate of conceptions among under 16s, by 2010. Since 1998, conception rates among the under 16s and under 18s have decreased by around 10%, however, it is too early to see if these government targets will be met. A further aim is to achieve a reduction in the risk of long-term social exclusion for parents and their children (through increased involvement in education, employment or training).

The second key policy initiative was the National Strategy for Sexual Health and HIV (Department of Health, 2001). This first ever strategy of this nature, over a period of ten years, has five main aims:

- to reduce the transmission of HIV and STIs;
- to reduce the prevalence of undiagnosed HIV and STIs;
- to reduce unintended pregnancy rates;
- to improve health and social care for people living with HIV;
- to reduce the stigma associated with HIV and STIs.

This strategy has obvious parallels with the work of the Teenage Pregnancy Unit (in reducing unintended pregnancies, and substantial investment), but differs in its focus upon all age groups rather than young people. The emphasis on HIV and STIs is very evident in this strategy and again illustrates how pregnancy and disease prevention are prominent in our understanding of sexual health. The remaining part of this section will now outline three areas of practice which have been influenced by these policy initiatives:

Improving the Evidence Base

Accessible compilations of the latest research evidence are valuable in informing practitioners of 'what works' with regard to sexual health promotion. In light of the strategies mentioned above, two comprehensive reviews have been published which are of relevance to sexual health. Firstly, Catherine Swann and colleagues (2003) looked at 30 separate reviews in relation to the prevention of teenage pregnancy. Their review presents a series of character-istics of interventions which were found to be effective in reducing teenage pregnancy:

- a focus upon high risk groups;
- recognition of interpersonal skills development, such as negotiation and refusal skills;
- accessibility of interventions in terms of location, opening hours and so forth;
- taking key opportunities for education and prevention, for example, if a teenager attends a clinic and receives a negative pregnancy test;
- encouraging a local culture in which the discussion of sex, sexuality and contraception is permitted.

Secondly, Simon Ellis and Anna Grey (2004) looked at 26 reviews into the prevention of STIs in non-clinical settings. Although applicable to all age groups, this has obvious relevance to the sexual health of adolescents. Their review highlighted characteristics of effective STI interventions as follows:

- having a sound theoretical base, for example, following behaviour change models;
- targeted and tailored (in terms of age, gender, culture, etc.), making use of needs assess-ment or formative research;
- provision of basic, accurate information through clear, unambiguous messages;
- use of behavioural skills training, including self-efficacy.

Good Practice Guides

In conjunction with the improvements in the evidence base, the two strategies have also re-sulted in the publication of brief and accessible good practice guides. Although they are too numerous to mention, two have been selected given their reference specifically to adolescent sexual health. Firstly, the Teenage Pregnancy Unit (2000) produced *Best practice guidance on the provision of effective contraception and advice services for young people*. This guid-ance highlights the features of an effective service for young people as follows:

> *an age specific focus, confidentiality, non-judgemental staff, accessible locations and opening hours, a friendly atmosphere and publicity in places where young people meet. To be effective, contraception and advice services for young people should be commis-sioned and provided against these criteria. Young people should be involved in planning and evaluating services. (Teenage Pregnancy Unit, 2000, p. 1)*

Secondly, *Sex and relationships education guidance*, published by the DfEE in 2000, pro-vides a wide range of useful information. This includes updates on policy development, the specific issues to be taught, integrating SRE into PSHE (personal, social and health edu-cation), and appropriate teaching strategies. As an illustration, the guidance states that all schools must have an up-to-date sex and relationship education policy, this should be inclusive of all pupils, and developed in consultation with parents and the wider community. In terms of promoting better sexual health, the guidance spells out areas that need to be focused upon in SRE. These include:

- young people need access to, and precise information about, confidential contraceptive information, advice and services;
- young people need to be aware of the risks of STIs, including HIV, and know about prevention, diagnosis and treatment;
- young people need to know not just what safer sex is and why it is important but also how to negotiate it with a partner.

In addition, the SRE guidance provides information on teaching techniques to meet these requirements. These include establishing ground rules, introducing 'distancing' techniques, making use of discussion and project learning, and encouraging reflection.

As a final note to this section, it is important to point out that a number of innovative interventions have been established in light of the improved evidence base and best practice guidance. However, as the evaluation of these interventions will take several years to report, we are currently uncertain about their true, long-term effectiveness. To cite an example, the recently implemented Youth Development Pilot Programmes are currently being evaluated in the United Kingdom. These pilot programmes, following their successful implementation in the United States, aim to prevent sexual ill-health alongside other risky behaviours, such as drug use and smoking. In addition to providing information and skills, these programmes aim to empower people with a greater sense of purpose, self-worth and opportunity for the future, thus decreasing the motivation to engage in risky behaviours.

Discussion point 8 – What is the case for abstinence education?

In light of the inconsistency in the sex and relationship education interventions reported in this section, it is important to keep a watch out for alternative approaches to promote sexual health. One such initiative, promoted widely across the United States, is abstinence education. Abstinence education has received federal funding for over 20 years. The principle behind this initiative is that by 'saying no' to sex until people are married will reduce teenage sexual activity, thus reduce teenage pregnancy and STI rates, and improve sexual health. Some young people wear a silver chastity ring until they are married (known as the 'Silver Ring Thing'). The polarized debate between abstinence education versus a comprehensive sexuality education is neatly typified by Simon Blake and Gill Frances (2001).

Supporters of abstinence approaches believe the following:

- Young people are irrational and driven by emotion. Because they are poor decision-makers, there is little point in developing their decision-making skills.
- Young people need to be told not to have sex otherwise they will choose to become sexually active.
- Young people need to receive a consistent message from school, the wider community and the media.
- The only way of avoiding danger and imminent disease is by abstaining from sex.
- It should be taught that sex is wonderful if it is preserved for marriage.

Supporters of comprehensive sexuality education believe the following:

- Children are decision makers and accessing good information is the key to making these decisions.
- Even with an abstinence approach, some teenagers may have sex before marriage and therefore need knowledge and skills about contraception, safer sex and other issues.
- The diversity of young people's experiences should be addressed. Abstinence messages do not meet the needs of many young Americans including those from within the Black communities, lesbian and gay young people and those in different family settings.
- Sexual health services for young people do not increase sexual activity, but increase use of contraception when they have sex.

Readers may like to ask themselves where they stand on this debate.

Despite the over 20-year existence of abstinence education in the United States, only relatively recently has it been systematically evaluated. Bearman and Bruckner (2004), in studying 12 000 young people over a period of six years, reported that STI rates were the same among those who had, and had not, pledged abstinence until marriage. Nine out of ten young people who took a sexual abstinence pledge went on to break it, and because they were so unprepared and felt guilty they were far less likely to use contraception or condoms. The authors report the problems of the abstinence campaign as follows:

> It's difficult to simultaneously prepare for sex and say you're not going to have sex...The message is really simple: 'Just say no' may work in the short term but doesn't work in the long term. (Bearman and Bruckner, 2004)

Summary of Section

- The government's Teenage Pregnancy Strategy (1999) and the National Strategy for Sexual Health and HIV (2001) intend to reduce teenage pregnancy rates and improve levels of sexual health.
- These strategies have led to improvements in the evidence base surrounding interventions preventing teenage pregnancy and STIs. In addition, a number of good practice guides have been compiled including reference to sex and relationship education in schools.
- Also, a number of recent innovative interventions have been established to promote better sexual health in adolescents. Innovations in school sex education far from provide an easy or complete solution to improving the levels of sexual health among young people.
- The government strategies and the associated activities are too recent to have been comprehensively evaluated.
- Abstinence education in the United States does not appear to improve the sexual health of adolescents, and the polarized debate continues over the pros and cons of comprehensive sex education in schools.

Conclusion

This chapter has provided a comprehensive account of the sexual health of today's adolescents. The approach has been to progressively deepen the reader's understanding of the key issues and debates. Opening with a definition of sexual health, the chapter has outlined the level of sexual health among adolescents, principally by drawing upon the widely available indicators of teenage pregnancy and sexually transmitted infection rates. The chapter briefly summarized the significance of these indicators, and highlighted some of the key sexual behaviours that may account for these trends (such as trends in condom use, concurrent sexual partnerships, etc.). With reference to the promotion of better sexual health, the chapter referenced theoretical literature to define some of the influences upon these sexual behaviours (such as knowledge, skills acquisition, cultural influences, etc.). Finally, the chapter has drawn upon the recent policy initiatives and innovative interventions that have set out to improve the levels of sexual health among adolescents. Through the discussion points, this chapter has also enabled readers to critically assess some of the theoretical and empirical literature that has been referenced.

In concluding where we are in terms of sexual health, the situation facing today's adolescents is clearly of some concern. With high levels of teenage pregnancy and rising STIs, it is obviously a public health issue that warrants attention. However, we must also acknowledge the physical and emotional pleasures that the majority of adolescents derive from sexual interaction. Also on a more positive note, with the recent substantial investment, it may be the case that the sexual health of adolescents will gradually improve. Until the results from the evaluation of the Teenage Pregnancy Strategy and the National Strategy for Sexual Health and HIV are known, it is impossible to be more certain about any such improvements. Although this evaluation remains a significant gap in the evidence base, there are also a number of additional areas which are in need of attention. In constructing this chapter, it has become clear that the following four aspects of adolescent sexual health require more research, and practice and policy focus.

1. *The positive aspects of sexual health* – sexual health should be viewed more positively, rather than exclusively around the teenage pregnancies and STIs that are frequently documented in the literature. We simply know less about the enjoyment, pleasures and benefits of sex and sexual behaviour. The balance between the negative and positive aspects of sexual health needs to be redressed.
2. *Puberty* – given the importance of the age at which young people start puberty, in terms of legislation, medical interventions, sexual behaviour, it is imperative that we are more certain about whether the age at onset is decreasing. Anecdotal evidence suggests this may be the case, but a large-scale, representative survey adopting a prospective design is required to scientifically test this hypothesis.
3. *Adolescent sexual health* – much of the evidence reported in this chapter has been drawn from the over-16 age group. There is a dearth of research evidence on young people in their early teens. Not only is it crucial to know more about the sexual behaviours of young people of this age group, but researching them in more detail will enable us to be more knowledgeable about the precursors for early sexual activity (which in itself has been shown to be linked to poor sexual health).
4. *Heterogeneity of adolescents* – adolescents are far from a homogeneous group. As illustrated earlier, the sexual health needs of young gay people, those from minority ethnic groups and those living in different socio-economic circumstances may all vary. Policy and practice could benefit from researching, in more detail, the sexual attitudes, lifestyles and behaviours of these groups.

Finally, it is appropriate to let an adolescent have the last word in this chapter. The following extract, taken from an actual case study published in *The Observer* (27 October 2002), neatly encompasses some of the key issues raised in this chapter. It is hoped that the following words illustrate how some of these issues operate in the real world. They also indicate the range of difficulties that are faced in improving an adolescent's sexual health.

CASE STUDY 5.1

Nicola Hughes (name changed), aged 15, talks about first sexual experiences, peer pressure, and sex education:

"I've spoken to quite a few of my friends about when they feel you should have sex. 'I lost my virginity when I was 12,' announced one. Most just say they'll do it when they're ready. 'I won't be ready until I'm 18,' said another friend. A couple of years ago, sex didn't seem like something we needed to worry about – but now our sixteenth birthdays aren't far away there's the worrying prospect of having to decide whether to sleep with your boyfriend or not.

One of my friends says: 'There are two extremes of peer pressure to do with sex: at one end you could be called frigid. Nobody would ever want to go out with you again because, especially in a lad's case, it would seem you don't know how to have a good time. And at the other end you could be called easy. It's a lot better to have a definite 'yes' or 'no' answer as to sleeping with someone or not. If we're unsure, then I think we should say no, as otherwise we might regret it. For example, one of my friends had sex with her boyfriend after just three weeks of going out, and after a two-month relationship they don't even say hi to each other. On the other hand, another friend had a nine-month relationship with her boyfriend, never quite having sex, and after breaking up they're still great mates.

From the age of eight, we've been aware of sex because of sex education classes in school. Each year the lessons become more and more graphic and humiliating. When we were 13 or 14, we had the typical video to watch, probably made before we were born, but this time they gave us quizzes to do and made us sit watching a poor friend of ours struggle to put a condom on a test tube. We all had turns at going bright red when the teacher told us some myths about sex – all of us believed at least one of them.

'You can't get pregnant the first time you have sex' was the one I thought was true. Another – 'you can't get pregnant when you're standing up' – seemed logical. Even though sex education was telling us to do one thing, television was, and still is in some ways, telling us to do another. There are at least two soap operas every weekday which inevitably involve characters having sex. Anna in Hollyoaks had a one-night stand with Alex and it resulted in them having a baby. And Jamie, who's a bit of a stud, gave everyone the clap. It was a bit melodramatic because every girl in Chester slapped him, but the point came across about what could happen. In some storylines sex is portrayed as the right thing to do, and in others it has its punishments." (Nicola Hughes, 15, a school pupil from Leicestershire)

Nicola describes a world where there is a lot of discussion and focus on sex, and yet a lot of confusion too. What could be done to improve this situation?

Further Reading

Social Exclusion Unit (1999) *Teenage pregnancy*, HMSO, London. Excellent review of related literature.

Department of Health (2001) *The National Strategy for Sexual Health and HIV*, Department of Health. Excellent review of related literature.

Ingham, R. and Aggleton, P. (2006) *Promoting young people's sexual health*, Routledge. Comprehensive insight into ways to promote positive sexual health among young people.

Moore, S.M. and Rosenthal, D.A. (2006) *Sexuality in adolescence: current trends*, Taylor and Francis, London. A detailed insight into theoretical and empirical research surrounding adolescent sexuality.

Wellings, K., Nanchahal, K., Macdowall, W. *et al.* (2001) Sexual behaviour in Britain: early heterosexual experience, *The Lancet*, 358: 1843–1850. The most recent insight into patterns of sexual behaviour derived from a nationally representative sample of young people in Britain.

Chapter 6

Substance Use in Adolescence

Rutger C. M. E. Engels and Regina van den Eijnden

Radboud University Nijmegen

- ■ Introduction
- ■ Facilitating Functions of Substance Use
- ■ Long-Term Effects of Early Substance Use
- ■ Unresolved Issues
- ■ Negative Health and Social Consequences of Drinking and Smoking
- ■ Practical Implications
- ■ Conclusion

Learning Objectives

After reading this chapter you should:

1 Be able to provide a framework describing the functions alcohol use and smoking have for young people.
2 Show empirical evidence illustrating the beneficial social functions of substance use, especially alcohol use.
3 Understand the functions of substance use in relation to the negative long-term and short-term consequences.
4 Appreciate that the development of prevention and policy measures needs to take account of the beneficial functions of substance use for some adolescents.
5 Be aware that smoking and drinking are quite different kinds of behaviours, with different precursors and functions.

Introduction

> ... that it be not given to Youths, as from 14 years of age unto 25, for wine is unto the most
> repugnant; because it doth above measure heat their hastie, hot, and agitating nature,
> and extimulate them (like mad men) unto enormious and outragious actions. ('Rules to
> live a long and healthy life' by Dr. T. Venner, 1650; in Hermus, 1983)

Alcohol, nicotine and other recreational drugs are major health hazards of our time.
Indeed, from a demographic point of view, statistics show that alcohol and drug-related
illnesses are on the rise, and that alcohol and drugs are often involved in traffic accidents,
domestic and public violence as well as in an array of criminal acts. However, national
surveys in Western societies, such as the United States and European countries have shown
that experimentation with potentially risky behaviours like cigarette smoking, marijuana use
and alcohol consumption is fairly normal among adolescents. Only a small proportion of late
adolescents reported never having smoked or drunk alcohol, so that, statistically speaking, it
is not 'normal' to totally abstain from smoking or drinking.

As a large number of people get involved in these activities in adolescence, we should have
a closer look at what role developmental tasks in the teenage years play in this. First, adolescent drinking is related to changes in leisure time preferences. By comparison with children
and early adolescents, mid-adolescents spend more time with friends outside the parental
home. Going out to pubs, discos and parties are considered to be important for the development and maintenance of friendships as well as romantic relationships. Since some leisure
time activities take place in settings in which certain risk behaviours (e.g. smoking, drinking) and the development of peer relations coincide, some risk behaviours can be assumed
to facilitate peer group integration (e.g. Engels, 2003; Engels and Knibbe, 2000; Engels,
Knibbe and Drop, 1999a; Maggs and Hurrelmann, 1998; Pape and Hammer, 1996; Shedler
and Block, 1990). In this respect, it is easy to understand the almost provocative statement of
Richard Jessor (1987, p. 335), who claims that behaviours such as drinking, smoking and sexual experiences are 'not necessarily irrational, perverse or pathological; for adolescents, such
behaviours can fulfil important goals and can be an essential aspect of psychosocial development'. So occasional drinking could be understood as a manifestation of developmentally
appropriate experimentation.

This assumption conflicts with earlier research indicating that drinking reflects psychological maladjustment. In these approaches, poor functioning in the family or at school is expected to result in low self-worth and distress as well as in poor functioning in peer networks.
Eventually, these youngsters will look for company in which they feel safe and secure, which,
more often than not, will be other maladapted youngsters. This line of argument assumes a
linear relation between substance use and psychological health, abstainers being regarded as
the best adjusted of adolescents.

Shedler and Block (1990) object to this and assume a curvilinear relationship between alcohol use and psychological well-being. Indeed, studies by Pape and Hammer (1996) indicated a
curvilinear relationship. For example, in a Norwegian longitudinal survey, Pape and Hammer
showed that *both* early and late male starters had lower self-esteem and greater feelings of
depression than those who started at the average drinking age. While this result seems fairly
obvious for early starters, an explanation is needed for the late starters/abstainers. It might be
that they do not drink because they do not participate in normal adolescent social activities.

One might argue that these relationships are different for other substances. However, Shedler and Block found that both abstainers and frequent users of marijuana reported serious difficulties. Adolescents who were more likely to be frequent users were under emotional stress and unable to form satisfying relationships. On the other hand, the authors describe the typical abstainer as '…a child which is relatively overcontrolled, timid, fearful and morose… not warm and responsive, not curious and open to new experiences, not active, not vital and not cheerful' (1990, p. 620).

Research on the functions of adolescent alcohol use may contribute to a more adequate prevention of misuse and its consequences than correlational studies. If, from an adolescent perspective, pub-going is more than just drinking alcohol, preventive efforts that do not take this into account are likely to have limited effects for two reasons: first, if alcohol is portrayed as something bad that should be prevented at any cost, youngsters will not accept this as *credible* because many of them also have other, more positive experiences. Second, young people will have more difficulties in *identifying* themselves with advertisements or educational promotion if users are described as antisocial, criminal or aggressive. In addition, strategies that reduce the availability of alcoholic beverages or cigarettes, for instance, could have negative side effects if drinking, or the setting in which it takes place, is relevant for adolescent development.

Facilitating Functions of Substance Use

Friendships

The transition from adolescence to adulthood is accompanied by intensified contacts with peers and an entrance into new social contexts and activities. The importance of achieving intimacy goals, such as closeness and trust, is redirected out from parents towards peers. There are two lines of research that provide evidence for the effects of alcohol use on youth functioning in peer groups and friendships.

First, research has shown that compared to drinkers, abstainers are less sociable, spend less time with their friends and are less likely to have a pal (Pape, 1997; Silbereisen and Noack, 1988), and have less adequate social skills (Pape, 1997). In addition, findings from a few longitudinal studies suggest that abstaining late adolescents and young adults are less likely than drinkers to develop a steady intimate relationship (Engels and Knibbe, 2000; Pape and Hammer, 1996). Thus, there is substantial support for the assumption that young people who drink alcohol are more sociable, more integrated into their peer group, have better peer relations and experience fewer feelings of loneliness (see Box 6.1).

Second, when youngsters are asked what motives they give for their drinking or smoking behaviour, they often mention social aspects (e.g. Kuntsche et al., 2005). It seems to make parties more fun, it makes one more relaxed, makes it easier to approach others, or to share feelings and experiences. The literature on drinking motives, for instance, illustrates that people who endorse enhancement (i.e. drinking to feel relaxed and at ease) and social motives (i.e. drinking to celebrate, to have a good time with friends), are more likely to report high drinking levels in social contexts (see review by Kuntsche et al., 2005). Research has shown that the expected reinforcing social elements of drinking are related to, and predictive of, frequency and quantity of adolescent alcohol use (e.g. Aas et al., 1998). Apparently in the eyes of the beholder (i.e. youngsters themselves), drinking is interconnected with sociability and associated with social interactions. Of course this does not mean that there is not some tolerance within peer groups. For instance, some smoking peer groups accept non-using members, because they have other qualities (Shucksmith and Hendry, 1998). It simply implies that *generally* people associate with others who exhibit similar behaviours and attitudes.

These lines of research indicate that substance use has social benefits, or at least, that young people perceive that to be the case. However, the overwhelming majority of studies used self-report data on social performance or relations. A limitation of self-reports is that there might be discrepancies in how people think they act in social encounters, and how others perceive them interacting. It is therefore essential to gather information from individuals' peers. If the social or psychological functions are primarily in the eyes of the beholder, and peer group members do *not* associate social skills or performance with substance-using peers, early adolescents' perceptions of the social consequences of their behaviour might well be distorted, and this could be challenged by the provision of correct information. Furthermore, though substance use is related to social benefits, it is also associated with antisocial behaviours, such as aggression, inattentiveness and

---

Box 6.1   Fragments from Interviews among Adolescents in Rotterdam, the Netherlands (Wits, Spijkerman and Bongers, 1999)

I: What do you like about drinking alcohol?

R: Nothing.

I: Then why do you do it?

R: Yes... for company, because I am not the only one, when I am alone I do not drink.

I: So, you only drink when you are with others. But I still do not know why you drink.

R: Why? Because everybody is drinking, and I am drinking with them.

I: What is so special about drinking with others?

R: There is nothing special about drinking with others, it is just ... when everybody is ordering beer, and I am ordering coke, it just doesn't fit. If everybody is drinking beer, I want to drink beer too.

I: Why is that?

R: See, they are my friends, and if they drink beer and I don't ... they wouldn't care, they wouldn't care at all ... I just want to drink beer if my friends do.(Boy, 17)

R: If a joint is circling in the group and others take a puff, it is hard to not join them.

I: Is it hard to tell them that you will not join them?

R: Yes.

I: Why is that?

R: Well... it is not hard to tell them that I will not join them, it is just hard to not join them!

I: What makes it hard?

R: That everybody is smoking dope, having a good time and being stoned and I am not ....(Boy, 14)

---

poor school performance. Therefore, it is relevant to get a more comprehensive picture of early adolescents by gathering information from their immediate peer group members.

We did this by asking adolescents in secondary education to evaluate their class mates on personal traits such as sociability, self-confidence, aggression or nervousness (Engels, Scholte and Van Lieshout, 2005). Thus, for every pupil in the study, we have ratings on their social behaviour by 25 to 35 classmates. We found that peers generally seem to perceive class mates who drink or smoke as self-confident and sociable.

Dating and Intimate Relationships

Love and romance are major concerns for young people. In this period of life, they have their first dates and sexual encounters. Although sexual experiences carry some risks, such as diseases and unwanted pregnancy, the development of intimate relationships is valuable for young people. For instance, they discuss their problems and worries with their partner and learn specific communication skills. In addition, young people with romantic experiences seem to exhibit higher emotional maturity and well-being. The initiation of intimate relationships can be seen, just like drinking, as one of the behaviours marking the transition from childhood to adolescence. Only a few studies have examined the effects of drinking on involvement in intimate relationships. These studies have shown that abstainers, or late starters, were less likely to have a steady partner compared to drinkers (Engels and Knibbe, 2000; Pape and Hammer, 1996; see also Engels and Ter Bogt, 2001). It is important to mention that the link between drinking and romantic relationships has to do with context. Pubs, discos and parties are places where young people go to meet the opposite sex and look for opportunities to establish a relationship or have romantic affairs. These are also the settings in which the majority of adolescent alcohol consumption takes place (Coleman and Hendry, 1999).

Even though engagement in risk behaviours is associated with size of social network and time spent with peers, levels of alcohol use alone appear to be directly related to perceived romantic skills. Thus, for appropriate entrance into the 'dating market', it not only provides the opportunity (going out with friends), but may also give adolescent users the feeling that it is easier to approach prospective romantic partners (Engels and Ter Bogt, 2001).

In conclusion, there is some evidence that alcohol use has a positive function for adolescents in terms of sexual and romantic experiences. Nevertheless, heavy alcohol use can also have negative consequences, such as impaired performance, loss of control, unsafe sex and even date rape.

Relationship with Parents

At approximately the same time as youngsters seek integration in the peer group, they are inclined to distance themselves from the social control of parents and other authority figures. The relationship with parents changes due to processes of maturation and autonomy. Many researchers have focused on the separation–individuation process of adolescents. The general view is that children separate themselves from their parents and search for the company of peers, but, at the same time, are inclined to keep good relationships with their parents (for instance, they still discuss important career issues with them). From this developmental perspective, some separation from parents is an important step in the growing-up process. Going out with friends becomes an important way of spending leisure time, particularly at weekends, away from the supervision of parents or other adults. Not surprisingly, these are the times when they consume alcohol.

There are, however, limited empirical findings available on the role of adolescent drinking in changes in parent–child relationships. Adolescents with attachment problems have a higher risk for substance use, or report more drinking problems in the past six months than securely attached adolescents (Anderson and Henry, 1994).

It is possible that young people drink alcohol because they already have poor relationships with their parents, or, that when children first start to drink, this becomes a reason for distorting that relationship. A longitudinal design enables us to disentangle the causal links between adolescent alcohol use and parent–child relationships. A study among early adolescents, who were interviewed three times in their first year of secondary education, tested whether or not alcohol use leads to deterioration in the quality of relationships with parents (Van Der Vorst et al., 2004). Indeed, there was some support for this hypothesis. Adolescents starting to drink reported a decrease in parental attachment, particularly if drinking was frequent and intensive. So, involvement in problem behaviours might affect the relationship between parents and their youngsters.

In terms of smoking, there is some evidence that many conflicts between parents and children can affect their relationship negatively, which in turn will increase adolescents' inclination to smoke (Duncan *et al.*, 1998). One of the explanations for this is that unsatisfactory relationships with parents are likely to lead to feelings of depression in the offspring, which, in turn, can increase the risk of smoking initiation. Furthermore, Engels *et al.*, (2005) showed that higher levels of suppressive parental control were related to higher rates of smoking for boys, while good parent– child relationships were generally associated with less smoking in the offspring.

In sum, there is some empirical evidence that engagement in smoking and drinking is associated with gaining autonomy and independence from parents: young people who start these behaviours are more likely to report conflicts with parents and deterioration in communication and emotional bonds with their parents.

Developmental Tasks

Research on stereotypes and self– other identification strongly relies on the assumption that people value positively peers who smoke or drink and may have self-consistency and self-enhancement motives for using cigarettes. They are more likely to start smoking if they perceive their self-image to be similar to a smoking stereotype (peer smoker), or if they value the characteristics of a typical smoking peer (stereotype) higher than their own image (Spijkerman *et al.*, 2004). In sum, people who associate admired characteristics (ideal self-images) or actual characteristics (real self-images) with the image of smoking or drinking peers are more likely to engage in these activities themselves (see Box 6.2).

By looking at how adults act, and how they are portrayed in the media, teenagers also learn about the norms and values of being an adult. Because drinking is a normative behaviour among adults in most Western societies, it is not surprising that youngsters adopt this habit: starting to drink is one of the ways to identify with the adult world, a reflection of norms and values in society. In addition, drinking distinguishes adolescents from younger children as well. In short, it is plausible to assume that drinking is related to other transitional behaviours, such as financial independence through a job, an interest in future positions in society, dating and mating and leaving the parental home (Pape, 1997).

Other psychological changes in adolescent lives are related to forming identity and getting a clear self-definition. Regarding identity formation, it appears that average levels of substance use in adolescents are related to a more mature and sophisticated identity status, while youngsters with low and high level of use are more likely to avoid confronting identity issues.

Psychological Well-Being

Drinking and pub-going can be seen as a collectively appreciated time-out situation in which it is legitimate to forget everyday problems. It facilitates the sharing of activities, experiences and emotions with peers. The exchange of common experiences and the knowledge that others are in a similar position have a positive impact on youngsters' well-being. For instance,

Box 6.2   Method Used to Measure Stereotypes of Daily Smoking Peers, Real Self-Images and Ideal Self-Images

Stereotypes of daily smoking peers were measured by asking the following question:

I think that someone my age who smokes on a daily basis:

	Absolutely not	Probably not	Maybe	Probably yes	Absolutely yes

a. does his/ her best at school

b. is sociable

c. listens to his/her parents

d. is self-assured

e. enjoys life

f. has many friends

g. is honest

h. is cheeky

i. has guts

j. dates often

k. is often away from home

l. belongs to the group

m. is popular

n. is cool

o. looks tough

p. looks nice

q. is interesting

r. is sexy

s. is sporty

The scale consisted of four reliable factors, i.e.: 'well-adjusted' (items a to g), 'rebellious' (items h to m), 'cool' (items n and o) and 'attractive' (items p to s). Real self-images were assessed by asking respondents to what extent these characteristics applied to themselves (1 = 'not at all' to 5 = 'very much'), and ideal self-images were measured by asking to what extent one would like to have the presented characteristics when being two years older (1 = 'not at all' to 5 = 'very much').

For more information on this instrument we refer to Spijkerman *et al.*, (2004)

engagement in social activities with friends seems to be associated with healthier emotional functioning. So, considering the potential advantages of alcohol-related settings, avoiding these might be related to loneliness, isolation and stress. Perhaps people who do not drink on a regular basis have fewer opportunities to relieve their daily stresses or to associate with peers.

It is widely believed that some alcohol provides short-term relief from the unpleasant effects of strain and conflict. The underlying causes of emotional distress among adolescents are diverse. Some adolescents, especially those who do not get on with their parents and are not committed to school and academic achievement, may be prone to seek out antisocial peers and to initiate drinking. Furthermore, low academic self-efficacy and a problematic family environment (e.g. divorced parents, living in deprived areas) are factors leading to stress and, eventually, to the initiation of alcohol use and to heavy drinking (Kumpfer and Turner, 1990).

Empirical findings are inconclusive regarding relationships between psychosocial well-being and substance use. While some studies have reported that low self-esteem, depression and stress are related to heavy drinking or problem drinking among young people, others have failed to demonstrate significant relationships. An explanation for this ambivalence is that the relationships might be more complex than these studies assumed. Windle and Windle (1996) emphasized that personal and social factors affect the relationship between stressors and problematic behaviours. For instance, research on general styles of coping and alcohol-specific coping styles has shown that coping strategies that are not problem-focused are related to alcohol misuse and heavy drinking, especially under conditions of stress. Another line of inquiry directs our attention to social support as a mediating factor. For example, when someone is not performing well at school and might become a drop-out, the amount of support s/he will get from parents and friends will affect whether problem solving is perceived to be possible to alleviate stress and negative feelings.

The case is somewhat different for smoking. Several longitudinal investigations have revealed that adolescents with symptoms of depression are more likely to start smoking (Breslau, Kilbey and Andreski, 1993). In addition, some longitudinal research has shown that low self-esteem is related to enhanced levels of smoking.

Some authors have suggested that the link between poor emotional adjustment, such as depression and low self-esteem, and smoking may be interpreted as a form of self-medication: nicotine may be used to withdraw from current problems and may alleviate emotional upsets.

However, there are other explanations for the association between emotional problems and smoking behaviour. In the course of adolescence, non-smoking youngsters are confronted with a rapid increase of smokers in their peer environment. Because several studies have shown that peer pressure is a relevant predictor of smoking onset, it is very likely that youngsters who have problems in dealing with peer pressures are more prone to yield to these pressures and begin smoking themselves. Furthermore, it is assumed that adolescents with emotional problems, such as depression or low self-esteem, are especially vulnerable to taking up smoking when they also lack the confidence and the skills to deal with peer pressures. For instance, in a 12-month prospective study, Petraitis and co-workers found strong negative associations between refusal self-efficacy and smoking onset (Petraitis, Flay and Miller, 1995).

In sum, there is mixed evidence concerning the link between psychological adjustment (i.e. depression, low self-esteem, stress) and drinking. However, there is ample evidence that poor psychological adjustment is related to smoking in young people.

Testing the Limits

Shedler and Block's research (1990) shows that teenagers who are neither curious nor open to new experiences are more likely to abstain from substance use in their adolescent years. Thus, since it is unusual for youngsters to remain abstainers, they could be perceived as fearing to lose control, and of lacking 'normal' sensation-seeking desires. There is some indirect support for this idea. It is widely known that certain forms of substance use and delinquent behaviours co-exist. For example, those who abstain from drinking are also less likely to smoke, to experiment with marijuana, to commit minor antisocial acts, to play truant and to rebel at school. Without arguing for a stepping-stone theory in which engagement in smoking and drinking leads on to hard drug use or delinquency, we think there is evidence that children who start drinking and smoking early are more involved in other experimenting behaviours (Engels and Ter Bogt, 2001). Thus, in some individuals, non-drinking is a sign of a relatively controlled and conservative lifestyle (see Box 6.3).

Long-Term Effects of Early Substance Use

Several prospective studies have found positive associations between the age of first use and alcohol problems later in life (e.g. Dawson 2000), yet other studies have found little evidence of continuity of drinking across the lifespan (e.g. Temple and Fillmore, 1986). Causal interpretation of the association is still controversial, as drinking onset and alcohol problems may have common origins in poor family support, personality traits or social environment. Early involvement in drinking is seen as part of a complex of problematic circumstances and behaviours, which are often ignored in scientific studies. Both the timing of initiation into drinking and the development of problematic drinking patterns later might be explained by a general vulnerability to problematic behaviours. In a longitudinal twin study, Prescott and Kendler (1999) showed that the age of drinking onset and later alcohol-related problems are caused by both nature and nurture.

As we all know, experimenting with smoking by adolescents is not without risk. Once adolescents become addicted to nicotine it is hard for them to quit and they are likely to develop a regular smoking pattern (e.g. Prokhorov *et al.*, 1996; Stanton, 1995). In our opinion, regular smoking habits develop through a sequence of small decisions, such as the decision to try a cigarette once, or to smoke with friends. Important in this regard is that smoking

---

Box 6.3   Should We Stop Paying Attention to Adolescent Drinking?

Although adolescent drinking is associated with several social and psychological benefits, this does not imply that we should stop worrying about adolescent drinking, or even encouraging youngsters to drink. In Western societies, in which a large majority of adults are drinkers, drinking to a large extent reflects social adjustment. However, in communities where alcohol use is prohibited by religious rules, such as in the Islamic world, the opposite is true and alcohol use may reflect poor adaptation. This illustrates how the degree to which the use of alcohol and other drugs is functional and beneficial largely depends upon existing social and societal norms.

It should be noted that socially acceptable drinking patterns, such as binge drinking during weekends, may have detrimental health effects as well as negative social consequences such as aggression, violence, sexual harassment, drunk driving or the development of problem drinking. Therefore, in our view, social and societal norms regarding alcohol use should be a topic of interest to policy makers and prevention workers. However, within the context of existing norms, one should have particular concerns for adolescents who do not engage in alcohol use for social reasons, but use it to combat feelings of stress and depression or a lack of self-esteem.

---

just a few cigarettes during adolescence increases the probability of developing nicotine dependence. Across studies, data consistently indicate that a large majority (two thirds or more) of adolescent smokers report experiencing withdrawal symptoms during attempts to quit or reduce their smoking (Colby *et al.*, 2000). Nevertheless, a considerable number of adolescent smokers want to quit smoking and many of them have tried. Unfortunately, relapse rates are high and few adolescents who try to quit on their own are successful. Experimenting with smoking leads to a 16-fold higher risk of adult smoking, and approximately 75% of adolescent daily smokers will continue to smoke as adults.

So, there is some evidence that heavy drinking in adolescence enhances the likelihood of alcohol misuse and alcohol dependence in adulthood. Smoking, even just experimentation with using cigarettes, increases the chances of nicotine addiction later in adolescence and adulthood.

Unresolved Issues

With respect to the social features of youth substance use, one might argue whether these effects should be attributed to the substance itself or to the situations in which young people use alcohol, drugs or cigarettes. From the age of about 14 years, a large majority of young people go out to pubs, bars, discos and parties with friends and on dates. Of course, attendance at these settings goes hand in hand with alcohol consumption: one of the strongest predictors of adolescent alcohol use is the frequency of pub-going. So this supports the hypothesis that these functions may be strongly related to context.

On the other hand, it is common knowledge that after a few drinks, people feel more free and confident to approach potential partners, for instance. For adolescents who drink exclusively at home (with or without their parents), alcohol use is not associated with social functioning in peer groups. In contrast, we found that drinking among these youngsters was associated with maladjustment and mental problems (primarily in boys, see Engels, Knibbe and Drop, 1999b).

So perhaps it is a combination of some of the properties of the beverage as well as the specific settings that is accountable for the relation between drinking and social benefits. This line of reasoning is more difficult for smoking, since we know that smoking cigarettes does not strongly affect individual emotional and social states (except perhaps in relation to stress reduction).

Most studies have used cross-sectional data to examine correlates of substance use. It is, therefore, difficult to draw conclusions with respect to the causal nature of different processes. Furthermore, the question remains: what are the effects of prolonged abstinence? For instance, adolescents who do not drink might be late maturers. Thus, some of the differences in social and emotional development may disappear if adolescents were re-interviewed in their mid-twenties. On the other hand, some adolescents who do not experience what for the majority of adolescents are important normative changes may encounter problems with the formation of peer relationships or with detachment from the family. Thus, future research should explore aspects of aetiology in more detail before conclusions concerning the relative position of abstainers, moderate users and heavy users can be made.

Abstainers are a very heterogeneous group and may have various reasons for *not* engaging in substance use. One group of abstainers consists of isolated youngsters with few peer contacts outside the parental home, who are dissatisfied because they want to spend time with others and belong to a peer group. Another group are young athletes, who might be abstaining because they want to maintain their healthy lifestyle, but could have a good social life nevertheless. In addition, for others abstinence could be a feature of a certain lifestyle. For instance, some religious groups have regulations that do not allow alcohol consumption, smoking or drug use at all. So those who participate in these movements may not drink but may still be adequately integrated into a social network. Indeed, they might encounter severe problems if they should break these rules. Another reason for not drinking is related to physical health. For instance, it is possible that young people with a chronic disease do not want (or are not allowed) to drink or smoke, but score higher on psychological maladjustment for other reasons.

Though there are substantial shortcomings in the studies on positive aspects of drinking, some findings do emphasize the social and developmental benefits of adolescent drinking. This implies that prevention efforts that do not take into account the positive aspects of drinking are likely to fail.

Negative Health and Social Consequences of Drinking and Smoking

In this chapter, only limited attention has been paid to the negative sides of substance use. Research on developmental and instrumental functions of adolescent risk behaviours is essential for the understanding of youngsters' reasons for experimentation and continuation of risky and unhealthy behaviour. However, investigation of the consequences of risk behaviours requires information about *both* negative and positive consequences. For instance, if an individual reports some positive consequences of risk behaviour, but perceives at the same time that the negative consequences outweigh the positive ones, this individual may be more likely to abstain from the risk behaviour (see Hendry and Kloep, 2002).

Box 6.4 Fragments from Interviews (Kloep *et al.*, 2001)

To the question 'Why do you drink?', young people from Sweden and Scotland gave the following answers:

Excitement and fun

If you are not sober you can have fun with everything. It feels so good to laugh, it can be silly sometimes, it is so nice to laugh out loud, you know. (Swedish girl, 16)

At a few dances, I've had quite a lot to drink. I would say that I've actually been drunk but only once to the point that I was being sick. Most of the time I just have enough to feel really, really good, you know. (Scottish girl, 17)

Sometimes you drink yourself stupid and everything changes to a wonderful world full of handsome guys. (Swedish girl, 15)

Easier to contact other people

It is difficult to come into contact – not with pals, but with birds, I mean, without alcohol... I met a girl at the school party, I was not sober then, but she has talked to me several times afterwards, last time was on Saturday. (Swedish boy, 16)

Sometimes they approach you and talk if they are pissed – though that is no fun, neither. In the beginning, it can be like this, they are smashed when you meet them, then they are sober again but nevertheless they come over and you feel shit-happy... it is often like that, drunk you meet wow shit-many friends like that. (Swedish girl, 16)

The most important reason to focus on the developmental functions of substance use is that the majority of young people do start drinking or smoking because of the positive consequences they perceive. The most significant motives adolescents have for their drinking are social and enhancement motives (Kloep *et al.*, 2001) (Box 6.4). Thus, adolescents drink because they want to have fun, to have a good time with friends and/or a partner or to feel good, and not to become involved in fights or car accidents.

However, there are also negative short-term or long-term consequences for adolescents. For instance, several studies have shown that adolescent alcohol use is related to drinking problems and alcohol abuse in adulthood. Pape and Hammer (1996) did find that those youngsters who drink heavily in their adolescent years are more likely to drink heavily in adulthood. However, only alcohol dependence in early and mid-adolescence is associated with problem drinking and negative alcohol-related consequences in adulthood, whereas social drinking is not. These findings parallel those of Beck, Thombs and Summons, (1993) who showed that the reasons people have for drinking rather than the drinking levels per se affect whether they become heavy or problem drinkers. Teenagers who drink to reduce feelings of distress might learn to perceive drinking as a coping mechanism and might be prone to higher drinking levels and problem drinking in late adolescence and young adulthood. These findings suggest that the functions drinking has for individual adolescents may affect what kind of drinking habits they develop later in life.

However, there is evidence for the direct negative consequences of binge drinking and alcohol misuse in adolescence, with drinking in adolescence being related to car accidents, suicide, homicide, delinquency, aggression and sexual assaults. The costs to society of underage drinking are enormous, as are the effects on individual adolescents and families. Nevertheless, a focus on the overwhelming number of studies on the short-term and long-term negative consequences of drinking does not lead to more insights into the reasons why young people take up and maintain drinking.

Furthermore, although it is essential to focus on alcohol misuse and its adverse consequences, it should be stressed that the majority of adolescent drinkers (moderate or not) do not become involved in sexual assaults, rapes or car accidents. The majority of adolescents drink at weekends together with friends and relatives, and do not seem to suffer from any severe short-term health consequences (except hangovers). Although many adolescents are indeed binge drinkers, their drinking patterns change significantly once they gain status in adult society. In other words, for many adolescents drinking alcohol has few if any negative consequences.

Practical Implications

Although research into the beneficial functions of substance use is considered to be preliminary, we would like to raise a few issues regarding the prevention of smoking as well as alcohol misuse and its consequences. Firstly, in Western societies, the vast majority of late adolescents have experimented with smoking and drinking. This implies that drinking and smoking are not only socially acceptable, but perhaps even normative. Therefore, health education which aims to discourage people from drinking at all can expect to have limited effects. Furthermore, insights into the positive aspects of drinking show that prevention focusing on the negative sides of alcohol while neglecting the beneficial functions are not convincing for target groups. So if one plans to reduce the prevalence of binge drinking or drunk driving, it is essential to think more comprehensively about the different motives people have for going out and drinking.

In addition, several review studies show the limited effects of school-based prevention programmes (Tobler et al., 2000). We think that one of the main reasons for this is that these programmes are based on wrong premises concerning the causes of juvenile drinking. The first premise is that drinking is rational behaviour and that people's cognitions (e.g. attitudes, ideas, beliefs, expectancies, self-efficacy) predict their drinking habits. However, recent studies show only limited effects of these cognitions on the development of drinking in young people over time (Jones, Corbin and Fromme, 2001).

Secondly, it is often assumed that peers constitute the main social force that drives young people into substance use. Nonetheless, recent longitudinal studies indicate that peer pressure is only marginally related to the development of drinking and smoking patterns over time. Furthermore, there is the assumption that people use and misuse alcohol, cigarettes and drugs because they lack social competence. However, the recent findings depicted above suggest that particularly sociable and well-integrated youngsters drink alcohol and/or smoke.

In addition, it is also quite remarkable that hardly any attention is paid to the role of parents in influencing young people's risk behaviours, either in prevention or in interventions. However, from several studies, we know that parental substance habits, parental norms, parenting practices, such as supervision, control and support, and quality of communication are related to consumption in adolescents.

So, although there is ample evidence that parents do matter, it remains a question why they are not more involved in primary prevention in many countries in Europe. One reason has to do with motivation and responsibility: many parents think that governments (mass media campaigns, laws) and schools should do the job. Furthermore, parents often do not realize that they can make a difference. We think, however, that there is enough evidence to concentrate prevention on parents and adolescents together.

Conclusion

In this chapter, we have provided some theoretical and empirical grounds for the argument that substance use can have positive functions for young people. Although many researchers, parents, policy makers and health educators primarily focus on the negative sides of smoking, drinking and drug use, we believe that if we want to truly *understand* the reasons why young people start using substances it is ineffective to concentrate exclusively on the negative consequences of drinking, smoking and other drugs. Instead, we have to consider both sides of the coin, to ensure that our interventions, educational programmes and promotional 'messages' take account of young people's perspective and are more sensitively attuned to the appropriate avenues for genuinely accessing adolescents who need help. We hope that the emphasis on the developmental meaning of substance use presented in this chapter has stimulated the reader to think about adolescent risk behaviours in a different way than before.

CASE STUDY 6.1

In the Netherlands, there is a popular multi-component school-based prevention programme focusing upon preventing youngsters from taking up smoking, drinking and marijuana use. The programme entitled 'Healthy School and Drugs' concentrates on secondary school children between the ages of 12 and 15, and 64–73% of all Dutch schools participate in the programme.

It is based on a model that states that intentions and behaviours are determined by attitudes, perceived social norms and self-efficacy (ASE), and programme elements can be effective if they have a positive effect on these three determinants. The participants consist of schools, their pupils and parents and health officials in a task force, and the programme consists of a series of educational lessons, school rules about the use of substances, the development and implementation of a detection system for early onset drug users, and the involvement of parents. Schools vary substantially in the extent to which they collaborate with the programme.

An evaluation study was conducted involving three control schools and nine experimental schools. The effects of the intervention were tested among pupils one, two and three years after the commencement of the intervention. No effects of the intervention on smoking initiation were found, few influences on alcohol use and there were even counterproductive effects for marijuana usage: adolescents in the experimental programme were more likely to be frequent marijuana users than those who were not enrolled in the intervention.

Clearly, the intervention did not work. Before you read on, try to find reasons why this intervention failed to be effective!

In our opinion, this might have to do with the portrayal of substances during the programme. Mostly they were portrayed negatively (in terms of long-term and short-term consequences) and the main message to pupils was to postpone starting to use drugs and alcohol. However, this did not coincide with their social and implicit knowledge (and often personal experiences) about the effects of smoking and drinking. Many youngsters associate positive qualities with peers who drink, as we have discussed in this chapter.

In our opinion, school-based prevention of alcohol and drugs will not be effective if it ignores the important social functions such activities have for the majority of adolescents. Future programmes that portray a more realistic picture of the functions of such substances – and their users – are more credible, and also perhaps more effective.

CASE STUDY 6.1 QUESTION

1. What are the obstacles to including both the positive and negative effects of substance use in a school-based prevention programme?

Further Reading

1. Engels, R.C.M.E. and Ter Bogt, T. (2001) Influences of risk behaviors on the quality of peer relations in adolescence. *Journal of Youth and Adolescence*, 30, 675– 695.
2. Kuntsche, E., Knibbe, R.A., Gmel, G. and Engels, R.C.M.E. (2005) Why do young people drink? A review of drinking motives. *Clinical Psychology Review*, 25, 841–861.
3. Pape, H. and Hammer, T. (1996) Sober adolescence: Predictor of psychosocial maladjustment in young adulthood? *Scandinavian Journal of Psychology*, 37, 362– 377.
4. Prescott, C.A. and Kendler K.S. (1999) Age at first drink and risk for alcoholism: A noncausal association. *Alcoholism: Clinical and Experimental Research*, 23, 101– 107.
5. Maggs, J. L. and Hurrelmann, K. (1998) Do substance use and delinquency have differential associations with adolescents' peer relations? *International Journal of Behavioral Development*, 22, 367– 388.

Discussion Questions

1. For which kind of groups do the costs of substance use outweigh the benefits, and why?
2. What can be done to ensure that public policy takes into account the conclusion that there are beneficial functions of substance use?
3. Are there cultural differences in the implications of our findings for prevention?
4. Do you think that the beneficial functions of substance use are similar for males and females? Discuss whether different approaches are necessary for young men and young women.

Chapter 7

Getting It Right in Health Services for Young People

Aidan Macfarlane

Independent International Consultant in Child and Adolescent Health

Ann McPherson

General Practitioner, Lecturer in Primary Care, University of Oxford

Authors of the 'Teenage Health Freak' series, www.teenagehealthfreak.org

- Introduction
- Who Provides Health Care for Young People in the United Kingdom
- What Young People Want from Primary Health Care Services
- The Pluses and Minuses of Primary Health Care Services in Meeting the Needs of Young People
- The Quality Issues Involved in Improving Primary Health Care Services for Young People
- Challenges for the Future

Learning Objectives

After reading this chapter you should:

1 Understand who provides health care for young people in the United Kingdom.
2 Be aware of what young people want from the health care services.
3 Have an understanding of the pluses and minuses of the primary health care services in meeting the needs of young people.
4 Have a sense of the quality issues involved in improving the primary health care services for young people.
5 Know how the primary health care services need to develop in the future so as to better meet the needs of young people.

Introduction

There are approximately 7.7 million teenagers aged 10 to 19 living in the United Kingdom at the present time, representing around 15% of the total population. Health service provision to meet the health needs of this age group has been given low priority over many years because: (a) young people have been considered to be a relatively healthy age group; (b) from a governmental point of view they had little voting power; (c) society and the media have both chosen to regard this age group as being 'risk' takers and relatively irresponsible about their health care behaviours; and (d) the pressures on NHS resources have been on other higher profile age groups, for instance newborn babies and the elderly population.

However, with the gradual realization that the health needs of young people aged 10 to 19 are significantly different from those of children aged 0 to 9, the continuing high negative media profiling of young people and their behaviours, the acceptance that teenagers actually grow into voting adults, and increasing pressure from health professionals themselves, the health of young people has now begun to be given a higher priority within Department of Health and government policies.

As a result, health services are beginning to look at the specific needs of young people and respond accordingly. It is the aim of this chapter to outline what the primary health care needs of young people are, and how health services can best develop in the future to meet these needs, accepting that NHS services will, and should, because of financial restrictions, be prioritized towards the most needy. However, investing in the future long-term health of adults by providing excellent health care for children and young people is economically sound and hugely cost-effective.

Who Provides Health Care for Young People in the United Kingdom

When considering the health services used by, and available to, young people, it is essential to first understand the huge range of people outside the NHS that young people use to obtain the relevant information and who are also responsible for managing the health care of young people in its broadest aspects. Most 'health maintenance' and 'illness care' in young people is dealt with by themselves and their parents. If these sources do not suffice then other non-medical sources are normally consulted – including friends, relatives, neighbours, teachers etc., before turning to professional medical resources.

There are also an extensive number of government agencies and services that are outside the NHS, many of which may be extremely relevant to the health of adolescents in one way or another. One problem with these agencies is that they themselves may not be aware of the fact that the health needs of young people are very different from both those of children and those of adults. Simply providing information to these agencies about young people's health needs is inadequate, and many of those coming into direct contact with young people will, in the future, require specific training, not only in health-related matters but also in being sensitive to young people's specific needs and how best to communicate with them.

Thus, 80% of all health problems are dealt with by people without referral on to *professional* health carers, with people on average consulting five different sources of non-professional information (family, friends, neighbours etc.) before contacting the primary health services. When the primary health services *are* consulted, the first line of health care is provided by the primary

Health Care Providers Outside the National Health Service

- Young people themselves
- Parents
- Other members of a family
- Nearby community sources
- Non-governmental organizations (e.g. Brook clinics)
- Friends
- Teachers
- Leaflets
- Books
- Magazines
- Television programmes
- Web sites (e.g. **www.teenagehealthfreak.org**)

Some of the National and Local Government Services Relevant to the Health of Young People

- Department for Education and Skills
- Youth services
- Youth Justice Board
- Connexions
- Prison services including young offender institutions
- Drug action teams
- Refugee networks
- Local education authorities
- Social services
- Probation services
- Family court services

health services followed by the secondary and tertiary care services. But again only about one in ten patients seen in primary care is referred on for secondary or tertiary care.

When primary health care services are used, the provision that may be obtained can come from a wide range of health-related professionals including school nurses, health visitors, public health nurses, practice nurses, therapists, psychologists, health promotion experts, counsellors, practice receptionists, pharmacists, general practitioners and dentists.

Likewise, although more young people aged 10 –19 years old are now being admitted to hospital than children under the age of 10 (excluding newborn babies as almost all births now take place in a secondary care setting), most young people will not be being admitted to hospital services that are specifically designed for them (Viner and Barker, 2005). Thus, the range of hospital doctors, let alone all the other related specialist hospital staff, who will have contact with young people will include paediatricians, endocrinologists, general and specialist adult medical doctors, obstetricians and gynaecologists, general and specialist surgeons including orthopaedic surgeons, accident and emergency department doctors, psychiatrists and many more besides.

What Young People Want from Primary Health Care Services

Questions relating to day-to-day health problems are not normally the first things that spring into young people's minds. Survey information indicates that, in the order of the overall concerns that young people have, school, appearance, and money all rate as areas of greater concern than 'health' as such. However, judging from the pages of teenage magazines, health-related issues are important to them (Balding, 2004).

Nevertheless when young people *do* want health information and care, they want it available to them when *they* need it, rather than having it pushed at them when health professionals feel that they should have it; in a format and language which they find accessible and understandable; non-authoritarian and non-condescending; and they want it, where possible, individualized to their own specific needs. The information that is available should be up-to-date and, where possible, evidence-based.

The first level at which such information can be provided, outside their family, is via books, television, the media in general and the Internet. Thus a number of web sites providing young people with health information are now available, the most successful of which is **www.teenagehealthfreak.org**, but also include **www.youthhealthtalk.org**, **www.mindbodysoul.gov.uk** and **www.childline.org.uk**.

The 1000 emails plus which **www.teenagehealthfreak.org** receives each month from young people provides an indicator of both the types of health concerns that young people have and also the concerns that they have which are not being dealt with elsewhere by other services. Analysis of 1500 emails show that their main concerns relate to serious sexual health questions (26%), next came concerns about diet and weight (7%), then with minor illnesses like headaches and nosebleeds (5%), relationship problems (5%), the effects of smoking 5%, body image (3.5%), and questions relating to pubertal changes (2%). Emails were categorized into 22 different groups. However, a large number of questions relating to bullying were analysed separately, as were questions which dealt with sexual nonsense ('My willie is three foot long. Will I hurt my girl friend?') and the emails that came from adults.

What Young People *Say* they Want from the Health Services

In examining the health services that are being supplied to young people, it is important to try and discover how well these match young people's expectations and needs. When questioned, what young people want from primary health care covers a range of issues, some of which are equally important to adult patients. For instance, almost all young people rate 'confidentiality' as the most important issue and their first concern (Churchill *et al.*, 2000). They then want to see a doctor who is interested and knowledgeable about their health needs and care, followed by 'same day appointments' and being able to choose the gender of the doctor that they see. Further down the list (see Table 7.1) is 'having a drop-in clinic available for young people' and 'a friendly receptionist'.

Another way of looking at what young people want from their primary health care services is to look at the kind of questions they want to ask of these services. Teenagers aged 10 to 19 years were asked to list the three questions they would like to ask their doctor or other health professional.

Table 7.1.   Priorities in provision of primary health care services among young people

	Percentages
Confidentiality (knowing that if you tell the doctor something, other people will not find out)	81
Having a doctor who is interested in teenage problems	51
Being able to see a doctor on the same day you make the appointment	39
Having a special teenage clinic which you can 'drop into' if you have a problem	39
Being able to choose to see a male or female doctor	33
Being able to ask for advice over the phone without having to give your name	32
Having a friendly receptionist	30
Seeing the same doctor or nurse on every visit	20
Being able to discuss problems with a nurse instead of a doctor	17
Being invited to a special health check with a doctor or nurse	17

From Churchill D, Allen J, Denman S, *et al.*, Do the attitudes and beliefs of young teenagers towards general practice influence actual consultation behaviour? British Journal of General Practice 2000; 50: 953–957.

The top ten topics and examples of questions were:

1. Contraception

- How do I know what is best for me?
- Where do I go?
- At what age can I take the pill?

2. Period problems

- Why are periods so painful?
- Why aren't they regular?
- What can I do about heavy bleeding?

3. Weight

- How can I lose weight?
- What is the ideal weight for my height?

4. Exercise/healthy eating

- What is the best form of exercise?
- How can I find out about a healthy diet?

5. Sex

- Where can I go to get good information about sex?
- Does sex at a young age increase the risk of disease?
- Should we get pushed into having sex?

6. Confidentiality

- Can I trust my doctor to keep what I tell him/her confidential?
- Is there anything they will tell my mum about?
- Do you discuss patients with your colleagues?

7. Sexually transmitted diseases

- How can I protect myself from AIDS?
- How can I tell if I have an STI?
- Is my vaginal discharge normal?

8. Acne

- Is there a cure for it?
- Does eating chocolate cause spots?
- Do any of the creams work?

9. Stress and depression

- Why do I feel so stressed out?
- Does anyone care about me?
- Why does love hurt so much?

10. Cancer

- How can I protect myself from cancer?
- What are the early signs of cancer?
- Can a doctor tell straight away if I've got cancer?

(Taken from Jones et al., 1997)

Not really surprisingly, the specific health concerns that individual young people have do not always match up with the concerns that others may have *about* the health of teenagers in general. The major health problems of young people as perceived by health professionals include: growth and puberty, nutrition, exercise and obesity, sexual and reproductive health, the common medical conditions of adolescence (e.g. acne, common orthopaedic diseases, functional/psychosomatic disorders, sleep disorders, fatigue and chronic fatigue syndrome), chronic disabilities, mental health and eating disorders, substance abuse, accidents and self injury.

What Young People Actually Consult about When they do Use Primary Health Care Services

Many young people, like their adult counterparts do not consult anyone about their health problems, though when they do consult health professionals their general practitioner (GP) seems to be the person they most use (see Table 7.2).

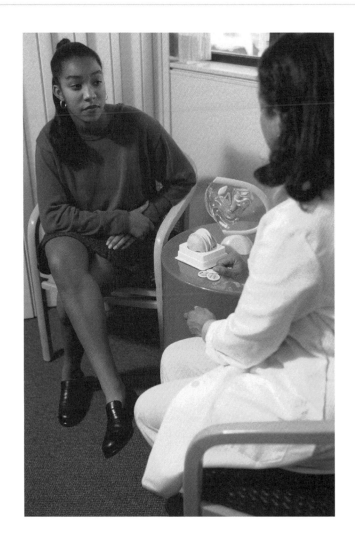

Table 7.2   Consultations for different conditions among 15–16 year-olds

Condition	No one	GP	School nurse	Clinic	Other
Spots/acne	39.1	50.8	1.3	4.8	4
Diet	49.8	30.8	8.6	3.9	6.9
Smoking	63.5	16	8.7	3.4	8.3
Pregnancy	34.3	25	4.3	30.2	5.2
STDs	58.3	18.2	9.2	7.9	6.3

LD Jacobson *et al.*, Teenager's views on general practice consultations and other medical advice, Family Practice (2000), 17, 156–158, by permission of Oxford University Press.

Percentages

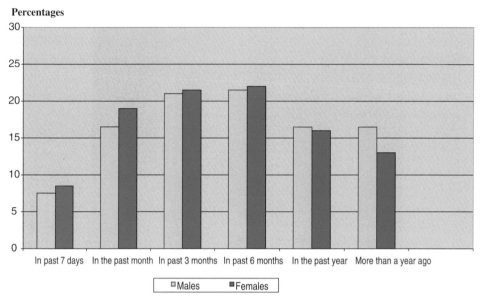

Figure 7.1   Frequency of visiting the doctor among 12–15 year-olds, by gender, 2003 (Balding, 2004). Reproduced by Permission of Schools Health Education Unit.

The next issue is how often young people visit their GPs and the results of surveying this shows that young people actually consult their doctors rather more frequently than most people expect (see Figure 7.1).

Furthermore, analysis of what young people consult their GPs about indicates that the reasons are not all that different from the reasons why adults consult, as shown in (Figure 7.2).

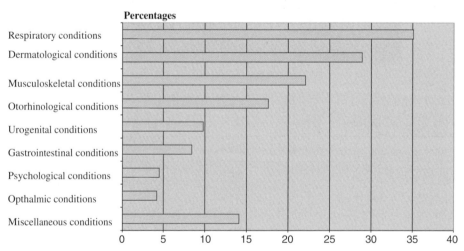

Figure 7.2   Reasons for consultation with a GP over a 12-month period (Churchill et al., 2000). From Churchill D, Allen J, Denman S, *et al.*, Do the attitudes and beliefs of young teenagers towards general practice influence actual consultation behaviour? British Journal of General Practice 2000; 50: 953–957.

The Pluses and Minuses of Primary Health Care Services in Meeting the Needs of Young People

The primary health care services in the United Kingdom have a number of great advantages, some of which are so obvious that they are easily forgotten. These advantages often relate to services provided for young people as well as adults and include: being free at the time of delivery; being relatively local; providing a degree of expertise (though not always specifically for young people's needs); being able to refer on to specialist services; continuity of care; and, hopefully, confidentiality.

Against this are the disadvantages of long waiting times for appointments; inconvenient surgery times from a young person's point of view; limited consultation time; possible lack of confidentiality; possible paternalistic attitude; and lack of skill in communicating with young people.

Overall, teenagers (like many adults) may have health concerns which they do not easily reveal to their GP, even though young people do visit their GPs on average two to three times a year, with around 70% of all young people visiting their primary care service in any one year. Other surveys do, however, show that adolescents are usually happy to discuss health issues with their GPs, although four out of ten found it difficult seeing their GP and six out of ten said that they would not know to register with their GP when they left home. Research also shows that the average consulting time that a doctor gives to an adolescent is eight minutes compared with ten minutes for an adult.

Furthermore, from a young person's point of view there are a number of other barriers to using the appropriate health services.

What Young People have Said are the Barriers to their Effective Use of both Primary and Secondary Care Services

- Lack of information
- Difficulties in achieving low visibility access for confidential issues
- Services are not seen as youth friendly because of:

  - concerns about confidentiality for those under 16 years of age
  - lack of expertise and continuity of care by professionals
  - failure to respect the validity of young people's views
  - young people in hospital having to be accommodated either in a children's ward or with a population they regard as elderly
  - some groups of young people have particular difficulty with access to services associated with issues such as disability, poverty, ethnicity, being looked after and sexual orientation.

Bridging the gaps: health care for adolescents. Royal College of Paediatrics and Child Health, 2003.

Primary Health Care Services and Meeting the Needs of Young People with Chronic Health Problems

Primary health care, along with other medical services will increasingly be seeing young people with long-term medical conditions, as better treatments for illnesses such as cystic fibrosis enable them to live on into adolescence and even adulthood. The implementation of the White Paper 'Our health, our care, our say' (Department of Health, 2006) will mean that more care covering chronic problems, including asthma, diabetes and so forth, will be carried out in the community. This will be an important challenge to the primary care services.

Communication Difficulties with Young People Consulting in Primary Care

Special skills are required to ensure that communication with young people is maximally effective and this is as true of all primary health care facilities as it is in hospital. In order to do this, it is necessary to understand the young person's cognitive and social development. One reason for difficulties in communication is the triadic nature of many primary health care consultations with adolescents, where the health professional often has to communicate with the young person and their parent(s) at the same time. Another reason is that attempting to communicate with a person undergoing rapid social and psychological change may mean that there are few shared values or understanding when trying to delineate best treatments and care management (Donovan *et al.*, 2004). Nevertheless, randomized controlled trials do indicate that training can improve GPs' communication skills and interactions with young people (Sanci *et al.*, 2000).

The Role of Primary Health Care in Health Promotion for Young People

There are a number of health-related issues where it would seem obvious that primary health care could, at least opportunistically, offer advice and help to young people in the field of health promotion and primary prevention. These areas include obesity, smoking, illegal drugs, alcohol abuse, sexual health and contraception, as well as mental heath problems including self-harm and eating disorders. However, the role of primary health care services in health promotion has to be seen 'in context' and is only a single cog in a much bigger wheel, the main elements of which are political intent. Nevertheless, it is essential, in order to ensure any kind of effectiveness, that all service provision for young people is seen to be 'singing from the same hymn book' and is able to refer young people between the multitude of services provided – as most appropriate and most effective.

The Quality Issues Involved in Improving Primary Health Care Services for Young People

With increasing devolvement of health care in the United Kingdom to local parliaments, it is beyond the scope of this chapter to give more than some examples of the Department of Health's initiatives in England in this area.

'You're Welcome' Quality Standards for the Service Provision of Health Care for Young People

All young people are entitled to receive appropriate health care wherever they access it. The 'You're Welcome' quality criteria have been developed by the Department of Health and attempt to lay out the principles that should help guide health services both in the primary health care services and in hospitals to 'get it right' and become 'user-friendly' to young people. The general quality standards are set out below, with how they apply to primary health care in italics (see Department of Health, 2005b).

General practices are required to provide primary health care services for a broad spectrum of the population, not *just* for young people. Many of the standards cited in this document are generic to the whole practice, for example, compliance with the Disability Discrimination Act and with child protection procedures. The following list therefore summarizes those standards that are specific to providing high standards of care specifically for *young people* in this setting.

1. Accessibility

- Young people can use the service outside school or college hours OR the service is provided very close to a school or college site.
- Under-16-year-olds can access the service without an adult making an appointment for them and be seen alone.
- Where there is a choice about service location, the location is accessible by public transport and is acceptable to young people.

Young people of any age should be able to make and attend an appointment without an adult. A mixture of urgent and routine appointments should be available outside of normal school or college hours. Some practices may be able to offer a 'drop-in' service.

2. Publicity

- Advertise, through posters and information booklets:
  - confidentiality;
  - about making an appointment oneself even if under 16;
  - about free contraception;
  - other local services for young people.

The practice leaflet, and any other practice information, should explicitly state that under 16 year-olds can be seen unaccompanied by an adult, and that they are entitled to a confidential service. Posters should be displayed in the reception area to this effect. Some practices may prepare a specific leaflet for young people.

3. Confidentiality and consent

- Ensure there is a written policy, including for under-16s, which all staff sign.
- Have staff meetings to discuss confidentiality annually (and other services).
- Make sure young people and parents understand about confidentiality.
- Use the confidentiality toolkit to help this process.

The practice has, and implements, a written policy on confidentiality and consent in relation to under-16 year-olds that is consistent with current Department of Health guidance. The policy ensures the provision of a confidential service for this group and includes a clear protocol for the management of child protection concerns and possible breaches of confidentiality.

Staff should take opportunities to explain the confidentiality policy and its implications to both young people and their parents at various ages both prior to, and during, adolescence. Young people attending with an adult should be given the opportunity to be seen unaccompanied for part of the consultation if they wish.

4. The environment

- Welcome young people appropriately.
- Make sure waiting rooms are young people friendly.
- Provide leaflets, magazines, etc., for young people.
- Refresh waiting room information every three months.
- Provide Internet access? Music?

Young people are welcomed on arrival and are not asked any potentially sensitive questions in public that might be overheard in the reception or waiting area. The waiting areas are 'young person friendly' and include up-to-date young people's magazines, leaflets and relevant posters about other local and national services.

5. Staff training, skills, attitudes and values

- All staff should have basic training in communication skills with young people.
- Clinical staff should be trained in consultation skills with young people, particularly in relation to mental health and sexual health.

All staff receive training on the practice's confidentiality policy. Practices should consider any significant events that occur in relation to the policy as part of their clinical governance procedures. All staff who are likely to come into contact with young people receive basic training on communicating easily with young people and on promoting young people friendly attitudes and values.

6. Joined up working

- Services should have knowledge of local and national services that young people can access.
- Keep parents in the picture, without breaking confidentiality.

The service has up-to-date information about the range of services available for young people in the local community, and appropriate referral mechanisms.

7. Involving young people

- Get feedback from young people themselves, for example, through:
  - surveys
  - focus groups

- talking during a consultation
- comments box.
- Get staff to imagine they are a teenager.

The views of young people are included and taken into account in any practice develop-ments and in patient satisfaction surveys.

8. Services offered

Young people can request the gender of the member of staff that they see, and this will be arranged whenever possible. Patient information leaflets tailored to the needs of young people should be used when available in preference to adult-orientated material. Routine sexual health services should be available as part of a holistic approach to care.

The second published government document outlining the services both for children and young people is the National Services Framework (NSF) for children, young people and ma-ternity services (DH and DfES, 2004). Many of the standards set out in this document have specific requirements of health services, and include:

- giving young people increased information, power and choice over the support and treatment that they receive, and involving them in planning their care and services;
- introducing a new health promotion programme;
- promoting physical health, mental health and emotional well-being;
- improving access to services;
- ensuring that all staff are suitably trained.

The NSF goes into detail to help support the implementation of these standards as they relate to the care of young people in primary care:

- The health and well-being of young people should be promoted and delivered through a coordinated programme of action led by the NHS in partnership with local authorities.
- Primary health care trusts should tailor their health promotion services to the needs of disadvantaged groups.
- Young people are actively involved in decisions about their health based on appropriate information.
- Primary health care trusts and local authorities work together with other agencies to de-velop links, so that information derived from an assessment can follow them and be avail-able to other services.
- All young people have access to appropriate services which are responsive to their specific needs as they grow into adulthood.

Challenges for the Future

There are, as the chapter has suggested, a large number of proposed developments within the national health services designed to meet the needs of young people. The single main barrier to implementing these is the lack of appropriately trained health professionals.

Training in Adolescent Health

The priority need at the present time is clear. Although other countries, such as the United States and Australia, have, over the last 10 years, begun to set up extensive specific training programmes in adolescent health and illness in academic centres, for instance at Rochester, Minneapolis and Boston in the United States, and in Melbourne and Sydney in Australia, no such academic centre or training course has been developed for doctors in the United Kingdom.

Apart from the field of adolescent psychiatry, training in the United Kingdom in the field of adolescent health is presently carried out in an ad hoc fashion by a handful of doctors in various specialities, for example, public health, rheumatology and primary care, most of whom have had little or no training in being a 'trainer'. As a result, training in the field of adolescent health and illness has been and remains extremely limited and if medical training is to meet the present and future needs in this field, there has to be a rapid expansion of the number of those trained to be trainers in the field (McDonagh *et al.*, 2004).

On the positive side, training methodologies and the content of a training programme in adolescent health and illness have already been well developed in Europe in an Internet-based programme – 'European Training in Effective Adolescent Care and Health' (EuTEACH) (**www.euteach.com**). The best elements of this programme now need to be used to develop training programmes in the United Kingdom in the field of adolescent health.

Therefore the need for training in adolescent health can be summarized as follows:

- Practising clinicians should comprehend that they have needs for training in adolescent health.
- 'Training in adolescent health should be mandatory for both undergraduates and the trainees of all the Royal Colleges whose members may be involved in the care of young people' (Bridging the gaps: healthcare for adolescents, RCPCH, 2003). All those working in the field of adolescent health and medicine should be encouraged to obtain a relevant qualification.
- At the present time in the United Kingdom there is no formal specific training in adolescent health/illness outside of mental health and primary health care.
- There is very little information available in general paediatric or adult medicine textbooks about adolescent health.
- Time and available training courses are two major constraints as seen by clinicians when trying to get further training.
- A new approach to training in adolescent health is needed. Such training needs to involve young people themselves both as adolescent actors and as assessors.
- Multi-disciplinary modular training programmes in general and specific aspects of adolescent health should be developed for allied health professionals.
- Existing nursing training modules in adolescent health should be developed and available throughout the country. Practical training in nursing young people should also be developed.
- There is an urgent need to train up trainers in the field of adolescent health.
- There are training programmes such as **www.euteach.com** available to train the trainers and these should be built on.

Taking into Account Young People's Views and Involving Young People in Developing Appropriate Services

It is important to make sure that young people's views are taken into account, although some young people may want to be involved in helping to develop appropriate services whereas others will simply want there to be good services available. There are many different ways of getting feedback including questionnaires, qualitative research and focus groups. It is essential, however, to ensure that the feedback views are collected in a rigorous way so as to ensure that it is simply not a question of '(s)he who shouts loudest gets their way'.

'One size fits all' is also not ideal and there should be as many different ways of delivering an appropriate service for young people as is financially feasible.

Youth involvement needs to be, when it comes to health, broader than just looking at the health services.

Figure 7.3 Youth Infusion (Sarah Schulman, **www.youthinfusion.com**).

The United Nation's Convention on the Rights of the Child (ratified in 1989 by 192 countries, with the exception of the United States and Somalia) equates freedom of thought, expression, and conscience with youth voice. Article 12 states, 'Parties shall assure to the child who is capable of forming his or her own views the right to express those views freely in all matters affecting the child, the views of the child being given due weight in accordance with the age and maturity of the child' (UNICEF online).

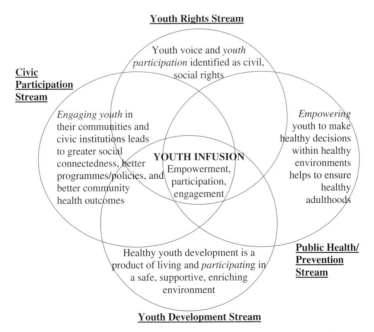

Figure 7.3   Youth Infusion (Sarah Schulman, www.youthinfusion.com).

The Role of Primary Health Care in Health Promotion

The main rationales behind health promotion to/for adolescents are: that there are health-related behaviours laid down during adolescence which continue into adult life (e.g. smoking, diet); that there are health-related behaviours during adolescence which have a direct effect on their immediate quality of life (e.g. drug-taking); and finally that there are health-related behaviours by adolescents which have effects both immediately and in the long term (e.g. exercise, sexual behaviours).

In order to promote health to young people there are three main strategic approaches, which are: the health promotion carried out by society as a whole on behalf of adolescents (e.g. banning cigarette advertising, making contraception easily available and free); the more personal level health education exhorting adolescents to behave in healthy ways (e.g. not to smoke, to use contraception, to eat a balanced diet, etc.); and finally the provision for young people of the most up-to-date health-related information in a format that they want, when they want it.

Primary care has a role in all three of these areas. First, all those working with young people in the field of health have a responsibility for being advocates on behalf of young people. This advocacy includes collecting and providing data concerning young people's health and using the information to lobby on their behalf with government and others. Second, as young people visit general practice on a regular basis, the consultation provides an ideal moment to bring up specific health subjects. Research indicates that this is more effective if done in relation to the reason for consultation, for example, if a young person consults because of a chronic cough, then asking about cigarette smoking, providing advice about ways of giving up and, at the same time, providing access to nicotine patches free may have an additive effect. Finally, the primary care services have a responsibility for providing health information for young people in an appropriate way for young people to use as they wish. This may be via leaflets or notices in the practice, or on a more global scale by using the electronic media, by developing national level web sites, for example, **www.teenagehealthfreak.org** and **www.youthhealthtalk.org** (see Box 7.4 below).

Role of Parents in Providing Health Care

Parents remain a vital primary health resource/provider (as well as in other areas of their lives) to young people into their late teens.

Firstly, the socio-economic background provision which parents are able to provide for their teenager will have a profound effect on their health, though this has been shown to be less influential as the teenager gets older and begins to become economically independent of their parents.

Secondly, parents remain a primary source of health information for young people in a number of areas into their late teens (though with drugs and sex young people may either feel that they are better informed than their parents or feel that they would rather not discuss these matters with them!).

Thirdly, parents remain the vital primary health care providers when their children are either acutely ill or when they have a chronic health problem.

In general terms, amongst health care professionals there has been a swing away from talking almost exclusively to parents about their teenagers, to now talking almost exclusively to teenagers *without* involving their parents.

In primary care, however, as well as considering the needs of the young person themselves, consideration should also be given to the needs of parents as carers in order to support them in their role as primary carers. This means that when issues arise with a young person concerning confidentiality and their parents being told, the health professionals should carefully weigh up the pros and cons of having the parents involved, and if this is considered to be beneficial, then to make every attempt to persuade the young person that their parents should be told. If, however, a young person is adamant, and not in danger or a danger to others, then confidentiality has to be maintained.

Factors which may Influence Communication with Young People in Primary Care

To understand what may lead to difficulties of communication between primary health care professionals and young people, it is necessary to look at some of the factors influencing this communication.

Parents: when contacts are for physical problems, parents being present may not matter as much as when they involve emotional or intimate personal problems. Although 'difficult' consultations may highlight problems with having a parent present, it has to be remembered that parents may also have a 'facilitating' role. Nevertheless, the need for a young person to see a doctor without a parent present sometime during a consultation cannot be overemphasized.

Lack of adequate training for the health professional: when dealing with an adolescent, particularly one with an embarrassing personal problem, a trusting relationship between the health professional and the young person may need to be developed before disclosure of the problem occurs. This takes time, training and experience and the relationship may need several visits to develop fully.

Confusion over where responsibility for care lies: the health professional may have difficulty during a consultation knowing how far it is the responsibility of a young person to disclose their problem and how far the health professional should go in obtaining the disclosure. Part of the confusion is over personal autonomy, that is, how much the health professional should feel responsible for adolescent patients, and how much they should respect the young person's ability to manage their own health problems.

The health professional's own feelings: these can be far ranging and include frustration, anxiety, anger, sense of failure, omnipotence and impotence. It may also be difficult for a health professional not to experience parental feelings for an adolescent – to be overprotective, and to fight the problems on behalf of the young person, rather than letting them work it out for themselves. However, the feelings may not always be negative and consultation with adolescents can be deeply satisfying if handled correctly.

The developmental process in the adolescent: the physical changes, the emotional changes and the changes in cognitive ability demonstrated by young people during puberty all mean that there is enormous variation in the ease of communication by and with individual adolescents. This means that the health professional has to be acutely sensitive as to what stage of development the adolescent has reached in these areas, has to be an accomplished concerned listener and have the ability to build up a relationship of trust and mutual respect.

The adolescent's views of primary care: when young people consider consulting their primary care services, their views of what they might expect may condition how they behave during the consultation. Research indicates that young people value a health professional who allows them time to overcome their initial fears and gain enough confidence to voice their concerns. This enables them to relax, something that occurs with health professionals who are caring, friendly, interested and are good listeners.

Box 7.4 www.youthhealthtalk.org

An example of making excellent health information directly available to young people themselves and their carers is the web site **www.youthhealthtalk.org**.

It is provided free on the Internet and is made up of a series of modules dealing with young people's health issues. For each health issue a sample of around 40 young people from different backgrounds, ethnic groups, and geographical areas is carefully selected to give the broadest possible range of views and opinions.

It presents video and audio clip interviews with young people about their views and opinions on what it is like having an illness, coming into contact with the medical services and how doctors and nurses can be helpful to young people.

Because it presents young people's comments about the services that they receive, it also provides excellent teaching material for a wide range of people caring for young people, including health professionals.

Here, for example, is a young man who has diabetes talking about what he wants from carers – whether at primary or secondary care levels.

"I think they should know that young people aren't completely oblivious to what's going on. And I think it's important not to patronize young people about their diabetes and to tell them what to do and how to control their diabetes. Because it's... it's the individual who controls it. And anything that you might tell them doesn't really,... doesn't do any help. It does probably more harm than good because it makes people want to rebel against what you, what advice you're giving them. And so I think, and there's no need to really boss people and tell them, 'Well, you shouldn't be doing this' or whatever. And I don't think that's, that's not good advice for somebody. I think just to be supportive. And if they do ever ask questions about it, about diabetes, never be afraid to tell them the truth or give them the answers that they want. Don't just say something you think they'll want to hear. Give them the truth. And I think that's going to be beneficial to young people. But, yes, I think the... the key thing is just not to patronize young people or treat them like sort of an outsider because they've got diabetes, or anything like that. Or, or like they've got a r-, a s-, the most, the worse thing is when people treat you like you've got a most serious, life-threatening disease. When it's not like that. I think it's just, it's just important to understand that it's their diabetes and you've got to let them, you've got to remember that it's those, those individuals who control it. And so just be understanding."

(The authors would like to thank all the members of the Royal College of General Practitioners working party on 'Adolescent Health' because the chapter relies on their ideas, thoughts and observations. We would also like to acknowledge that the section on 'Factors which may influence communication with young people in primary care' relies heavily on observations made in *Difficult Consultations with Adolescents* by Chris Donovan and Heather C. Suckling with Zoe Walker, Janet Bell, Tami Kramer, and Sheila R. Cross, published by Radcliffe Medical Press, 2004).

Further Reading

Coleman, J, and Schofield, J. (2005) *Key data on adolescence*, Trust for the Study of Adolescence, Brighton.

Donovan, C., Suckling, H., Walker Z. *et al.* (2004) *Difficult consultations with adolescents*, Radcliffe Medical Press, Oxford.

McPherson, A., Donovan, C. and Macfarlane, A. (2002) *Healthcare of young people: promotion in primary care*, Radcliffe Medical Press, Oxford.

Chambers, R. and Licence, K. (2004) *Looking after children in primary care: a companion to the Children's National Service Framework*, Radcliffe Medical Press, Oxford.

Chapter 8

Being Different: Adolescents, Chronic Illness and Disability

Peter J. Helms

Department of Child Health
University of Aberdeen

- Introduction
- Chronic Illness and Adolescent Transitions
- Adolescent Risk-Taking
- Impact of Chronic Disease on Identity and Self-Esteem
- Parenting Adolescents with Chronic Illness
- Death and Dying
- Legal Aspects
- Challenges for the Health Care Team
- Conclusion

Learning Objectives

After reading this chapter you should:

1 Comprehend the effects of chronic illnesses on young people and their families during the transition from childhood to early adulthood.

2 Understand and recognize the different effects of these illnesses depending on their actual and/or perceived severity and whether there are any obvious physical changes which may make the affected individual seem different from their peers.

3 Identify the complex interactions among the diseases themselves and the developmental tasks during adolescence, such as risk-taking, peer relationships and independence from parents.

4 Understand the role of parents and health care professionals, which are keys to successful negotiation of the child/adult transition.

5 Understand the complex nature of these disabilities, including issues of control, vulnerability and identity and find ways to contribute to young people's successful coping with these illnesses.

Introduction

Adolescence encompasses a period of life when physical, psychological and sociological maturity and independence are intermingled and when chronic illness and disability impose additional challenges for the individual and for his/her family. According to most definitions, adolescence refers to the chronological ages between 10 and 20 years, encompassing 12–15% of the whole UK population. Within this age group, adolescents with a disability or chronic disease have been referred to as 'the forgotten tribe' as their needs are often missed in the transition from paediatric to adult services. They have gained the reputation for being difficult and less rewarding to manage than younger children and mature adults (Viner, 2005).

Different chronic diseases have rather different clinical courses and hence have differing impacts on the affected individual. For the non-clinically trained professional one of the first tasks must be to gain an understanding of the main features of the disease or condition, including its manifestations, its medium- to long-term prognosis, particularly if life threatening, and the types of treatment on offer together with any unavoidable side effects. Diseases such as cystic fibrosis, the most common life-threatening genetically determined disease in white populations, are progressive, although it is not usually until the last 2–3 years of the illness that quality of life is seriously impaired. This is quite different from the situation in other serious genetic disorders such as muscular dystrophy where the loss of physical function and decline in life quality follows a more linear trajectory throughout the limited lifespan of these individuals. Recent improvements in mortality and morbidity for a number of chronic previously life-threatening disorders such as cystic fibrosis have led to a shift away from viewing health strictly in terms of survival towards quality of life and the effects of the illness on normal daily activities.

The traditional medical model, based on the need to understand the underlying disease mechanisms, describes illness as a sequence flowing from aetiology to pathology to manifestation. However, this model fails to reflect the full range of problems which may affect normal daily functions such as attending school or seeing friends, problems that are not always generated by the views of young people themselves, as illustrated by comments of an 11-year-old girl with severe asthma: "School is pretty much okay, sometimes the teachers go a bit over the top in making sure you're alright, you know, you just want to be treated a bit more like a normal person" and "your friend would say 'would you like to come round' and their mum will say 'well, I don't know' 'cause they get worried that if you have an attack they wouldn't know what to do, so they don't want you come round just in case."

In this context the World Health Organization suggests a more comprehensive health model with the sequence flowing from disease to impairment to disability to handicap (*International classification of impairments, disabilities and handicaps*, WHO, 1980). As Figure 8.1 shows, this latter sequence allows distinctions to be made between impairments (psychological, physiological, anatomical, structural), disability (restrictions or lack of ability to perform normal activities) and handicap (disadvantage in comparison with a peer group). This more patient-centred model can be used to assess the impact of disease on daily living and assess aspects of disease not reflected in traditional clinical measures of illness, such as severity scores and the use of medicines and health service resources.

The transition from loss of function to reduced performance and ultimately restricted ability and handicap are clearly influenced by both the physical effects of the disease, such as breathlessness associated with asthma or the inability to walk with muscular dystrophy, and how the disease is perceived by the affected individuals, their families and peer groups. What, for example, would be a very minor degree of breathlessness in a sedentary adolescent with asthma could become a severe and limiting handicap for a young aspiring elite athlete. Lack of understanding of the condition and its management could also result in inappropriate and discriminatory treatment by the young person's peers and adult mentors. Attitudes and behaviour of parents and health care professionals can also have either deleterious or positive effects.

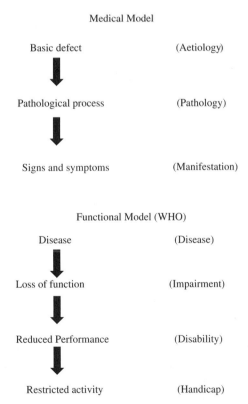

Figure 8.1   Two main disease models: the medical model focuses on biological mechanisms whereas the WHO model focuses on the impact on the individual.

Chronic Illness and Adolescent Transitions

The impact of chronic illness can be considerable and amplified by the challenges of the child–adult transition and even apparently minor illnesses can have a significant impact resulting in isolation, stigmatization and handicap. As Focal Theory (Coleman and Hendry, 1999) points out, most young people approach the many challenges of the adolescent transition by tackling them one at a time. If these developmental tasks are exacerbated by added complications due to a chronic illness, coping becomes more difficult. Some conditions such as acne, eating disorders and scoliosis (lateral curvature of the spine) have their origins in adolescence and together with already established chronic health problems present another complication interacting with the adolescent's transition towards adulthood. Kidney disease, for example, is aggravated by poorly controlled insulin-dependent diabetes whose peak incidence occurs in early adolescence (12–14 years). The prevalence and impact of disease can also vary by gender, partly due to physiological and hormonal influences and partly to gender-specific social and behavioural changes. One example of this is the reversal of the male predominance for asthma (Figure 8.2) and the greater likelihood of severe progressive respiratory disease in adolescent girls.

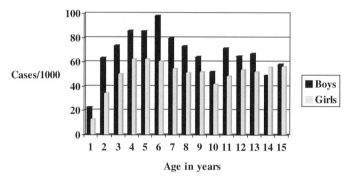

Figure 8.2   Children and adolescents presenting to general practitioners for asthma (Scottish Continuous Morbidity Recording (CMR) practices 1998–1999).

Adolescent Risk-Taking

Although it is commonly believed that most young people are healthy, more than half will visit their general practitioner at least once every year and approximately 30% have some type of chronic health problem. Most of these problems could be classified as minor, in strictly medical terms, but they may have a very real impact on quality of life and behaviour in association with the other changes occurring during the move from childhood to adulthood.

Adolescence is a period of transition during which risk-taking behaviours and their consequences begin to appear, as evidenced by a number of features of health care use. The most common reasons for hospital admission in males during late adolescence (15–20 year-olds) are head injuries and open wounds. Deliberate self-poisoning increases with age and 30% of all legal abortions are performed under the age of 20. Young males between 16 and 24 years of age account for almost 60% of driver fatalities while they represent only 10% of

licensed drivers. The development of lifestyle behaviours such as smoking, drinking, diet and physical activity clearly have implications for lifetime health in the whole population and are even more acutely focused on those with chronic disease. Growing up involves the adolescent in a variety of learning experiences, experimentation and 'testing the boundaries' of rules and accepted social practices. A desire to take part in 'risk-taking' is normal in the transition to adulthood (see Kloep and Hendry, 1999). However, potentially unhealthy behaviours compound existing chronic health problems such as asthma or diabetes.

Impact of Chronic Disease on Identity and Self-Esteem

Illness behaviours in children and adolescents reveal that high expectations of encountering one health problem are usually associated with high expectations of encountering other difficulties. Self-assessments of health are also influenced by competence in important

areas of life such as success in school and participation in sports and exercise. For children with chronic disease the expectation of encountering a range of somatic and psychological symptoms is likely to influence disability and handicap. In this regard it has been found that perceived health problems and limitations associated with disease are more prominent than those actually experienced by young people. Studies in young adolescents with cystic fibrosis (Brown, Rowley and Helms, 1994) have shown that although they appear to cope very successfully with their disease they perceive themselves as being more vulnerable to the psychosocial effects of the disease than their actual life experiences demonstrate. There may also be a discontinuity between the clinical severity of the disease and the adolescent's own perceptions of their health status. This discontinuity is important for health care professionals and carers to appreciate that what appears to be a mild disease in strictly clinical terms may have a sizeable impact on the adolescent's perceived quality of life and behaviour. On the other hand, those with very severe clinical disease may have adapted to the associated limitations on their lives and consequently do not perceive their own situation to be as limited and as adverse as viewed by their medical attendants. Although many young people with a severe handicapping disease appear to cope very well with the consequences of their disease, Brown, Rowley and Helms (1994) found a disparity between perceived vulnerability and subsequent experience, indicating an uncertainty about the effects of the disease and/or a lack of understanding about the goals and outcomes of medical treatment.

The hopes and aspirations of adolescents with chronic illness and disability are no different from those of their able-bodied peers. However, as Wilkinson (1981) has pointed out, their expectations are often low, with their concerns focusing on their physical appearance and attractiveness and whether they could cope with the perceived tasks of parenthood.

In this regard the attitudes of their parents are important as they may believe that their child may never be able to establish a long-term relationship with someone else who could begin to provide the previous caring role of the parents. It is a natural parental concern to want to protect their children but, in so doing, they may reduce the likelihood of their child's ability to establish and develop mature relationships with others. Some parents, for example, insist on choosing their children's clothes and take the opportunity of dressing them in younger fashions than their years in order to make them less physically attractive to members of the opposite sex. This may also be part of a strategy to keep their children dependent and in order to maintain control over what would otherwise appear to be a dangerous and unknown future. Despite these problems, many adolescents with chronic disease and disability will realize their aspirations, although the frequency of pre-marital sexual intercourse is generally considered to be lower than their healthy peers with the principal limiting factors being disease, activity and associated pain and fatigue, rather than their physical appearance. They may also have suffered the affective neutering effects of lack of privacy in dealing with their personal hygiene and in the frequent impersonal body contact given by health professionals, thus creating a detached attitude towards physical intimacy.

Social isolation of young people with severe chronic disease is common and many may have very little contact with their peers outside their own family and during school holidays. Young people may feel unattractive because of the physical manifestations of their chronic ill-health and the fact that they may be delayed in their transition through puberty, appearing younger than their actual years. Peer pressure and the need to be accepted as 'one of the crowd' are other influences which are particularly strong in girls and young women. Having to take medication throughout the day often draws unwanted attention, together with features of the disease that cannot easily be disguised, such as constant coughing, sputum production and altered physical appearance. These are some of the reasons often cited by young people for poor adherence or compliance with regular treatment or the avoidance of situations likely to provoke symptoms and adverse comments from their peers.

It is important to encourage the expectation that the child and adolescent will join the world of work at some point in the future. Blum (1995) has shown that the early inclusion of children with chronic disease into regular chores in the home, including routine responsibilities, is important in fostering confidence. Missing as little time as possible from school, overcoming problems with transport, the use of computers and integration with peers are all-important in this regard. White, Gussek and Fisher (1990) point out that work experience, careers counselling or an advisory panel of employees are just as important for young people with chronic disease and disabilities as they are for able-bodied children and young people. It is essential not to 'shield' young people from these important issues and choices just because they carry the additional challenge of chronic illness or are considered to be handicapped in some way. As one 13 year-old with persistent asthma put it: "Well I'm wondering if it will ever go away because it could affect your job because you want to be a builder or something", and as commented by a mature 11-year-old girl: "Well sometimes you sort of wonder about things, like what effects it has as you grow older, what actually makes you have it or whether it passes through the family and things like that."

Parenting Adolescents with Chronic Illness

For most families living in fully developed economies the threats of severe chronic illness and of premature death are rare, thus making the burden of serious chronic and life-threatening illness in those so affected harder to bear and accept. The scenarios outlined in Case Studies 8.1 to 8.3 illustrate the tensions that can arise between the emerging autonomy of the young person and the role of parents, and encapsulate some of the issues and tasks facing young people having to cope simultaneously with the difficulties of a severe disability and the challenges of growing up.

In one of the few European studies on the topic of parenting in adolescence, Shucksmith, Hendry and Glendinning (1995) showed that parents of adolescents tend to be mostly permissive, trying to encourage their children's striving for increasing independence. However, some parents of chronically ill or disabled children find this transition difficult to achieve. All responsible parents invest huge amounts of time and emotional energy into child rearing, but these efforts are redoubled by the presence of acute disability and chronic illness. Most parents experience some feelings of loss at the passing of childhood and the changing relationship with their children as they make the transition to adult life. Such loss can be avoided if parents choose to use the presence of chronic illness to maintain their child in a dependent role (see Case Study 8.1).

CASE STUDY 8.1

Mark, aged 12½, has had mild intermittent asthma, mainly precipitated by viral infections, since he was three years of age. He has never required hospital admission and whenever presenting for assessment he has had normal lung function with no chest deformity or any signs of persistent chronic disease. He is in early puberty and growing normally, being above the average for his age. Mark has an older sister aged 20 who is in her last year at university. His mother, Elizabeth, works occasional night shifts as a nursing auxiliary in a nursing home and his father is a long-distance lorry driver, often away from home during the week. Mark rarely takes part in any medical consultation and his mother Elizabeth usually speaks for him. Mark has had a history of school refusal in his early years but this appears to have resolved. He dislikes physical activity and his mother has

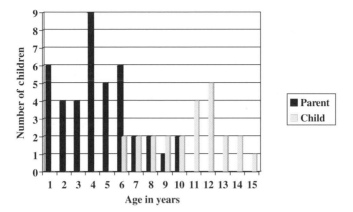

Figure 8.3   Distribution of parental/child responsibility for asthma therapy by child age (data adapted from Kaarsgaren, Zulstra and Helms, 1994). Reprinted from Respiratory Medecine, Vol 88, Issue 5, Kaarsgaren RJ, Zulstra RF, Helms P., Asthma medication in children, 383–386, Copyright 1994, with permission from Elsevier.

negotiated with the school that he does not take part in anything other than very light physical activities in the gym. She usually takes him and collects him from school herself. She also takes full responsibility for Mark's asthma treatment.

The child may not acquiesce to this situation of mutual dependency or may experience a need to establish independence by deliberately failing to comply with the recommended therapeutic regime. In potentially life-threatening and life-limiting illnesses, adherence to the recommended treatment can become a source of conflict. Parents are aware of potential dangers of poor treatment adherence and risk-taking behaviours such as smoking and drinking, but many young people find it difficult to link present behaviours to long-term consequences, and use their condition as an opportunity for adolescent rebellion (see Case Study 8.2). Adherence to treatment, however, is a major concern, as failure to maintain regular therapy can have serious immediate and long-term consequences for the health of the affected individual. Asthma remains a rare but real cause of sudden death in adolescence. Thankfully, such situations are rare and the transition to self-management and responsibility usually occurs somewhere between 10 and 13 years of age (Figure 8.3).

CASE STUDY 8.2

Susan, aged 14, has severe persistent asthma and frequent exacerbations, hospital attendances and short two- to three-day admissions. Her attendance at follow-up clinics is sporadic with frequent failures to attend. Her inhalation technique is poor and although she claims she is taking her medicine regularly this is not borne out by the very infrequent collection of her repeat prescriptions from her general practitioner. Her mother, who usually attends with her for her rare follow-up visits, often gets into conflict with Susan when the subject of symptom control and medication is discussed. Susan is a sociable girl, always receiving text messages on her mobile phone, even during her hospital and clinic attendances. Both parents are regular smokers and although Susan claims that she does not smoke herself she often smells of cigarette smoke during her assessment visits. She feels that her mother and the doctors and nurses at the asthma clinic are fussing unnecessarily about her and that she can look after herself if everybody would just leave her alone.

A few parents live vicariously through their own children and impose their own goals on their children's achievements. This becomes obvious, for example, in parents pressurizing their children into sports competitions (see Hendry and Kloep, 2006). In the case of chronically ill children, parental ambitions can lead to a denial of the underlying illness and a refusal to accept the consequences and come to a reasonably balanced approach to its management (see Case Study 8.3).

CASE STUDY 8.3

John, aged 13, has had chronic severe asthma since he was five. He is currently taking maximum inhaled therapy with a good inhalation technique and rarely misses his daily treatment. As a consequence of his chronic disease, his pubertal development is late and he is the least mature and smallest in his school class. He has particular difficulties with exercise-induced symptoms. He has two younger sisters, his mother is a part-time primary school teacher and his father, James, is an engineer in the oil and gas industry. James, aged 42, is often away from home with frequent trips abroad. In his younger days, James played club rugby and remains an enthusiastic supporter of his local team. He often takes John to cup matches and internationals. John attempts to play rugby at school but is not enjoying the sport because of his small size, his sexual immaturity, in comparison to his peer group, and the distressing symptoms he experiences on the pitch. James feels that his son needs 'toughening up' and that sport participation and dealing with the associated challenges is an important part of growing up. In his view, what John needs to show is more determination and that overcoming his reluctance to participate will be the making of him. He refuses to accept that his son's asthma is as bad as the doctors and his mother claim.

Death and Dying

For the young person in the final stages of life, particularly after carrying the burden of chronic illness and handicap, a number of challenges arise. The relative rarity of death in

Table 8.1   Some chronic illnesses/conditions affecting adolescents

Life-limiting	Potentially life-threatening	Physically/socially limiting	Unpleasant/inconvenient
Muscular dystrophy	Asthma	Scoliosis	Eczema
Cystic fibrosis	Diabetes	Inflammatory bowel disease(Crohns and ulcerative colitis)	Hayfever
Severe cerebral palsy	Epilepsy	Autism	Alopecia (hair loss)
	Severe acute allergy (Anaphylaxis)	Asperger's syndrome	Psoriasis
			Acne

Key Themes Relevant to Adolescents with Chronic Disease

Challenges for parents in 'letting go'
Improving and maintaining adherence (compliance) to therapy
Dealing with peer pressures
Establishing trust with health care professionals
Transition to adult care

childhood and adolescence in post-industrial affluent countries means that even professional specialists rarely encounter death in this age group. The broad spectrum of diseases involved also makes generalizations difficult as each situation is unique.

Young people and families facing death of a loved and cherished member will usually have had long-term relationships with a number of trusted health care professionals. It is this group of professionals who are likely to be involved in the palliative care of the young person once the often difficult decision has been made that a well-managed death is the best option. Rather than viewing the transition to palliative care in terms of what treatments can prolong life or what can be withdrawn, the emphasis needs to be on what treatments could improve the quality of what life remains. Young people should be involved in such decisions although, just as in adulthood, some individuals may have difficulty in coming to terms with their situation.

For parents and siblings who are likely to have invested huge physical and emotional resources into the care of the young person facing death, the situation can be extremely painful and difficult to accept. For the young people themselves it is often the fear of the process of dying rather than death itself that is prominent. This may also be accompanied by feelings of inadequacy and guilt in somehow failing to match the huge investment put into them by their parents and carers (see Case Study 8.4).

CASE STUDY 8.4

Louise, aged 12, was first diagnosed with cystic fibrosis at the age of two and by the time I met her she had developed irreversible lung disease with an estimated life expectancy of six months or less. She came from a very close-knit family with an older sister and a mother who had made huge efforts to maintain Louise in good health. Her mother, Jane, had given up work some years previously in order to care for Louise and always stayed in hospital with her during her frequent admissions. At the time, a heart/lung transplant programme was being introduced for children with end stage lung disease and Louise's parents were pressing to have her assessed for the programme. Louise appeared to go along with this plan and a request for review by the transplant team was in preparation. Early one evening, when both Louise's parents were at her older sister's parent/teacher evening, Louise began to talk about her situation.

She assessed her current quality of life as very poor and that she was nearing the end of her life. She was not frightened to face death itself but was frightened about the process of dying. She did not want to be considered for a heart/lung transplant as she had had enough of hospitals and treatments and did not want to put herself and her family through any more pain and distress. In all of this her main concern was how her parents, particularly her mother, would cope after her death: "I have been such a big part of her life, I don't know what she and Dad will do when I am not here. Mum and Dad have spent so many hours looking after me. I don't want to disappoint them but I really do not want to go through with the heart/lung transplant idea."

At an appropriate interval after death (two to four months) parents and siblings should be given the opportunity to meet a representative of the caring team so that any remaining questions relating to the underlying cause and implications for the future can be addressed. Siblings may find feelings of guilt and loss mingled with relief and anger and parents may unreasonably blame themselves for all that has happened. In addition, many parents will find a huge void in their lives and have problems replacing the many hours previously taken up in caring for their child. Parents also need help to recognize that their lost child can never be replaced and that their grief will be rekindled at important anniversaries including the anniversary of death and birth, Christmas and culturally relevant religious festivals and family holidays.

Legal Aspects

Ratification of the United Nations Convention on the Rights of the Child by the UK government in 1991 has been reflected in national legislation and has significant consequences for parents, young people and their carers (see above). The Children Act (England and Wales 1989, Scotland 1995) enshrines some of the rights of young people and responsibility of their carers. This legislation supports previous legislation on the age of majority. Although 18 years is commonly regarded as the age of achieving full adult rights and responsibilities, children of any age able to understand what is being proposed for them, whether it be medical or surgical treatment or custody arrangements, must be involved in the decision-making process. The age at which a child must be included in these important decisions does not have a lower age limit but certainly by the age of 12 children and young people need to be involved in consent for any medical interventions proposed for them. Confidentiality must also be maintained unless there are overriding reasons why this should not be so. Young people have the right to have confidential information about them withheld from their parents/guardians if they so desire. At some stage the child becomes competent to make his or her own decisions, a competence that is not strictly based on age, but rather on ability. It is also argued that the greater the risk to the child of any intervention or procedure the more he or she should be able to demonstrate the ability to understand the consequences of the decision. Several reports have been written and recommendations made subsequently and it has been suggested that a charter such as that suggested by the British Association for Community Child Health should be made available in settings where young people are being seen by health care professionals (see below).

Themes from UN Convention on the Rights of the Child

- Consider the best interests of the child, particularly in family disputes
- Keep up the standards of services and facilities
- Respect and support parents/carers
- Seek the child's view
- Maintain privacy and confidentiality
- Provide access to relevant information
- Protect from violence
- Protect the right to education
- Protect rights of disabled
- Protect rights of minorities

A Suggested Confidentiality and Privacy Charter

We will:

- see you on your own, in private, if that is what you want.
- always keep what you want to tell us confidential (unless there is a very good reason why we should not). If we do have to tell someone else we will tell you who and why.
- give you all the support you need if we are going to tell someone else.
- make sure all our staff know about these rules on confidentiality.

Challenges for the Health Care Team

It can sometimes be a challenge for the caring team to achieve a balance between a patho-logical over-acceptance of the illness by both child and parents and the other end of the spectrum – denial of the severity of the disease and the resultant harm by failing to comply with the best possible medical treatments.

The health care professionals dealing with young people and their families may also become enmeshed in this situation by either acceding to the parental behaviour or appearing to take sides in the resultant conflict. Parents may also become involved in conflicts with the health care team and seek second opinions often moving from one group of carers to another until they find a team that does not appear to be concerned by or challenge the enmeshed behaviour.

A pattern of transitional care is commonly adopted for children in their early teens and is an important step towards full independence and regular follow-up in an adult-oriented service. Transfer to the adult service would traditionally take place somewhere between 16 and 18 years of age. Parents often find it difficult to allow their children independence, particularly when they have hitherto been largely responsible for their medical management. Unless responsibility for day-to-day management is transferred to young people there is a danger that the medical management itself may become part of the natural testing of boundaries and the young person's need to establish independence (see box above), as the examples in Case Studies 8.1 to 8.3 show. In severe conditions such as cystic fibrosis a responsible attitude to therapy can quite literally mean the dif-ference between early death and extended survival in relatively good health. Parents are aware of this fact but for many young people present behaviour is not often linked to long-term consequences.

Establishing trust between health care professionals and young people, transferring re-sponsibility for disease management and communicating the desirability of adopting a healthy lifestyle to young people themselves are prerequisites for long-term future health (see Case Study 8.5 for an example).

Siersted et al. (1998) found that ease of access to health care professionals and their accessibility are of paramount importance, as many chronic health problems may go unrecognized in young people because of communication problems with medical and health care professionals. Viner (1999) comments that this can be compounded by the unease that some medical practitioners experience when dealing with young people who are confused and unwilling to take conventional routes to health care. Young people may also become irritated with repetitive exhortations to take their treatment and this may have the opposite effect to that intended. As one 11 year-old commented concerning her contact with a particular health care professional: "She keeps on telling you things you already know over and over again".

A successful transitional programme (see also Chapter 9) anticipates possible obstacles and manages a smooth transition to adult care. Failure to do this can result in patients not attending regular follow-up sessions, with the consequent implications for poor disease management and disease progression. The favoured model in the United Kingdom is a transition programme coordinated between paediatricians and adult physicians. It must be remembered that the transition programme is a process and not a single event and that it requires support by fully documented protocol so that no details are overlooked. Such a programme is, of necessity, multidisciplinary, although usually coordinated by an individual, often a nurse specialist who works in both paediatric and adult clinics.

CASE STUDY 8.5

Colin, aged 13, has had inflammatory bowel disease since he was six and has required follow-up in the Specialist Paediatric Gastroenterology Clinic ever since. His mother Ann has become very involved in his day-to-day management and has become a local organizer for the regional support group for children with inflammatory bowel disease. Colin is in early puberty and, when seen with his mother at a clinic visit, appears to be less communicative than usual and Ann appears to be irritated by Colin's apparent rudeness. Dr Mackenzie, the Paediatric Gastroenterologist, who has known Colin and his family since his diagnosis, feels that Colin needs to be seen on his own, at least for some of the outpatient visit, in order to prepare him for the transition to the adult gastroenterology service in a few years' time. Indeed, he suggests that Colin should be given the opportunity to be seen on his own at this visit and he invites Ann to leave the consulting room for a few minutes while he talks directly to Colin about his future management. Ann is subsequently asked to come back into the room and is invited to stay on her own while Colin leaves, in order for any other issues to be discussed. At first, Ann appears rather shocked and hurt by what has just been done but agrees after further discussion that this would be an important step for Colin to take and that he really does need to become more involved and more responsible for his own management.

Conclusion

Young people travelling through a challenging and sometimes turbulent period of their lives who carry the additional burden of a chronic illness require and deserve a knowledgeable and sympathetic health care team if they are to be afforded the best chance of lifelong health. Parents and carers also need to be supported through this period so that they can assist young people to negotiate the transition to responsible adult independence. An awareness of the issues facing young people is an absolute requirement in order to ensure that they can successfully manage their own medical problems and understand the contribution they themselves need to make in order to maintain physical and mental health.

The challenges for carers of young people, their parents and guardians in facing the challenges of chronic illness and handicap are considerable. Nevertheless, we should be aware of Rutter's (1996) argument that experiences which are difficult enough to challenge the individual's psychosocial resources, but are possible to cope with, can be compared to vaccinations which create antibodies and strengthen the immune system against future infections. By analogy, he calls these challenges 'steeling experiences', small 'injections' that prepare the individual to cope with more demanding challenges in the future. This is where carers can be effective. Listening to young people themselves and understanding their perceptions can be both helpful for them and instructive and rewarding for those charged with their care. The principles of empathy, understanding and honesty are no different from those necessary for dealing with persons of any age or level of competence.

Further Reading

Brook C.G.D. (ed.) (1993) *The practice of medicine in adolescence*, Edward Arnold, London.

British Association for Community Child Health. (1995) *Child health rights. A practitioners' guide*, British Paediatric Association, London.

Macfarlane A. and McPherson A. (2002) *The diary of a teenage health freak*, Oxford University Press, Oxford.

Macfarlane A.(ed.) (1996) *Adolescent medicine*. Royal College of Physicians, London.

Royal College of Paediatrics and Child Health (2003) *Bridging the gaps: health care for adolescents*, RCPCH, London.

Discussion Questions

1. Over and above all the normal demands of parenting a teenager, there are additional demands for parents of young people with a chronic illness or disability. Discuss how dependency between parent and teenager can be both a strength and a weakness.

2. Should death education become part of the school curriculum? How would you teach it?

3. It is not surprising that both parents and members of the health care team can become involved in denying the severity of a medical condition in a young person. How can this problem be addressed?

4. How would you decide when a young person can be deemed competent to make their own decisions about their medical treatment and care?

Acknowledgment

Comments from young people courtesy of Dr Leisl Osman.

Chapter 9

Transitions for Young People with Complex Health Needs

Janet McDonagh

Clinical Senior Lecturer in Paediatric and Adolescent Rheumatology,
Division of Reproductive and Child Health, University of Birmingham

- Introduction
- Transition – the Evidence of Need
- Managing Transition Effectively
- The Potential of Transitional Care
- Conclusion

Learning Objectives

After reading this chapter you should:

1 Understand the importance of transition in adolescent health care.
2 Recognize the interdependence of health transitions with educational, vocational and social transitions during adolescence.
3 Be aware of the key principles of transitional care.
4 Be able to present strategies for effective management of transition during adolescence.
5 Have a grasp of the positive benefits of coordinated transitional care.

Introduction

Transition is an integral component of adolescent health care. All young people will hopefully make the transition from childhood to adulthood and, along the way, move from the family home to live independently and move from school to work or further education and/or training. Another transition they will negotiate will be from paediatric to adult services including health care. Adult health care differs in many respects from paediatric health care and young people with and without chronic illnesses will need preparation and skills to become new and effective adult users of health services.

Differences between Paediatric and Adult Health Services

- age range (!)
- cultures of care
- recognition of growth and development
- consultation dynamics
- communication skills
- generic issues
- role of parents
- role of family
- role of peers
- educational issues
- vocational issues
- confidentiality issues
- tolerance of immaturity
- procedural pain management
- spectrum of diseases
- impact of disease
- legislation
- service provision.

The transitions which characterize adolescence, that is, educational and psychosocial, are interdependent and have implications for health transitions, directly and/or indirectly. The linkages between them are, however, becoming looser and less age-related as a result of the changing sociocultural trajectory, for example, the average age of leaving the parental home and/or marriage is now well into the twenties and thirties respectively. Many young people make these transitions successfully. Some, however, will find them difficult for various reasons and this group potentially includes those young people with chronic illnesses and/or disabilities. With rapidly evolving medical technology and improvements in therapies and medical care, there are increasing numbers of young people with chronic illnesses and/or disabilities surviving into adulthood where previously they died in childhood, for instance, cystic fibrosis, inherited metabolic disease, congenital heart disease, cancer, transplantation, haemoglobinopathies, cerebral palsy and so forth. Some of these conditions have not previously been a concern of adult services, but with increasing survival they have become so, often with associated morbidity. Morbidity in adulthood of other conditions such as diabetes and juvenile idiopathic arthritis (JIA) is also increasingly recognized.

Transition – the Evidence of Need

Health transition is a *process*, which begins in paediatric services and is completed in adult services following the *event* of transfer. Transition is a young-person-centred, multidimensional, multidisciplinary, holistic active process that attends to the medical, psychosocial and educational/vocational needs of adolescents as they move from child- to adult-centred services. Transition starts when the decision to begin or prepare for transition is made. Ideally this should be as early as possible. The middle phase is that of transition readiness when the adolescent, their family and the providers are prepared to begin, continue and finish the process of transition. The final or end stage occurs when the adolescent or young adult not only transfers to adult care but is actively participating in adult health care activities, for example, self-management and decision-making.

Key Principles of Transition

- An active, future-focused process
- young-person-centred
- inclusive of parents/caregivers
- early start
- a resilience framework
- multidisciplinary
- inter-agency
- involves paediatric and adult services in addition to primary care
- provision of coordinated, uninterrupted health care:
  - age and developmentally appropriate
  - culturally appropriate
  - comprehensive, flexible, responsive
  - holistic – medical, psychosocial and educational/vocational aspects
- skills training for the young person in communication, decision-making, assertiveness, self-care and self-management
- enhancement of sense of control and interdependence in health care
- the maximization of lifelong functioning and potential.

The literature is very persuasive on the need to improve transitional care provision and the latter has been the subject of two important reviews in recent years (While *et al.*, 2004; Beresford, 2004). Some of the key themes of this evidence are discussed below.

Experience of Young People Themselves

Unfortunately the evidence from the perspective of the young person is that transfer to adult care is not a positive event and is associated with significant concerns and anxieties (While *et al.*, 2004; Beresford, 2004; Shaw, Southwood and McDonagh, 2004a). Although reporting a reluctance to transfer to adult care, some young people also report favouring changes towards more adult-orientated care during adolescence (Shaw, Southwood and McDonagh, 2004a; Boyle, Farukhi and Nosky, 2001; Zack *et al.*, 2003).

Increasing Numbers and Morbidities

Approximately 10–20% of adolescents now report a significant ongoing health care need related to a chronic health condition. In addition to increased survival rates, there is evidence of increasing incidence, prevalence and/or recognition of diseases specific to the adolescent age group (e.g. cancer, diabetes). There are childhood conditions as yet unmatched by dedicated adult services (e.g. autistic spectrum disorder, attention deficit hyperactivity disorder). There is also evidence of increasing morbidity of childhood-onset disease in early adulthood (e.g. problems with spina bifida complicated by hydrocephalus (Tomlinson and Sugarman, 1995), transplant loss (Watson, 2000), second malignancies, osteoporosis and so forth). Of patients with a renal transplant transferred to adult nephrologists, 35% had lost their graft within 36 months of transfer (Watson, 2000). Adolescence is a key time for educational transitions and can be associated with negative outcomes. Burchardt reported that although there is no difference in the scope and/or level of aspirations among disabled 16 year-olds and their non-disabled counterparts in the United Kingdom, there is a significant divergence of experience and aspiration in early adulthood (Burchardt, 2005). Unemployment is not always found to be related to educational

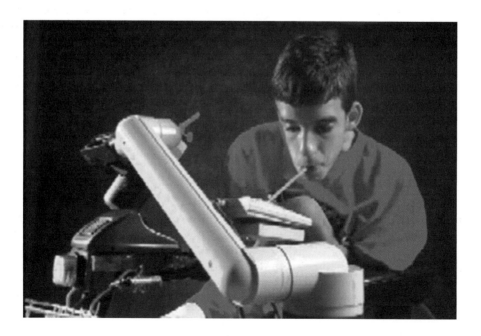

achievement or disability and raises the possible contribution of other factors of vocational readiness which are likely to originate during adolescence, for instance, expectations of self and/or others, knowledge of resources and/or rights, self-esteem, work experience and so forth.

Loss To and Lack of Follow-Up after Transfer

Indirect evidence of the need for transitional care is provided by the reports of loss to and/or lack of follow-up of young people following transfer to adult services; for example, up to two thirds of young adults with diabetes have no medical follow-up after leaving paediatric care (Pacaud *et al.*, 1996) and are potentially subject to higher rates of disease-related complications. In a UK study of a cohort of patients two years after transfer, 51% of transferred patients were still attending compared to 92% two years prior to transfer (Kipps *et al.*, 2002). Tomlinson and Sugarman reported 100% follow-up until age 16 of young people with spina bifida complicated by hydrocephalus but only 40% in young adulthood with the associated concern discussed earlier (Tomlinson and Sugarman, 1995).

Limited Service Provision

In addition to the above, there is evidence of need for service development. Studies have reported no adolescent or transition clinic provision in a significant proportion of speciality clinics, for example, 82% of rheumatology clinics (McDonagh *et al.*, 2000). Furthermore, there is limited provision of dedicated adolescent inpatient units to support such services (Viner, 2001). Limited service provision is particularly pertinent to adolescent onset disease, which only presents during adolescence and may be diagnosed within paediatrics, and yet local policies may dictate transfer to occur shortly after diagnosis, sometimes before control of the disease is achieved.

The *differences* in service provision between paediatric and adult services also need to be acknowledged, as there may be an actual reduction in services following transfer despite the fact that most young people with disability have ongoing health problems. Young people themselves may have difficulties in appreciating why they may no longer be entitled to services previously offered by the paediatric team (e.g. hydrotherapy), despite remaining with the same consultant and within the same hospital (Shaw, Southwood and McDonagh, 2004a). The situation is not helped by the lack of information made available to young people and their parents about future options and opportunities and the sorts of services and support that will become available on transfer (Shaw, Southwood and McDonagh, 2004a).

The Differences between Paediatric and Adult Health Care

Paediatric and adult health care are two very dissimilar systems (see above), which serve distinctively different populations with divergent health care needs, and therein lies the evidence of the challenges of transition! These differences are readily perceived by the young people themselves and contribute to their concerns regarding transfer. The different cultures of care between paediatric and adult services need to be acknowledged by both health care providers as well as in transition programme content in order to prepare the young person and their caregivers for these differences.

Potential Delayed Adolescent Development into Young Adulthood

Integral to the provision of adolescent health care, including transitional care, is a working knowledge of the reciprocal influences of adolescent development on the health of the individual young person. Development should be used as a lens to look at adolescent health in its entirety, acknowledging the interrelationships of physical, cognitive and psychosocial development on health and illness. The potential for delayed development needs to be recognized when considering those with chronic illness and/or disability in order to ensure age and developmentally appropriate care in paediatric AND adult settings.

Managing Transition Effectively

Although the philosophy of transition has been accepted both nationally and internationally for over a decade, the challenges of translating policy into practice remain. Legislation, policies and policy guidance do not guarantee change or improvements. Despite national consensus of the importance of transition, a US-based study of 4332 young people with special health care needs revealed that half had not discussed transition and of those who had, only 59% had a plan and only 42% had discussed transfer to adult care (Lotstein *et al.*, 2005). In a multicentre transitional care research project in the United Kingdom, only two of ten participating centres had a written transition policy at the start and although an easy-to-use template was provided in the study resources, no additional centres had developed a policy at the end of the three-year study (McDonagh, Southwood and Shaw, 2006a).

There are many evidence-based strategies to support effective management of transition for young people with special health care needs, and these will now be considered (see below).

How to be an Effective Manager of Transition for Young People

- Remember to look outside the health box.
- Be adolescent friendly in approach and place.
- Communicate, educate, anticipate, collaborate!

Looking Outside the Health Box

Since the transitions adolescents face are interdependent as discussed above, it is important for practitioners to look outside the 'health box' and adopt a truly holistic view of transition. Evidence to support this comes from the young people themselves who perceive that health professionals (and in particular doctors) lack awareness of the wider impact of illness during adolescence (Shaw, Southwood and McDonagh, 2004a; Klosterman *et al.*, 2005; Beresford and Sloper, 2003). In a series of focus groups involving young people with juvenile idiopathic arthritis (JIA), participants wanted information and support not only about their condition but about a wide range of topics including psychosocial issues, bullying, vocation, disclosure of their condition to future partners and/or employers, independent living, sexual health and adult relationships (Shaw, Southwood and McDonagh, 2004a).

By definition, transition is multidisciplinary and inter-agency. Transition practitioners need to look outside their immediate team and consider the role of the young people themselves, their peers, their families, primary, secondary and school health, education and vocational services, youth and social services in addition to voluntary agencies.

Be Adolescent Friendly in Approach and Place

Provider behaviour is a key determinant of adolescent satisfaction with health care. Being empathic and non-judgemental are keys for success! The assurance of confidentiality is imperative for gaining the trust of young people and must be explained and confirmed at the outset of all consultations with adolescents. The rights of young people with respect to confidentiality must also be explained to their caregivers or parents. Posters addressing confidentiality issues are a useful resource in waiting areas. Engaging in small talk is one means of earning adolescent trust reported by young people and facilitates the acknowledgement of the wider impact of illness as mentioned above (Klosterman et al., 2005). Other strategies include asking for the adolescent's opinion and not withholding information (Shaw, Southwood and McDonagh, 2004b; Klosterman et al., 2005). Young people are also clear in their desire for honesty and respect from health professionals in addition to confidentiality (Shaw, Southwood and McDonagh, 2004b; Klosterman et al., 2005).

Time is an important factor to consider in the provision of age and developmentally appropriate settings for transitional care. Adolescent clinic appointment times need to be longer than both paediatric and adult clinic appointments due to the necessity to be unhurried with adolescents and the complexity of adolescent health service delivery. Some of the time demands can be countered if continuity of health professionals between visits can be assured (Klosterman et al., 2005) although young people debate how often you need to see a particular professional before an effective therapeutic alliance is established (Beresford and Sloper, 2003). Continuity of care is also helpful for parents/caregivers as they start to anticipate the young person becoming more independent managers of their own health (Shaw, Southwood and McDonagh, 2004b).

Unfortunately there is still a lack of provision of dedicated facilities for adolescents in hospitals in the United Kingdom. Young people often feel 'out of place' in both paediatric and adult environments, reporting that they find paediatric environments patronizing, adult environments distressing, and both environments isolating (Shaw, Southwood and McDonagh, 2004a). Young people ask to be valued and to feel normal with provision of age-appropriate, dedicated adolescent areas (Shaw, Southwood and McDonagh, 2004a). Dedicated adolescent environments was one of three components of transitional care considered by a panel of users and providers in a Delphi study for best practice but feasible in only a few UK centres (Shaw, Southwood and McDonagh, 2004b). A recent policy document has summarized the key attributes of young-person-friendly health services and will provide an important benchmark to build future services upon (Department of Health, 2005b). The direct involvement of young people in the planning and design of services is vital to ensure success!

Communicate, Educate, Anticipate, Collaborate!

The core skills for any adolescent health practitioner can be summarized by four simple but challenging words: communicate, educate, anticipate, collaborate! Each of these areas will now be discussed in turn.

Communicate!

Communication between young person and health professional should be interactive rather than interrogative. Strategies can be considered as being one of two types: one is unidirectional, characterized by the giving of facts, opinions and/or advice. If such strategies are used by professionals, the young person has to interrupt and/or assert themselves to enter such conversations. This is in contrast to the preferable interactive bidirectional strategies which incorporate assessment of the understanding of the young person as well as some skills training in the form of problem-solving strategies and posing hypothetical situations. In the latter form of communication there is a clear expectation of the young person participating and responding. The use of 'the third person' is another developmentally appropriate communication strategy particularly for sensitive topics, for example: "some young people with your condition get very fed up with it and start harming themselves. Have you ever tried to harm yourself?" It is important always to seek their permission to ask these more sensitive questions with an explanation of why you are asking them, for example: "I want to ask you some personal questions. This is standard practice in our clinic and these questions are to help give me a picture of your overall health and who you are. Is that OK with you?" It is also important for practitioners to be sure they understand clearly that what has just been said is what the young person meant to say. A useful strategy is to simply paraphrase what the young person has said and repeat it back to them to ensure clarification.

Beresford and Sloper (2003) reported a range of practical, attitudinal and behavioural factors influencing communication between young people with chronic illnesses and their doctors. These included perceived attitudes towards adolescents; communication skills of the adolescent *and* health professional; the type of information needed; a perceived lack of interest in the wider impact of chronic illness; presence of parents and students/trainees; duration and frequency of contact and gender of the doctor (Beresford and Sloper, 2003). Such findings support the inclusion of communication skills training as a core subject in future adolescent health training programmes for health professionals.

Educate!

Salient information, that is age and developmentally appropriate, is an integral part of disease education, self-management and informed consent for young people with chronic illnesses. Such information is requested by both young people and their parents but is not always available or perceived as satisfactory by them (Shaw, Southwood and McDonagh, 2004a, 2004c). Often information is provided for parents or young children only and not written specifically for the adolescent age group. The range of information needs requested by young people is potentially wide and often extends beyond the medical aspects of the condition (Shaw, Southwood and McDonagh, 2004a). Similarly, information about drug therapy requested by young people includes rationale and risk-benefit discussions and not just details of daily regimens and side effects (Shaw, Southwood and McDonagh, 2004a). Knowledge is important for effective, appropriate disclosure to potential partners or employers, an unmet transitional need reported by adolescents themselves (Shaw, Southwood and McDonagh, 2004a). Effective information has been reported to improve quality of life, adherence with health regimes and coping with chronic disease. Despite these, knowledge deficits are well recognized in both adolescent and adult populations of childhood-onset disease including long-term clinic attendees.

Understanding the implications of a chronic condition and its therapy for other aspects of health is important for young people. For example, understanding the implications of a chronic illness and/or disability for sexual and reproductive health is a key aspect of transitional care and yet not always well addressed during adolescence by health professionals. Sexual health is important for many reasons, not least for the development of a sexual identity, consideration of physical limitations, heredity, pubertal effects, teratogenicity and suchlike. Young people with chronic illnesses and/or physical disabilities are reported to be at least as sexually active as their peers (Suris and Parera, 2005; Valencia and Cromer, 2000; Suris *et al.*, 1996). However, their level of contraceptive knowledge/use tends to be lower than their able-bodied peers (Valencia and Cromer, 2000) and they experience more negative consequences of their sexual behaviour in terms of sexually transmitted infections and abuse (Suris *et al.*, 1996). The maturational challenges of having a chronic illness during adolescence may also lead to young people engaging in risky behaviours as a means of achieving developmental goals such as peer acceptance and independence.

Another integral component of education is the provision of information. It is not just *what* information we provide but *how* we provide it. Development of resources should always be based on a needs assessment directly involving young people themselves and not just on professional judgement. Ideally multiple methods are available including some which are kept up to date and can be accessed anonymously. In several studies, young people have expressed their wish for professionals to be honest and not to hold back or be gatekeepers of informational resources (Shaw, Southwood and McDonagh, 2004a, 2004b; Klosterman *et al.*, 2005). The use of modern technologies such as the Internet and text-messaging have obvious benefits, with many excellent web sites available (see below).

Adolescent-Friendly Health Information Sites

UK-based

www.teenagehealthfreak.org

www.youthhealthtalk.org

www.childrenfirst.nhs.uk

www.need2know.co.uk

www.connexions.gov.uk

www.lifebytes.gov.uk

www.mindbodysoul.gov.uk

International

www.doctissimo.fr
www.ciao.ch
www.teenhealthfx.com
www.goaskalice.columbia.edu

Skills training is another important aspect of adolescent health education and is very much in keeping with the resilience framework, so integral to transitional care (Olsson *et al.*, 2003). Diabetes self-management education and coping skills training programmes have been shown to improve metabolic control, self-efficacy, and quality of life in adolescents (Anderson and Wolpert, 2004). One key opportunity for the development of self-advocacy within the health care setting is feeling confident to choose to see the health professional alone. This was reported to be one of the five main methods of 'demonstrating transition' by providers of health care for adolescents with sickle cell disease in the United States (Telfair *et al.*, 2004) along with encouraging patients to accept more responsibility, providing literature, making the patient more financially responsible and having family conferences to discuss transition (Telfair *et al.*, 2004). Independent visits have been shown to be important as one determinant of attendance at one adult Grown-Up Congenital Heart (GUCH) clinic appointment (Reid *et al.*, 2004) and as an associated factor with improvement in health-related quality of life in adolescents with JIA (McDonagh, Southwood, Shaw, 2006b). In a Delphi study involving adolescents with JIA, parents of adolescents with JIA and a range of health professionals involved in their care, one of six features of what was considered best practice and feasible in the majority of UK hospitals, was giving adolescents the option of being seen by professionals without their parents (Shaw, Southwood and McDonagh 2004b). Young people may be unaware of their rights to choose to be seen independently and it is therefore important to proactively inform them with inclusion of such information within clinic literature and advertising with posters in the waiting room and suchlike. Their rights to a chaperone (other than their parent) must be explained in addition to the assurance and explanation of confidentiality as detailed previously.

Promoting self-management in young people with chronic illness can be challenging for parents and health care providers alike! Discrepancies have been reported between parents and health care providers in the perceived 'right age' for self-management practices, such as independent visits and self-medication (Geenen, Powers and Sells, 2003). Similar discrepancies have been reported in the perceived importance of discussion of sexual health and substance use issues with young people with special health care needs, with health care professionals perceiving significantly greater importance (Geenen, Powers and Sells, 2003). Professionals need to be aware of the potentially competing aspects of the parenting role during transition, that is, protecting their son's/daughter's health while supporting their growing need for independence, privacy and autonomy. Optimal care may or may not be achievable, depending on a young person's level of development.

As a result, negotiation of compromises between parent and young person are frequently required!

A final consideration with respect to education is the education of professionals involved in transition. Telfair *et al.*, reported that although the majority of providers agreed that a transition programme was necessary for adolescents with sickle cell disease, few actually did anything to demonstrate their involvement in the transition process (Telfair *et al.*, 2004). There is a need for increased guidance, education and training of professionals both at practice and policy level. The current background of limited training opportunities in adolescent health training for both paediatric and adult care providers will impact on delivery of transitional care in the United Kingdom. Although considered best practice, professionals knowledgeable in transitional care were considered only feasible in a few hospitals in a UK Delphi study (Shaw, Southwood and McDonagh 2004b). In a survey of staff in a major UK paediatric hospital, 60% of respondents reported that they had received no prior specific training in adolescent health with no significant difference in these needs observed between doctors and other health professionals (McDonagh *et al.*, 2006).

There is now evidence that training in adolescent health is beneficial! Sustainable, large improvements in knowledge, skill and self-perceived competency were reported in a randomized control trial within primary care in Australia, which were sustained at five years (Sanci *et al.*, 2005). Furthermore, positive outcomes of such training often include higher rates of desired clinical practices, for example, confidentiality, screening, greater number of adolescents seen and a greater tendency to engage in continuing education in adolescent health. The potential of using transitional care as an invaluable model to teach patient- and family-centred care, differences between paediatric and adult care, dyadic vs. triadic consultations, cultural competencies and shared decision-making should not be underestimated.

Anticipate!

The essence of transition is an early start! Every encounter with an adolescent is a potential opportunity for health promotion and/or skills training. In the context of chronic illness, the transition to secondary school is a useful means of explaining transition to a young person – they are not going to stay in primary school forever – and likewise they will not stay in paediatric services forever either! Starting transition planning at age 11 in an evidence-based transition programme in adolescent rheumatology appeared to be advantageous (McDonagh, Southwood and Shaw, 2006b).

In a national survey of health professionals, 77% of them felt that individualized transition plans were *important/very important* for adolescents with JIA (Shaw, Southwood and McDonagh, 2004c). However, a significant proportion of patients in several studies have no documented plan for transition to adult care (Robertson *et al.*, 2006; Lam, Fitzgerald and Sawyer, 2005). In a 10-year audit of admissions of young adults aged 18 years and over to a major Australian paediatric hospital, 51% of surgical inpatients and 28% of medical inpatients had no documented plan for transition to adult care (Lam, Fitzgerald and Sawyer, 2005). In addition to lack of planning, disease complexity was reported to have contributed to the increased admissions (Lam, Fitzgerald and Sawyer, 2005).

Young people are very clear as to their desire to be involved in planning and/or goal-setting with their health care team. In transitional care, as with the rest of adolescent health care, it is important that health professionals engage the young people themselves when providing such care. When individualized transition plans, developed with the young people and with their parents respectively, were implemented in a programme of transitional care, they were successfully completed by 95% and 92% of adolescents and their parents respectively, and successfully identified their needs (McDonagh, Southwood and Shaw, 2006a).

Finally, anticipatory guidance is an important component of transitional care. Adolescents often have more diverse and serious health concerns than expected by health care providers and these emphasize the need for a proactive, anticipatory guidance approach in consultations involving adolescents. Further support for the provision of such guidance includes the prevalence of risk-taking behaviours reported in young people with chronic illnesses and/or disabilities (Suris and Parera, 2005; Valencia and Cromer, 2000; Suris *et al.*, 1996). A useful screening tool to help in anticipatory guidance is the HEADSS mnemonic (**H**ome, **E**ducation, **A**ctivities, **D**rugs, **S**ex, **S**uicide), now in several formats in the literature (McDonagh, 2005). Improved documentation of HEADSS issues in case notes of young people recently transferred to adult care has been reported following the implementation of a transitional care programme (Robertson *et al.*, 2006). This in part was attributed to the raised awareness of adolescent health within participating centres (Robertson *et al.*, 2006).

Collaborate!

The most important person to collaborate with is the young person themselves! Research has identified differences between the views of young people and the views of the adults close to them, suggesting that adults cannot be used as reliable proxies for young people's views (Waters, Stewart-Brown and Fitzpatrick, 2003). In a study considering both adolescent and parent proxy ratings, 50% of parents of adolescents with JIA (n=303) either overestimated or underestimated their child's pain, functional ability, global well-being and/or health-related quality of life (Shaw, Southwood and McDonagh, 2006). Parents and young people also tend to agree about easily observable behaviours compared with less overt phenomena (Shaw, Southwood and McDonagh, 2006).

Collaboration with and inclusion of the parent/caregivers is of similar importance. Family connectedness, family role models, family concern for the well-being of the child and autonomy at home are all factors identified that foster resilience in young people and should be encouraged and affirmed (Patterson and Blum, 1996), especially during adolescence and transition. The challenge of negotiating the appropriate extent of parental involvement is an integral component of adolescent health irrespective of the presence or absence of chronic illness and/or disability. In a UK survey of professionals involved in the care of adolescents with JIA, a third reported parental difficulties (including parental overprotectiveness) during transition and perceived these to influence the success of transition (Shaw, Southwood and McDonagh, 2004c). Parents therefore also need a preparation period for transition and transfer. Such service provision has obvious resource allocation in terms of clinic space and/or time in addition to staffing levels, particularly for those practitioners not working within a multidisciplinary team.

In addition to collaboration between providers and the young person and their family, effective collaboration across the paediatric–adult service interface is a key to success. Telfair *et al.* reported differing opinions between paediatric and adult providers for adolescents with sickle cell disease (Telfair *et al.*, 2004). These differences were in relation to transition expectations and programme need especially among female providers, those practising in urban areas and providers who treat both adolescent and adult clients in comparison with their counterparts (Telfair *et al.*, 2004). Often the paediatric providers are more concerned than their adult counterparts and this is reflected by the paediatric origin of much of the transitional care development and research to date. However, transition by definition includes the adult services and both opinions and perspectives must be acknowledged and respected.

Due to the holistic nature of transition, care will, by definition, require a collaborative, multidisciplinary and multi-agency approach. The heterogeneity of these 'virtual teams' has major implications for effective communication within and between services. Documentation of relevant information is important in view of both the multidimensional and multidisciplinary nature of transitional care. Unfortunately in a national audit of case notes of recently transferred young people to adult rheumatology services, there was limited documentation of key transitional care issues in the case notes (Robertson *et al.*, 2006). Young people and their parents have expressed specific fears regarding this transfer of information (Shaw, Southwood and McDonagh, 2004a). Despite participation in a multicentre transitional care research programme, there was unfortunately no improvement in the number of patients for whom copy letters and/or medical and/or multidisciplinary team summaries were sent to the adult team prior to transfer (Robertson *et al.*, 2006).

The Potential of Transitional Care

In the context of the increasing survival and/or recognition of childhood-onset conditions in adulthood, transitional care can be argued as a responsibility rather than an optional extra of health professionals involved with such young people. This is particularly true for paediatric and adolescent specialists, being advocates of age and developmentally appropriate care, irrespective of chronological age. This message, however, has to now be effectively communicated to our adult counterparts who will potentially be involved with these young adults for much longer than paediatric specialists were. Although objective data is limited, the benefits of transition have been reported in terms of improvement in satisfaction, disease control and adherence to appointments post transfer. In diabetes clinics there was a higher rate of adherence to appointments in units where the young people had met the adult doctors prior to transfer (Kipps *et al.*, 2002) and improved control (Orr, Fineberg and Gray, 1996). Young people have reported a preference in meeting adult doctors prior to transfer (Shaw, Southwood and McDonagh, 2004a; Kipps *et al.*, 2002) and there is an evolving evidence base to support the development of young adult clinics for 16–25 year-olds to acknowledge this particular period of emerging adulthood (Dovey-Pearce *et al.*, 2005; Anderson

Web-Based Transition Resources

United Kingdom

www.transitioninfonetwork.org.uk

wwwg.dh.gov.uk/transition

www.dreamteam-uk.org

www.transitionpathway.co.uk

www.youngminds.org.uk/publications/booklets/adulthood.php

Australia

www.rch.org.au/transition

United States and Canada

www.door2adulthood.com

http://hctransitions.ichp.edu

http://depts.washington.edu/healthtr/index.html

http://chfs.ky.gov/ccshcn/ccshcntransition.htm

www.communityinclusion.org/transition/

and Wolpert, 2004). The first large objective evaluation of an evidence-based coordinated transitional care programme in a chronic illness (JIA) has reported significant improvements at 6 and 12 months for adolescents and their parents compared to baseline in terms of health-related quality of life, knowledge, satisfaction with health care and vocational readiness (McDonagh, Southwood and Shaw, 2006b). There are numerous models of good practice from around the world to support further developments in this area, examples of which are listed below.

However, there remain many more questions than answers in the arena of health transition. Do different models of transition care produce equivalent medical and psychosocial outcomes? What is the economic cost evaluation of such models? Which patient characteristics (medical, social, psychosocial) identify those who need a transitional programme? What constitutes transition readiness? What defines 'successful' transition? Are there critical periods during the transition period wherein the timeliness of interventions would be more effective than others? What is the role of primary care in transition? What are the core subjects for transitional care training for health professionals? Does the effectiveness of parental support correlate with transition outcomes? Is there a relationship between family characteristics and the young person's development of transition readiness and/or achievement of transition outcomes? Can transitional care influence long-term outcomes? What are the most appropriate outcome measures for evaluative research? Finally, such research must involve young people and their families and/or carers as well as paediatric and adult care providers in health, education, social services and the voluntary sector if the true picture is to be realized.

CASE STUDY 9.1

Alex is due to turn 18, four years since the onset of his juvenile idiopathic arthritis (JIA), originally diagnosed and currently managed by the rheumatology team at the local children's hospital. Unfortunately, despite maximal drug therapy, he has yet to experience disease remission. He continues to have pain, stiffness and swelling in multiple joints, both large and small despite twice weekly injections of etanercept, once weekly methotrexate injections, daily anti-inflammatory tablets and daily prednisolone tablets. The latter medication has caused facial acne, which upsets him. He left school at 16, not sure what he wanted to do but has recently started as a clerk in a local bank. He is very anxious about time off work as he enjoys it, and has missed his last four rheumatology clinic appointments. He had previously lived with his mother. She remarried last year and has since had a new baby but unfortunately Alex does not get on with his stepdad and has recently left home and moved in with his girlfriend. He is currently not in contact with his mother and is currently no longer receiving the injection therapy, as it was his mother who had done these injections. He had increased his steroid tablets without advice to try and stop his arthritis getting worse off these drugs. This was proving unsuccessful, however, and he was increasingly worried as to how long he could manage at work. He is sexually active but does not use condoms as he finds these difficult to use because of the arthritis in his fingers and his girlfriend is on the pill. He is aware that the transition policy at the children's hospital states that adolescents are transferred to adult care usually between the ages of 16 and 18 years but the adult hospital nearest his home is not at all convenient to his work.

Consider and discuss the following key transition management issues in relation to Alex for the rheumatology team to address:

A. Health

1. Negotiation of a mutually convenient appointment at the children's hospital.
2. Training in self-injection techniques and reinstating etanercept and methotrexate.
3. Review of drug management and discussion of need to induce disease remission, acknowledging that new therapies will require new funding which will require negotiation with adult service.
4. Discussion of steroid (prednisolone) therapy including a risk-benefit discussion and importance of talking about dose changes with either his GP or the rheumatology team.

5. Suggestions for topical therapy for acne.
6. Introduction of sexual health issues including locally available adolescent-friendly sexual health services, sexually transmitted infections, importance of condoms and potential alternative strategies, for instance, asking his girlfriend to put them on when he is unable to manage.

B. Vocational issues

1. Discussion concerning disclosure to employers, rights under the Disability Discrimination Act.
2. Occupational therapy assessment connected with hand function, work place.

C. Social issues

1. Exploration of avenues for potential reconciliation with his mother whilst assuring confidentiality.
2. Receipt of benefits, which he is eligible for.
3. Driving assessment to assist with transport issues.
4. Development of links with youth advocacy services in community.

D. Transfer to adult care

1. Discussion concerning transfer to young adult clinic involving both his paediatric rheumatologist and new adult rheumatologist in a hospital nearer his place of work with a late afternoon appointment to improve adherence and facilitate completion of transition.
2. Email and text-message contact with the team member he knew best (the occupational therapist) during transfer period until successful transfer achieved and confirmed.
3. Involvement of primary care team to provide additional support during this period.

Conclusion

Transitional care is an area ripe for development in terms of service, education and training and research. Recognition of the non-categorical nature of transition in the context of chronic illness and/or disability with subsequent sharing of knowledge and expertise between specialities will aid the 'walking of the (transitional care) talk'. In so doing, we can help improve the health-related quality of life of all young people with chronic illness and/or disability, enabling them to 'survive and thrive', and reach their true potential!

Further Reading

Department of Health (2006) Transition: getting it right for young people. Improving the transition of young people with long-term conditions from children's to adult health services, Department of Health Publications, London **[www.dh.gov.uk/transition]**.

Eiser C. (1993) *Growing up with a chronic disease*, Jessica Kingsley Publishers, London.

Michaud, P.-A., Suris, J.-C. and Viner R. (2004) The adolescent with a chronic condition. Part II: Healthcare provision. *Archives of Disease in Childhood*, 89, 943–949.

Office of the Deputy Prime Minister (2005) Transitions: young adults with complex needs, ODPM Publications, Wetherby, UK **[www.socialexclusion.gov.uk]**.

Royal College of Nursing (2004) Adolescent transition care: guidance for nursing staff, London **[www.rcn.org.uk]**.

Royal College of Paediatrics and Child Health (2003) Bridging the gaps: health care for adolescents, RCPCH, London **[www.rcpch.ac.uk]**.

Suris, J.-C., Michaud, P.-A. and Viner R. (2004) The adolescent with a chronic condition. Part 1: Developmental issues. *Archives of Disease in Childhood*, 89, 938–942.

Discussion Questions

1. Sally is an adolescent with insulin diabetes since the age of 4 years old. What are the potential effects of her chronic condition on her psychosocial and cognitive development at age 11, 14 and 17 years?

2. Who are the key players in transitional care and describe their potential role in the care of Sally?

3. What are the key transition skills which Sally will need to actively participate in health care as an adult?

4. What support will Sally's mother potentially require as Sally grows up and which professionals could provide this in the United Kingdom?

5. At age 16, Sally is informed of her transfer to the adult clinic. What are the concerns likely to be of (i) Sally (ii) Sally's mother (iii) Sally's paediatric endocrinologist (iv) the adult endocrinologist?

Chapter 10

Health Promotion and Health Education

Donna Mackinnon

Health Scotland, Health Education Board for Scotland

- Introduction
- Promoting Adolescent Health
- Towards a 'Youthist' Agenda
- Bridging the Gap Between Providers and Users
- Conclusion

Learning Objectives

After reading this chapter you should:

1 Be aware why adolescents are a priority focus for health promotion and education.
2 Understand that a variety of individuals have a contribution to make in promoting adolescent health including non-health personnel and non-professionals.
3 Recognize the key differences and needs among young people and the variety of influences which play a role in their health and well-being.
4 Understand why health initiatives must resonate with adolescents' own lives and take account of the meanings they themselves give to their health and health behaviours.
5 Describe ways in which young people can become partners in the health promotion and education effort and the reasons why it is important.
6 Understand why the available evidence must inform the design and implementation of interventions but also recognize how much more evaluation is required, especially on activities with socially excluded adolescents.

Introduction

This chapter considers the difficult task of providing health education and health promotion for adolescents and emphasizes that approaches for adults are by no means immediately transferable to young people. It looks at some of the issues that occur when targeting young people as they go through key transitions en route to adulthood. The chapter also considers the difficulties in providing health education and promotion for socially excluded and vulnerable adolescents.

The first section of this chapter considers the nature of health promotion and health education and why young people constitute a key target. Some of the main areas where health promotion and education take place are examined; school-based health education, youth work settings and use of the media and information technology. It is suggested that a multi-site approach to young people's health may present the most benefits and that a variety of individuals (including non-health professionals) have a contribution to make. This chapter stresses how young people are all different. Such heterogeneity is shown through consideration of the different influences on their health as well as the key differences in their health behaviours. Young people's lives and health needs are complicated not least because the factors that have been found to promote their health have also been shown to hinder it e.g. their peers, family and the school.

Undoubtedly, a lot of data on many aspects of young people's lives and health exists. However, a great deal has been developed from the perspective of adult-defined health concerns and issues. The second section of this chapter emphasizes the need to move towards a 'youthist' agenda. The evidence indicates that where young people have been asked their views about their health and well-being, a different perspective has often become clear. Some key questions are addressed. What does health mean to young people? Why do young people take 'risks'? What do young people themselves want to meet their needs? The discussion attempts to move away from problem-focused approaches and curricula towards a consideration of the contemporary youth experience – what it is like to be young today – and an approach which prioritizes their mental well-being and resilience.

The final part of the chapter looks at how young people can become partners in the health promotion effort and examines how this can be achieved through more participatory approaches. The importance of evidence in health promotion and education is confirmed here when we ask ourselves how we know what we are doing is working. The chapter concludes that if health initiatives are to be meaningful to young people they must resonate with their own lives, take account of the meanings young people themselves give to health and health behaviours and also recognize differences within the youth population.

Promoting Adolescent Health

Health education and *health promotion* are terms that are often used interchangeably. Although exact definitions of the terms remain contested there are differences in the activities and goals of each. Health promotion finds its roots in the longer established health education and grew in prominence in the 1980s. The Ottawa Charter, established in 1986 at the first health promotion international conference, defined health promotion as the process of enabling people to increase their control over their health and to improve it. Therefore a central principle of health promotion is empowerment. More recently empowerment has been viewed as less of an individual and behavioural orientation and more of a collective community-based activity. The primary goal of health promotion is to prevent ill-health and also to enhance positive health and well-being. This can involve a number of processes such as the provision of practical facilities like screening, immunization and health improvement programmes. In effect health promotion consists of prevention of ill-health, protection of health and education about health. There is an emphasis on the physical, mental and social elements of health. It is fair to say that health promotion has a politically driven impetus and social action on health is driven by policy.

Health education has a more *communicative* aspect, imparting information and increasing knowledge as well as aiming to motivate people to promote their health. A central aim is to stimulate a healthy environment and there is an emphasis on individual- and behavioural-focused activities. Often health promotion efforts assume a topic-based approach with programmes devised for each, for example, smoking, alcohol, and coronary heart disease. However, behaviours and topics are clearly linked and such an approach can result in a duplication of effort. The other main tack has been settings-based work such as the voluntary sector, workplace, community and the school. This has allowed for a coordination of efforts in the topic areas. In addition a more arena-based approach can facilitate national–local links.

Why Target Young People?

By and large young people are a healthy sector of the population. West and Sweeting (2002) have argued that there is even a trend towards 'equalization' to the effect that little social class patterning of health is evident for a period. As noted in Chapter 1, they do not show the signs of life course wear-and-tear. Yet young people are one of the primary targets of health promotion efforts. Linked to this is the political drive to tackle adolescent behaviours. Therein is a desire to prevent young people from engaging in disorderly, risky behaviour that is often perceived as threatening to adults and wider society. As the discussion in Chapter 1 highlighted, the focus is on adolescents as *a risk* as well as *risk-takers*. There is also the need to be seen to be tackling potentially negative future outcomes that will lead to an unhealthy adult population, such as the rising obesity rates among children and adolescents. Indeed the prominence of adolescents in the health improvement agenda can be seen in terms of a perceived need for action and control in the present and arising out of a concern for the future.

Clocking Up More Miles

A life-course perspective in health promotion has resulted in concerns over the consequences of adolescent behaviour for later health. The evidence is strong that the risk factors for disease in adulthood, such as coronary heart disease, often find their origins earlier in the lifespan. Although in comparison to older generations less social class patterning of health is evident among young people, it follows that action taken in adolescence may pre-empt health inequalities at a later time. Moreover, as with adult society, it remains that young people who are in vulnerable, excluded or the most impoverished groups still experience many of the poorest health outcomes or threats to their health. Indeed marginalized groups have been identified; young people in care, homeless young people, those leaving care, travellers and young offenders (Tisdall, 2002). The evidence also suggests that these young people have the highest rates of severe chronic illness, the poorest diets and are the heaviest consumers of tobacco, alcohol and illicit drugs. In effect, while adolescence is one of the healthiest periods in the lifespan with regard to morbidity and mortality, some young people are already stocking up more miles on the clock.

Tackling Risk-Taking

A related reason for focusing on young people lies in the way in which young people's behaviour has been problematized and adolescence has been viewed through a 'storm and stress' lens – a time of natural upheaval with all those hormones coming to the fore! Scarcely a day goes by without alarming statistics being highlighted on youth drinking, drug-taking, obesity or sexual risk-taking. Moreover, the clustering of engagement in a number of risk behaviours has caused adult concern. *Moral panics* around young people's behaviour are not new. Academics have traced them as far back as Victorian society when the word hooligan first appeared in the press to refer to a group of young people. Problematizing young people's behaviours has resulted in problem-focused approaches and curricula in health promotion and education in an attempt to reduce those statistics!

Rites of Passage

During the transition to adulthood young people are faced with new situations that lead to them having to face a number of choices including choices about their behaviour. Experimentation is integral to adolescence and is a key feature of the transitional period of youth when adult identities begin to form and risk behaviours are tried out. Smoking, drinking, drug-taking and sexual activity are all part of the 'rites of passage' that young people try out as part of experimenting with different self-identities. In particular drinking alcohol is associated with becoming an adult and social participation by young people. Additionally they are entering

an adult world that is highly sexualized. But as discussed later in this chapter, young people regard experimentation and risk-taking behaviours differently to many adults for whom such behaviours in young people are seen as a problem. Moreover, recent changes in the youth experience of the transition to adulthood has seen some researchers arguing that young people are now subjected to many more 'windows of risk' which could increase their vulnerability to potentially health-damaging behaviours (Furlong and Cartmel, 1997).

New Challenges

It is now widely accepted that the nature of young people's transitions to adulthood is altering. The challenges young people face in making the transition to adulthood are now very different from even a decade ago, let alone a generation ago. Related to this acceptance is more recognition that a 'storm and stress' view is too narrow given wider societal changes and their effects on young people's experience. Whereas in the past transitions to adulthood were relatively straightforward and predictable they are now much more heterogeneous and complex; consequently they are more individualized and less of a group experience. Young people are spending unprecedented amounts of time in the company of their peers and it is claimed that their leisure time and social relationships have taken on new meaning and significance for their identity formation (Hendry *et al.*, 1993). Navigation of transitions (such as changing educational establishments, leaving home, becoming a young parent) is a key feature of young people's lives today and managing change successfully is an important aspect of health and well-being in youth, but also an important foundation for future health and well-being as an adult. Young people who fail to make successful transitions are at serious risk of exclusion and poor mental and physical health in their adult lives. Providing reliable, trustworthy information and confidential health and well-being advice is therefore paramount at this time.

Where and How do Health Professionals Target Young People?

The School Setting

Schools have been seen as a prime site for health promotion for many years but there has been renewed acknowledgement of their potential for health education and health promotion initiatives. Commentators have offered an analysis of the strengths and weaknesses of the school as a health-promoting setting in various countries. Some of the key strengths and weaknesses are summarized in the table below (Table 10.1).

As the table indicates, schools may allow for the means to improve young people's health and well-being in ways which will also bring about benefits to their educational achievement. They present a significant target audience given that attendance is compulsory. In a study of parental experiences of providing sex education for their children, Walker (2001) concluded that parents did have the skills as educators but that they found the experience uncertain and embarrassing particularly when dealing with sons. Health education in the school setting can allow parents to opt out but can also facilitate their efforts. Studies have shown that parents are interested in their children's health education. Also, there is evidence to suggest that schools

Table 10.1   Key strengths and limitations of the school setting

Strengths	Limitations
Reaches significant numbers. Most young people attend school for a minimum of 11 years	Some young people slip through the net through truancy, exclusion, illness, etc.
Teachers come ready trained to facilitate learning	Teachers may not have received adequate training and support for more sensitive issues
Teachers may already have a rapport with the young people they are in contact with on a daily basis	Schools can be regarded by many young people as institutional places of authority and hence fears over confidentiality may exist
Links with other learning topics/subjects such as modern studies, may help promote transferable skills such as communication and self-reflection	Existing pressures on the curriculum may mean health education is not a priority in the standards and targets staff have to meet
Schools are viewed positively by most parents in the delivery of health education	Schools can be used as an opt-out for parents
	Education and health professionals often use different discourses which can inhibit understanding and partnership working
Offers a curriculum structure which is geared to appropriate age and aptitude levels	Different understandings of what constitutes a successful outcome in health education can exist, e.g. a reduction in smoking rates or increased knowledge

Source: Young, 2004; Scriven and Stiddard, 2003

are more effective in terms of academic achievement if good relations are developed with parents (Denman, 1998). Such links would surely see benefits in health education. However, there are difficulties in the school as a setting, not least because of the pressures that already exist on staff with regard to the curriculum and the need to meet educational standards in core subjects.

Positive developments for the school as a setting for health improvement lie in the health-promoting school concept in Scotland and Northern Ireland, the Welsh Network of Healthy Schools and the National Healthy School standard in England. As Young (2004) suggests, such a unifying whole school approach may result in schools being able to consider health in the *informal curriculum* as well as in the formal curriculum, in other words not just through traditional educational/informational approaches but also through promoting a healthy ethos. This is important not least because schools can give conflicting messages to young people. Messages about healthy eating and the benefits of physical activity may not be backed up with healthy food options in the canteen or vending machines or the availability of bicycle facilities and changing areas. Moreover, health promotion stresses empowerment but the institutional setting of school has a control ethos and health education in schools may present a clash with the home culture. We could also ethically question the 'captive audience' aspect of the school setting – how often do young people give their informed permission for school-based interventions as opposed to their parents or teachers?

School Staff

Gordon and Turner (2001) have explored the views of staff and pupils on whether staff should be health 'exemplars' – role models. These researchers found little support for this from either staff or pupils. The pupils in their research felt that even if teachers were to practise healthy behaviours this would not serve to encourage them to adopt the health behaviour displayed. Staff rather represented a group the pupils wished to differentiate from and they did not identify with them. Both staff and pupils in the research did show agreement that staff could give legitimate advice on health. Pupils did feel that staff should not openly demonstrate negative health behaviours if they were also articulating negativity about those behaviours, that is, being contradictory. However, the strongest feelings from both staff and pupils on staff as 'exemplars' was not with regard to physical health but rather that staff should embody good interpersonal behaviours such as showing respect, rapport and calmness. The health-promoting school concept looks beyond teaching to emphasize community links and a more multifaceted outlook. It also includes all members of the school community. Yet as Young (2004) has asserted, school-based health education alone is insufficient to change young people's behaviour and a multifaceted approach is required in view of the variety of influences on young people's health. One such important influence is the media.

The Media

Young people are expert media consumers and are quite shrewd about which media are better for different types of information. It has been suggested that young people in the United Kingdom aged 6 to 17 spend as much as five hours a day consuming/using media forms with some evidence pointing to even higher levels (Batchelor and Raymond, in Burtney and Duffy, 2004). In surveys young people have consistently cited the media as a main source of information. Young people have also been found to have very high levels of recall of advertisements in comparison to other populations and they are much more critical when discussing content (Batchelor and Raymond, in Burtney and Duffy, 2004). Using the media to promote their health would seem to be ideal in targeting this population, but do health promotion advertisements work? The answer to this is yes, but not on their own.

Health educators must be realistic about what the use of the media can achieve. It can be important in drawing attention to issues, putting them on the public agenda and imparting information. There is evidence to suggest that they influence attitudes. Sustained campaigns, in particular, have been shown to contribute to wider societal shifts in attitude, for instance, drink–driving campaigns. However, such attitudinal shifts take considerable time to manifest. Moreover, with regard to a result in behavioural change, the effects of health advertisements are too difficult to determine and isolate. Change is only likely to be instigated where motivation already exists. Also, the link with more local health promotion efforts is paramount. Use of the media must be backed up at grass-roots level. There is little benefit in imparting information about stopping smoking if there is no community cessation support based work in progress and vice versa.

Active Consumers

The primary positive element in using advertising to promote health messages lies in challenging young people to reflect and giving them more knowledge. Far from being passive consumers of health messages, young people are very active consumers, constructing their own meanings and understandings. These meanings have been shown to be mediated by their own lives and personal experiences. Like other health promotion initiatives, media campaigns only succeed when accurately informed by the evidence around young people's lives. In fact, research by MORI has indicated that a majority of young people, 68%, think that young people would be the best people to write adverts about healthy living, (MORI, 1998 cited in Burtney and Duffy, 2004). In addition, research suggests that the tone of an advert aimed at young people is as important as the actual content. The importance of tone has also been shown in an examination of young people's views of health information online.

Using Information Technology

Information technology continues to transform how information is exchanged and the Internet, in particular, is increasingly being recognized as a potentially powerful tool for improving health. It allows people to take responsibility for their health and also allows professionals to offer an alternative type of service which can have both global and local content. Research carried out by Mackinnon and Soloman (2003) considered young people's needs, experiences and attitudes towards the provision of health information online (see also Gray *et al.*, 2005). Many young people viewed the Internet as their main source of information. It was seen as more fun than books or leaflets and more up-to-date. Moreover it was seen as an ideal source of information due to perceived anonymity. However, the research noted that Internet access, preferences and use varied with age and this is important when we develop resources.

   Advertising and the use of new information technology do play a valuable role in targeting young people. In particular multimedia will undoubtedly gain in significance as a new learning environment for health promotion. But clearly information on its own is insufficient. For example, information campaigns about HIV have been shown to result in increased awareness levels but people still engage in unprotected sex. Similarly messages on drug use may be limited in effect for young people who do not perceive their use as dependency. Moreover, Duffy and colleagues (2003) have prudently pointed out that not all young people have the expertise to appraise the information that is presented or have the capacity to change any negative health situations even if armed with information. These authors also note that less than 10% of the world's population has Internet access and indeed the majority have yet to make a phone call. Indeed, settings such as the school and using media and new technology may not reach the very types of people who require the most support.

In the Community and Beyond

We should also consider how we can access young people who are outside of the statutory school system; how can we get the health-promotion message across to hard-to-reach and excluded young people? Here it becomes clear that a number of individuals have a contribution to make to health promotion with young people. Outreach workers, youth workers in drop-in cafes and centres and community educators all have considerable contact with young people. Increasingly, youth health issues are being identified and responded to by a wide range of youth organizations, both statutory and voluntary. Research into the needs of youth workers and organizations has illustrated that regardless of their remit, health is a major area of concern, particularly mental health (Smith, Cunningham-Burley and Backett-Milburn, 2003). Indeed, other research studies into adult professionals with a broad remit in relation to young people have reported that rather than a topic-focused approach on priorities such as drugs or sexual health a more inclusive approach is required (Aggleton *et al.*, 1998).

In a mapping of health promotion for young people, Peersman (1996) found that different risk activities are interlinked and also that they tend to cluster amongst vulnerable young people. It makes sense then to employ a more joined-up, holistic approach to young people's health promotion and health education than we may with adults, if their needs are to be met. For example, young people have indicated in research elsewhere that a more holistic view of drinking and drug use which takes their wider lives into consideration should be adopted in education (Potter and Hodgkiss, 2002). Furthermore, one size does not fit all, given the individual, community and social differences that play a role in young people's health and health behaviours.

The Heterogeneity of Youth

Young people are often portrayed as a relatively homogeneous group. Why is this? They are no more the same than all adults are. They do not all share the same views, nor exhibit the same behaviours. There are many influences on their health needs and behaviours. In a systematic review of the evidence around young people's views and health interventions, Shepherd and colleagues (2002) have drawn our attention to the ways in which key influences on young people's health can act as both facilitators and barriers. They assert that these influences operate at three main levels: individual, for example, age and gender; community, such as friends and family; and societal, which includes economic and environmental circumstances. These influences can be seen through participation in health-compromising behaviours and in the meanings young people attach to such behaviour, relationships and life situations at this time.

With reference to gender, Wight and Henderson (in Burtney and Duffy, 2004) have noted that the meanings young people give to sexual relationships derive from same sex peers and thus a difference develops between young males' and young females' understandings. Young females consistently show higher rates of smoking in Britain than their male counterparts. They are more receptive to messages about healthy eating but engage in less physical activity outside of school (Shepherd *et al.*, 2002). Ethnicity too sees differences. Wight and Henderson (in Burtney and Duffy, 2004) note that age at first intercourse differs considerably between ethnic groups and therein between genders. Minority ethnic adolescents may have particular health promotion needs, relating not just to language but also parental and cultural expectations. For example, in her study of the housing and mental health care needs of Asians, Radia (1996) asserted that in different cultures there are different beliefs as to what will help treat mental health issues, for example, the use of a *hakim* who uses traditional herbal remedies or a spiritual healer. Where in Western culture, body and mind have often been seen as separate entities, Radia (1996) notes that in many ethnic cultures they are regarded as one and need to be treated as a whole. Hence a number of interventions may not be culturally sensitive.

Peers, Parents and Place

During adolescence peers take on a renewed significance for young people, not just as counterparts in age but also as advice and support providers. Young people see friends as one of the most important sources of information on health topics such as sex and drugs. While friends differ from peers (they are selected), studies continue to show that having friends or a best friend that smoke increases the likelihood of a young person smoking. Although peer pressure does play a role in influencing some adolescents, particularly younger age groups, peer identification/influence has increasingly been favoured as an explanation. Similarly, while parental beliefs can affect young people's health behaviours, the influence points more to parental behaviours as predictors, for example, parental smoking.

As noted earlier, an adolescent's economic and social background has been highlighted as contributing to engagement in health-compromising behaviours – storing up more miles. The median age of first sexual intercourse has been found to be lower in working-class young people. It is interesting to note that young people who are ascribed social class via parental occupation also show clear distinct differences in levels of risk engagement when it is their own career expectations which are considered (Glendinning et al., 1992). While educational level is related to social class, research has found that it constitutes an independent effect. For example, lower educational aspirations and expectations have been linked with earlier sexual activity, lower rates of using contraception and more unwanted pregnancies (Wight and Henderson, in Burtney and Duffy, 2004). Overwhelming evidence indicates the relationship between poverty and poor nutrition and activity levels. Clearly access and the cost of food and leisure play a role. Yet access and cost levels do not just impact on economically deprived populations, where an adolescent lives is also a factor.

While increasing evidence exists on the impact of gender, class and peers, health promotion has not always been quick to address the influence of place and local culture on young people's attitudes and behaviours. But there are clear urban and rural differences in delivering the health needs of young people. As Shucksmith and Hendry (1998) argue, location constitutes a significant dimension of social relationships. These authors caution against spatial determinism but note that local influences impact on young people's cultures. Rural differentiation is also highlighted in other studies, which found that diverse local cultures played a role in young people's beliefs and expectations, for example, on the subject of sexual activity when living in a remote area characterized by religion and where marriage is revered, or the fear which comes from acquiring a reputation or being subject to stigma (Mackinnon, 2005; Hendry et al., 1998).

Clearly, interventions need to consider these differences and see adolescents as individuals with different ethnicities, genders, social classes, locales and ages. Indeed, Internet research highlighted the adolescent need to be seen as an individual. Young people felt that this mode offered the opportunity for more personalized data, with tailored, individual approaches for their own weight, fitness level and stressors (Mackinnon and Soloman, 2003). The next section of this chapter explores the complexity of young people's lives further when it looks at young people's perspectives on their health needs and their behaviours. It is suggested that alongside an awareness of diversity, young people's views must be taken into account in health promotion and education given their own understandings and meanings.

Summary of Section

- Adolescents are a priority focus for health promotion and education because of adult concern over future repercussions of their risk behaviours. These behaviours are thought to be more clustered at this time.
- Provision of health information is necessary but it is inadequate on its own, not least because not all young people have the ability or capacity to access it or act upon it.
- Health promotion and education requires different approaches and different people for a diversity of adolescents.

Towards a 'Youthist' Agenda

Many young people have sophisticated understandings of health, their behaviour and the wider socio-economic environment in which they live. To assume they all need to be targeted as passive recipients of a professionally driven health promotion agenda is to deny their role as active agents in their own lives. (Shepherd et al., 2002, p. 14)

How do adolescents make sense of health and what do they want heath promotion and education to do in order to answer their health concerns? A recent review has indicated that little is published which takes the young person's perspective as its primary concern and considers how young people construct their worlds (Shucksmith and Spratt, 2002). Certainly, young people are surveyed, perhaps almost to the point of saturation, but such research has for the most part been focused on young people responding to a predetermined list of questions, questions already predefined by adults. In the rare studies where young people have been consulted on their thoughts on health, research has indicated that rather than highlighting the prominent issues of drugs or smoking, young people place considerable emphasis on body image, on social relations and social activities for their well-being (Aggleton *et al.*, 1998; Shucksmith and Hendry, 1998; Shucksmith and Spratt, 2002; Mackinnon and Soloman, 2003). Drawing on a study into rural youth concerns, Hendry and Reid (2001) report that the main health concerns were a lack of self-confidence, worry about achievement, concern over interacting with others and dealing with emotions and depression. Although concern over health topics such as drugs was evident, these authors point to the prominence of social relationships in young people's feelings about health and well-being.

A strong theme from research into young people's health is young people's desire to act autonomously and have control over their personal decision-making. Hendry and Reid (2001) found that young people wish to maintain their ability to make their own minds up after obtaining reliable information (see also Hendry *et al.*, 1998). In some of these more consultative studies young people have expressed a desire for *interactive* material which involves discussion and more interactive methods of education. These indicate that young people have expressed a need for:

- a chance to discuss implications freely without foregone conclusions;
- information based on the context of their lives;
- tailored resources for different genders and ages;
- single sex group work where desired;
- up-to-date, relevant and non-judgemental information.

Like the conclusion reached by Shepherd and colleagues noted above, Shucksmith and Spratt's (2002) review confirms that young people's knowledge about how to maintain their own health has been found to be adequate or even high. However, this knowledge is not necessarily reflected in their behaviour. For example, these authors illustrate how young people have good nutritional awareness and know the benefits of physical activity but in practice other more powerful sociocultural influences come into play. In effect, knowledge would appear to be less of an attribute in health lifestyles than the social context in which the behaviours are carried out. Aggleton (1996, p. 89) has drawn our attention to the idea of 'cultures of risk' as the way different young people make sense of health and health concerns:

> *Such cultures encompass understandings of the self as in relation to health. They also generate norms and expectations about appropriate and inappropriate health-related behaviour, and position young people differently in relation to health risk. Each has its own values, be these explicitly defined or otherwise and each is linked to specific states of physical and mental well-being.*

It is important then to understand and address the meanings that young people themselves attach to their behaviours and to acknowledge that they can often show contradictions in their attitudes and ambivalence. For instance, Allbutt, Amos and Cunningham-Burley (1995) found that young people held ambivalent and contradictory attitudes towards smoking. Regardless of whether they smoked, they expressed positive and negative images of smoking. How young people view themselves, their processes of self-labelling and identity clearly needs to be explored further.

Why Do Young People Take Risks?

As the discussion noted earlier, adolescence is a period of heightened risk behaviours and the majority of young people use risky behaviour as a mode for trying out or establishing identities. There is evidence to suggest that the majority view their behaviour as very different from more problematic risk-takers and that their risk practice is social practice, key social interaction moments in becoming an adult. As Hendry and Kloep (1999) have asserted, very few risk behaviours are conducted alone, without the audience required. In particular, alcohol use is a majority activity and perceived as a part of growing up. Shucksmith (in Burtney and Duffy, 2004) has noted that risks can seem worth it to young people when they perceive a pay-off in terms of developing their autonomy, asserting their identity and affirming their nearly adult status. As such we need to acknowledge the voluntaristic nature of young people's behaviour. In other words more focus in health education and research needs to be on what benefits young people perceive to arise from smoking, substance use, engaging in sexual activity – in behaviour adults have deemed risky. Shucksmith and Hendry (1998, p. 54) noted the importance of individual choice:

It is clear from this study that young people did believe they had a degree of self-agency, both in terms of selecting their reference group and also in making individual choices about health related matters, often in resistance to wider group norms.

That is not to say that choice is an open house:

...there are clear structural determinants of young people's health behaviours and risk behaviours. Despite this young people have agency and can make choices, but the menu of choices is restricted according not just to structural constraints but to a localized cultural development and norm setting process. (Shucksmith and Hendry, 1998, p. 54)

In order to reduce negative health outcomes, develop and implement effective strategies and support young people in making healthy choices, we need to take account of the broader context of young people's lives and their perspective. What young people prioritize, what they believe to be important and carry out does not always correspond with our adultist viewpoint, not least because young people often act within a different time frame.

Young People's Viewpoint

Research has indicated that young people think and act in a more immediate time frame than adults. Examining young people's drinking, Coffield (1992) found that young people find it very difficult to think of themselves as 50 years old. Indeed, for young people possible consequences from health-compromising behaviour seem to exist far into their futures and hence are less relevant to them. The threats of sexually transmitted diseases from unprotected sex, heart disease from smoking and abuse of substances which may appear at least a decade on from where they are now, take on much less meaning for young people. This is also evident in research which has considered young people's definition of what health is. For younger age groups, health is a distant and negative concept implying illness, hospitals and doctors and, as one argued, you don't need to worry about health till you're old. Older young people were found to be more likely to include emotional well-being in their definition of health and see health in more positive terms (Mackinnon and Soloman, 2003). Hendry and Reid (2001) found that young people felt adults underestimated and even trivialized the impact of relationships with regard to their emotional health. Relationships were seen both as a source of anxiety and a factor in the ability to deal with other health concerns. Young people state very similar reasons for engaging in certain behaviours to those of the adult population, primarily because they enjoy them and for sociability. However, there are some particular reasons. To sum up, young people take risks because:

- they don't necessarily see them as risks;
- risk behaviours constitute important social interaction/practices;
- they often operate in a different time frame;
- they perceive them as having rewards;
- they see such behaviours in the adult world they are about to enter.

Health education has often taken a different tack and problematized young people's behaviour, viewing it as dangerous and something to be reduced, eliminated or controlled. Recent evidence from both adults and young people themselves is pointing to the need for a different approach which stresses positive development and promoting young people's resilience, in line with the recognition that there are links between what young people do and what they feel (Shepherd *et al.*, 2002).

Promoting Well-Being and Resilience

Shepherd and colleagues (2002) argue that good mental health can be viewed as a resource for meeting one's full potential. Furthermore, they assert that mental well-being underpins other aspects of a young person's health and as such it should be a priority given the challenges and choices faced at this time. But moving from a problem focus, which primarily identifies and responds to risks, towards promoting good mental *resilience* may also mean that we accept that young people will experiment and thus they should be equipped with social and emotional competence skills that will meet their own development. It is also a recognition that young people's mental and emotional health needs need to be taken seriously rather than perpetuating a storm and stress model. Young people themselves find such a model dismissive and want to be taken seriously over mental health issues (Shucksmith and Spratt, 2002). It seems their concerns are warranted as there is evidence to suggest that psychosocial disorders among adolescents have been on the increase (Rutter and Smith, 1995).

The research into young people's concerns about mental well-being all point to the same factors for promoting positive feelings: family and friends, having someone to talk to, doing well (personal achievement) and feeling good about themselves. Likewise, negative feelings derive from lack of self-confidence and not feeling good about themselves, peer and family conflict, worry about achievement and not doing well. Shucksmith and Spratt (2003) point out the irony that adolescence is a time of moving away from the family and asserting self-control through experimentation which may involve risks, but at the same time family networks and strong friendships are still needed for support. Similarly, Aggleton and colleagues (1998) found that young people placed importance on social relationships with family and friends for their sense of well-being. In the research reported by Hendry and Reid (2001), the importance of close, supportive ties was continually stressed by young people as helping to enhance their sense of self and health. Although much weight is often put onto self-esteem and it has been shown to be a protective factor particularly against self-harm and suicide, it is not all-encompassing. Indeed, studies have challenged the idea of a direct relationship between self-esteem and health behaviours such as alcohol and drug use, smoking and early sexual experience (West and Sweeting, 1997; Glendinning, 1998).

What is Resilience?

A host of definitions exist on resilience (see Olsson *et al.*, 2002 for a concept analysis) but a common understanding is that it is a process of adapting to adversity. Hence it is not a personality trait. Rather than *avoiding* risk experiences resilience implies successfully *coping* with them. Resilience theory is not too far removed from other development theories such as attachment theory and there is the underlying belief in meeting needs as an adolescent develops. There are also links with emotional literacy, for example, good interpersonal skills and the ability to empathize with others. Kloep and Hendry (1999) conclude that learning to cope with risk experiences aids young people's feelings of being in control. This is a similar premise to Rutter's (1996) concept of 'steeling experiences'. Small exposures to negative experiences can help young people deal with future risks and hence can serve as a resource adolescents can draw upon. For Newman (2002), managed exposure to risk is essential if young people are to learn coping mechanisms and problem-solving abilities. As such he cautions that the experiences that promote resilience may not always be socially acceptable!

Although some young people will demonstrate resilience without interventions, the difficulty of translating the theory into practice is especially shown when targeting young people whose lives have been very unpredictable or who face serious problems, such as homeless young people and those leaving care. In addition, there are gender differences in the promotion of resilience. For young females, parenting styles that stress reasonable risk-taking and independence have been noted as pertinent. For males, it seems that male role models who spend time with them and take an interest appear to be important as do higher levels of supervision. Indeed, very often people in contact/working with young people are promoting resilience through their efforts while not describing it as such. Newman (2002) has produced a very comprehensive review of resilience and has identified key factors that promote resilience in adolescents such as support from family, good educational experiences, opportunities to exert agency and valued social roles such as part-time employment or voluntary work. In particular Newman (2002) has noted the importance of non-professionals in promoting resilience. For example, a parent substitute or a mentor who is committed.

Mentoring: Significant Others?

Recently Philip, Shucksmith and King (2004) have studied the impact of *mentoring* in different settings. These authors have found that most young people find the experience of mentoring to be positive and that it contributed to their confidence, skills and development in a variety of ways. The young people studied felt that mentoring relationships differed from those with other adults. The 'ability to have a laugh' and the friendly nature of the relationship made the experience distinct. Mentors who shared similar backgrounds and experiences were found to be especially valued. Mentoring was found to help young people come to terms with relationships which were difficult, especially familial ones. It was also found to assist young people in exploring their identity and their own skills in supporting others. These researchers also found that the mentoring experience was a positive one for the mentors who valued working with young people as opposed to on them. Some regarded their role as a bridge between the young person and more formal professional adults. The study did find difficulties in mentoring. For example, young people expressed fears about being let down or their confidences breached and therefore were guarded. Also, the process of ending a mentoring relationship could undermine any benefits accrued, as could negative peer groups. The research concluded that while mentoring cannot overcome all problems of vulnerable young people, it nonetheless constitutes a useful part of interventions. Philip and colleagues (2004) also concluded that different mentoring approaches are needed to suit each young person's circumstances. It is a similar contention to that of Philip and Hendry (1996) who advocated that different social relationships and networks besides that of the traditional model of one older adult to one young person can be influential.

A Mentoring Typology

Previously, Philip and Hendry (1996) devised a typology of mentoring which illustrates the diversity of mentoring. Classic mentoring where a one-to-one relationship is established with an experienced adult providing support and advice to a young person; individual–team mentoring where a group gets support from an individual or small number of individuals; friend-to-friend mentoring where friends provide the setting for young people who are particularly distrustful of adults; peer group mentoring where a friendship group has a mentoring role and may share a common issue, for example, drug misuse; long-term relationship mentoring with 'risk-taking' adults which, although akin to classic mentoring, has an adult who has had a history of challenging authority/adult society. Like peer education interventions, youth mentoring stresses young people as active participants. Also like peer education, mentoring has suffered from a lack of evaluation. Nonetheless more and more commentators have suggested that the presence of an adult mentor can make a real difference in helping young people through transitions and may be an important strategy to promote resilience, especially with disadvantaged young people.

Thus far, the evidence of incorporating resilience promoting strategies into services to young people indicates good effectiveness. However, as Newman (2002) concludes, whilst we have a good understanding of the processes which promote resilience, we also need to know the ways in which we can influence these processes, that is, practical applications require much more development. In addition effective resilience strategies are likely to be part of a broader strategy that includes varied institutions and agencies.

Summary of Section

- Young people's perceptions of health differ in comparison with the underlying 'adultist' principles of health education curricula.
- Research indicates health promotion and education need to take account of the meanings young people themselves attach to their behaviour and locate it in the wider social context.
- Most curricula are problem- and topic-focused as opposed to stressing positive development. The promotion of resilience in health promotion is a key way forward.

Bridging the Gap between Providers and Users

This section offers suggestions as to how providers and users may be brought together more effectively, for instance, using participatory approaches such as peer delivered health promotion and education. The underlying premise is that health promotion interventions cannot work if young people do not engage with them. But how do we respond to young people's perspectives? The UN Convention on the Rights of the Child (1989) asserts that children and young people have a right to be heard on matters that affect them and their views should be taken account of. How can we provide young people with appropriate information about how they can maintain their health, make decisions and at the same time involve them in shaping the decisions and services that affect them? Once we've listened, what do we do next?

Peer-Delivered Health Education

Young people always share information amongst themselves, use similar discourses and spend considerable time together. *Peer education* has arisen from a wish to capitalize on what is a naturally occurring process (Milburn, 1995). Given that exchange of information on health matters takes place anyway and it allows for more youth participation, this type of approach is indeed attractive. It lacks the authoritarian element of other approaches. It can also reach more vulnerable young people than other approaches. Peers also rank high on young people's hierarchies of credibility (who they believe most), particularly if they are able to draw on personal experience. However, definitions and meanings of peer education are diverse and vary between different professional groups. Milburn (1995) has criticized a lack of theoretical clarity around peer education and moreover has voiced concern over just how far power is unbiased in the peer educated–peer educator relationship. Doubts also exist over the impact of peer education and what can be deemed as effective. A lack of evaluated peer education

Table 10.2   The strengths and limitations of peer education

Strengths	Limitations
Can reach vulnerable groups of young people	Can have a limited audience with face to face work
Young people relate to peers as educators seeing them as credible sources of information and more empathetic	Conflicts between coordinators of programmes and peer educators can arise
Peer educators are seen as less likely to break confidences	Peer educators may not receive adequate support
May help in development of emotional literacy, self-esteem and social and cognitive development	Peer educators are often selected/rejected by authority figures if seen as 'appropriate' role models
Can strengthen personal development and confidence of the educators	Allows adults/parents to opt out
Makes use of existing social connections and networks which are acceptable to the target group	

Source: Milburn.K, A critical review of peer education with young people with special reference to sexual health, Health Education Research (1995), Vol. 10, No. 4, pp.407–420, with permission from Oxford University Press, Harden, Weston and Oakley, 1999.

projects has also added to the inconclusiveness of how valuable the approach is. Nonetheless, reviews of peer education have begun to be published and some common strengths and weaknesses have been identified as noted in the Table 10.2.

Similarities between young people can add to credibility of information given and make a message more persuasive. The importance of the accuracy of that information is evident. Also, different social mechanisms are at work in different settings. The information presented in a school setting is not necessarily transferable to outreach. The jury seems out on peer- vs. teacher-led activity with researchers finding it difficult to identify the features that make a peer education approach effective. The approach may best be summed up as having value in its potential, or as Milburn (1995) describes, as a working hypothesis.

Empowerment and Participation

Although empowerment implies participation, a person can participate but not be empowered. To be empowered a young person must not only participate but know that their participation and voice is being noted and may result in action. Giving young people a say and increasing their participation and control over their health and well-being is not as straightforward as mere good intent. Certainly, participatory approaches may encourage ownership by young people and they are more likely to feel in control of their health and to engage in health promotion. Yet Shucksmith and Hendry (1998) point to the shortage of young people's experiences and views around empowerment in research or indeed proof that they perceive it as desirable. Tokenism is always a danger. Youth consultation can be a tick box exercise. The benefits of empowering young people are akin to those noted for peer-led approaches. Also, like peer-led approaches, outcome measures of participatory health promotion activities remain to be clarified.

There are various types and models of participation and the Health Education Authority (McNeish, 1999) has commissioned a useful series of studies on participatory approaches to health promotion. Some are organizational models, but perhaps a most relevant typology lies in Hart's ladder of participation (1992, 1997; McNeish, 1999). The figure below (Figure 10.1) outlines his 'rungs'. These approaches are not exhaustive and the ladder has been criticized for its hierarchical manner. However, Hart has argued that the top level is not always the most appropriate for a given programme and different contexts come into play. The top five levels do represent viable choices.

On the lower rungs are the least participatory approaches, which for Hart are symbolic. We've all been at a conference or at a meeting where a few young people are present but with little meaningful engagement. The higher levels constitute more meaningful participation. Whilst the second level seems the most appealing, the lack of adult involvement may lead to an activity being perceived as less valuable and its potential less realized. Also, participation is not feasible for all young people, especially for those with serious problems in their lives, and all abilities. Where young people do desire participation, attention to diversity is again important. A chosen model may have to be age appropriate, gender differentiated or culturally sensitive. Some young people face more barriers to participation than others because of their life circumstances and life experiences, for example, homeless young people, young offenders and disabled young people. Nonetheless there is no doubt that young people can participate in decisions about their lives, about service provision, about their communities, in research and the influence of policy.

<table>
<tr><td>

Youth-initiated, shared decisions
Support / involvement of adults sought for influence or to promote success

⇑

Youth-initiated, youth directed
Limited, if any, adult involvement

⇑

Adult-initiated, shared decisions
Young people involved from onset, moving beyond consultation only

⇑

Consulted and informed
Young people's opinions taken seriously even if activity designed and run by adults

⇑

Assigned but informed
Adults define message but encourage young people to understand and desire informed consent

⇑

Tokenism
Good intent but limited number of young people there for their presence

⇑

Decoration
Young person has little understanding or involvement but wears costume/T-shirt

⇑

Manipulation
Adults using youth voices to carry their own messages

</td></tr>
</table>

Figure 10.1   Hart's Ladder of Participation (Hart, 1992, 1997; McNeish, 1999).

So, How Do We Know What We're Doing Works?

In order to know if what we are doing works we need to clearly know what we are trying to achieve – our desired outcomes. Why we are trying to achieve certain outcomes, our rationale, should be clarified. Taking heed of as much existing evidence as possible in designing the interventions focused on young people can go a long way to an effective final result. But we also need to be able to measure our outcomes as it is the only way to know if something works! Burtney and Duffy (2004) have reflected well on how we can know if health initiatives targeting younger populations work. They highlight the importance of evidence both in planning and implementing health promotion. They note that what works is not always what seems to be obvious to us. Also, just because an intervention has worked in some cases it doesn't follow it will always work. Hence we need to identify processes. Sometimes an activity will work because of an individual youth worker's perseverance or particular rapport. Strategies and interventions are not always realistic or culturally appropriate when simply transferred.

   Burtney and Burtney (2004) have also noted that we don't always do what does work! Even if the research evidence is strong in a particular area, in the real world health professionals may not have the resources, the time or the policy backing. Moreover, sometimes we simply do not know what works. For example, as West, Sweeting and Leyland (2004) point out, despite continuing interest in the health promoting school, there are limited studies that have investigated the ways schools influence pupils' health behaviours and this is particularly evident in comparison to the large quantity of work which is available on school effects on educational outcomes. In addition, we may have to be innovative. When we are piloting, evaluating our activities takes on added significance. Uncertainty over what works does not excuse us from aiming to achieve effective outcomes and attempting to harness our work to the evidence available. Moreover, there remains a key evidence resource for establishing if what we are doing works, namely young people themselves through consultation, participation and feedback.

Summary of Section

- Health promotion interventions cannot work if young people do not engage with them.
- Participatory approaches may encourage ownership by young people and they are more likely to feel in control of their health.
- We need to take heed of the existing evidence as much as possible in designing and implementing interventions but we must also evaluate our activities.

Conclusion

It is vital to understand young people's health against the background of the society in which they live and the wider adult and societal influences upon them. Young people need to be provided with information to help them make decisions during the period of transition to adulthood in which they face new challenges and choices. It would be naïve to suggest that if young people develop appropriate knowledge, skills and attitudes then they will necessarily make healthier choices and engage in less risky behaviours. The wider social and cultural environment plays a vital role and the differences therein need to be apprehended. The health needs and behaviours of vulnerable and socially excluded young people, of males and females, urban and rural residents, different classes and ethnic backgrounds have been identified as distinct, although much still needs to be done on the needs and health of vulnerable groups. We also need to be sensitive to age. The needs of a 12 year-old and an 18 year-old differ substantially as should the resources to meet them.

   Whilst structural influences are at play in young people's attitudes and behaviours, these do not negate the element of choice that is also evident. Health promotion must also regard young people as the best source of information with regard to their own lives and promote continuing consultation and participation on the strategies, practice and research which concerns them.

Undoubtedly how young people feel about themselves and their lives is linked to what they do. Resilience initiatives should be supported which promote the mental well-being and emotional competence of young people. However, we still have much to learn around participatory approaches and resilience interventions such as peer education and mentoring. Defining evidence of effectiveness is by no means solely an issue for those focusing on adolescents but exists for health promotion and education in general. The importance of evidence should be highlighted as appearing along a continuum, from informing initial activities to monitoring and evaluating in order to discover what works when promoting young people's health.

Summary of Chapter

- Young people are not all the same. They have different needs and a variety of influences play a role in their health and well-being. Health promotion and education requires different approaches and different people for a diversity of adolescents.
- Health initiatives must resonate with adolescents' own lives and take account of the meanings they themselves give to their health and health behaviours. Young people should be involved as partners and have ownership.
- The available evidence must inform the design and implementation of interventions but much more evaluation is required, especially on activities with socially excluded adolescents.
- Adolescents are a priority focus for health promotion and education because of adult concern over future repercussions of their risk behaviours which are also thought to be more clustered at this time.
- Provision of health information is necessary but it is inadequate on its own, not least because not all young people have the ability or capacity to access it or act upon it.
- Young people's perceptions of health differ in comparison with the underlying 'adultist' principles of health education curricula. Research indicates health promotion and education need to take account of the meanings young people themselves attach to their behaviour and locate it in the wider social context.
- Most curricula are problem- and topic-focused as opposed to stressing positive development. The promotion of resilience in health promotion is a key way forward.

Is Sex Education Good for Young People?

Different groups in society have contrasting views of the values of sex education for young people. Here we present three arguments for and three arguments against:

NO, early sex education is not good for young people for the following reasons:
1. It is embarrassing for early pubescent teenagers to have lessons about the details and mechanics of sex, even if these lessons do help to deter unprotected sex.
2. Stressing the need for 'safe sex' sexualizes the world of childhood and can actually encourage adolescent sex activity. Young teenagers should not have 'safe sex', they should not have sex at all!
3. The increase of detailed and explicit sex education has been accompanied by a massive increase in adolescent pregnancies. Clearly, sex education does not work.

YES, early sex education is good for young people for the following reasons:

1. Young adolescents are sexual creatures. It is stupid to keep them ignorant of something so central to their lives.
2. Whether we like it or not, many aspects of society present sexual images to the young. This makes it all the more vital to explain the sexualization of society to children. It is better that they get correct information from teachers, than incorrect information from pornography.
3. Scandinavian countries have the most comprehensive sex education programmes in the world: they also have the lowest rate of teenage pregnancies. Manifestly, sex education does work.

1. How valid are these arguments? Do you support the pro- or anti-statements? Why?
2. How can teachers offer non-judgemental sex education to teenagers?
3. How can parents become involved in sex education programmes?
4. What issues should be addressed in sex education?

Further Reading

Aggleton, P. (1996) *Health promotion and young people*, Health Education Authority, London.

Bradshaw, J. and Mayhew, E. (2005) *The well-being of children in the UK*, Save the Children, London.

Breinbauer, C. and Maddaleno, M. (2005) *Youth: choices and change. Promoting healthy behavior in adolescents*, Pan-American Health Organization, Washington DC.

Catan, L. (2004) *Becoming adult: changing youth transitions in the 21st century*, Trust for the Study of Adolescence, Brighton.

Shucksmith, J. and Hendry, L.B. (1998) *Health issues and adolescents: growing up and speaking out*, Routledge, London.

Discussion Questions

1. Discuss the reasons why some young people still engage in risky behaviours, such as unprotected sex, even though their awareness of the risks may be high.
2. How can risk behaviours have positive consequences for young people?
3. What are the barriers to employing participatory approaches with young people?

Chapter 11

Conclusion

John Coleman

Department of Educational Studies, University of Oxford

Leo B. Hendry and Marion Kloep

Centre for Lifespan Research, University of Glamorgan

- Introduction
- Health and Social Change
- New Thinking on Risk
- Young People, Health and Public Policy
- Engaging Young People in Clinical Services

Learning Objectives

After reading this chapter you should:

1 Understand how social change has impacted adolescent health.
2 Be aware of different notions of risk.
3 Know about recent policy developments relating to adolescent health.
4 Understand some of the principles behind the engagement of young people in clinical services.

Introduction

This book has covered a wide range of themes and issues to do with adolescent health. While the early chapters have addressed particular topics such as sexuality or eating disorders, the later chapters have considered services relevant to the health care of young people. Authors of the various chapters have raised controversial questions, and have included topics for discussion and debate. Many of these are of considerable significance for our understanding of young people, and for our approach to health care and health promotion. Such questions include, for example, how to judge the competence of a young person to make decisions about their own treatment, what position to take with regard to abstinence education, and what role parents should play with adolescents who have complex health conditions. We hope that the inclusion of questions like these will make the book both more interesting and more valuable for readers who care about adolescence and health.

In this final chapter we wish to explore a small number of themes that have broad relevance to all of the issues we have considered in this book. Thus we will look at some of the major social changes of the last few decades, and see how these have affected young people. We will discuss the question of risk, and review some of the differing views and attitudes to this complex topic. We will outline some recent policy initiatives relating to adolescent health, and we will end by suggesting some of the most important issues to be taken into account when seeking to engage young people in clinical services.

Of course, not all of the key questions about adolescent health can be answered conclusively. Some will inevitably remain up in the air. Throughout the book we have offered some suggestions, but some of the more controversial issues will always be matters for debate.

- What is a healthy lifestyle for a young person?
- Do adolescents need to take risks in order to grow and develop?
- In what ways do adult and adolescent definitions of health differ?
- Is adolescent health getting worse?

Readers will no doubt continue to ponder on these topics, considering them in the context of their experiences with young people. With this in mind let us now turn to some of the broader themes that underlie much of the material in this book.

Health and Social Change

Throughout the book there have been a variety of references to social change and its impact, or potential impact, on the health of young people. To take some examples, in the introductory chapter we illustrate how levels of both smoking and drinking have increased in recent years, whilst Lowry, Kremer and Trew (Chapter 2) raise questions about changes in the amount of physical exercise and sport taken by young people. J. Coleman (Chapter 3) draws attention to suggestions that the mental health of adolescents has declined over the last two decades, and L. Coleman (Chapter 5) documents major shifts in sexual behaviour. As we have noted, most of these changes appear to indicate a deterioration in the health of young people, and are at the root of the adult concerns about adolescent health discussed in Chapter 1.

In the concluding chapter it is appropriate that we examine these concerns in more detail, but before we do so, let us briefly review some of the social changes that have impacted on young people. The first and possibly the most obvious social change to affect young people has been the extension of the period of education and training, and the consequent delay of entry into the labour market. This change has been profound as it has meant that, today, almost the total cohort of 16 to 18 year-olds remains outside employment, and in addition, increasing numbers of 19 to 22 year-olds are in the same position. In the United Kingdom currently 45% of this age group are in some form of higher education.

This change has created a group of young people who remain dependent on families or the state for their financial support, and for whom the route to adult independence is less and less structured. The consequence is the creation of an age cohort who are in an 'in-between' position, a stage that has become known as 'emerging adulthood' (Arnett, 2004). Individuals who are 'emerging adults' are neither adult nor teenager, and most importantly, health services are not designed for this age group. It will be obvious that the lack of services and the ambiguity of status for those inhabiting this 'in-between' state may have serious consequences for health.

A second social change of importance to the discussion is the increase in disposable income available to this age group. While this may sound paradoxical in light of the fact that fewer young people are now in employment, and students in further and higher education are running up debt, it is the case that many adolescents have more money available to them than was the case 10 or 20 years ago (Coleman, 2002). The implication of this is that substances, including cigarettes, alcohol and cannabis, are all more accessible to this age cohort. There has been much debate about the reasons why there is a greater use of substances among young people today. It has been suggested that it could be to do with increased advertising, with the growth of supermarkets as a point of sale for alcohol and cigarettes, or with changing patterns of leisure. All these may be playing their part. Nonetheless, greater disposable income for young people is likely to be influential in determining the health status of adolescents today.

In a broader sense relationships between the generations are changing, so that there is greater equality between children and adults. This is part of a move towards growing equality in society generally. The UN Convention on the Rights of the Child was adopted in the UK in 1991, 40 years after the proclamation of the Universal Declaration of Human Rights (for adults!). In the world of social research, scientists over the last 15 years have begun to carry out research with children and young people as partners, encouraged to bring their own experiences and knowledge of the world to the research endeavour.

This growing sense of equality goes hand in hand with the promotion of individualism and an encouragement towards self-expression. Equality also brings with it a belief in equal access to goods and experiences, and one contributory factor in the increased use of substances by young people may well be a wish to share as widely as possible in what are seen as adult pleasures. As many writers have suggested (e.g. Jenks, 2003), society has to accept a trade-off between promoting individualism and the need for social control. Nowhere is this more apparent than in adult attitudes to adolescent sexuality and substance use. Here policy makers struggle to find ways of limiting what are seen as risky behaviours, often passing laws and framing policies that fly in the face of what is actually happening in the real world. As L. Coleman (Chapter 5) and Mackinnon (Chapter 10) graphically illustrate, health education will have no impact unless it is firmly rooted in the day-to-day experiences of the young people towards whom it is targeted.

Finally, we cannot discuss social change and its relation to health without mentioning the role of advertising and the media, as well as that of new technologies such as the Internet. It is often said that we live in a consumerist culture, where advertising, TV and film, as well as the print media and the Internet, promote certain values and brands that have a major impact on our lives. Where young people are concerned there are a number of ways in which this is apparent. One obvious area is that of food, nutrition and body image. As Faulkner (Chapter 4) makes clear, the promotion of the 'thin is beautiful' message for women creates anxiety and pressure, leads to dieting and food control, and may well cause eating disorders. There is also a broader issue of the advertising of junk food, and the sheer scale of the consumption of chocolate, sweets, drinks such as Coke, and snack foods, all of which may be contributing to the increased numbers of children who are overweight.

A further area of concern where young people are concerned is the 'sexualization' of society. The degree of change in this area of our lives since the 1960s has been remarkable. Sex is evident in every media channel, and children and young people are bombarded by images and messages about sex on TV, in the films they watch, through teenage magazines, in the advertisements they see and in the music they listen to. This preoccupation with sex in the media cannot but have an influence on the attitudes and behaviour of young people. It is no surprise that teenagers are becoming sexually active at an earlier age today than was the case in the 1970s and the 1980s, and the high level of conceptions and the rise in STIs among young people (see Chapter 5) must also be associated with society's attitudes to sexuality.

We have outlined some of the social changes that may affect the health of young people. In a number of chapters in this book attention has been drawn to changes in health behaviours that appear to indicate a deteriorating situation. Substance use is increasing, it is possible that mental ill-health is increasing, and there is more evidence of risky sexual behaviour. How can these things be linked together? Clearly a consumerist culture plays its part. As we have shown, eating behaviour, sexuality and substance use all may be affected by the messages promoted by advertising and embedded in the material that is portrayed by the media.

Health may also be affected by the amount of income that is available. We drink and eat more if we have the money to pay for these things. Changing patterns of leisure activity are important too. Sports facilities and the time spent on sport in school have been reduced over the last two decades, with an obvious effect on health (Chapter 2). Furthermore, there are few alternatives to commercial leisure on offer for young people. Existing leisure opportunities are usually organized *for* young people rather than *by* them, and thus do not encourage the development of organizational and creative skills (Hendry and Kloep, 2002).

Lastly, we should note two implications for health of the changes that have occurred for those between the ages of 16 and 22 or 23. First, because of the changing nature of the labour market, qualifications have become more important. This in turn has enhanced the importance of examinations, and caused increasing levels of emotional stress among this age group. This may well go some way to explaining the increased levels of mental ill-health among young people. Secondly, as we have indicated above, services are not designed with this age group in mind. The transition between paediatric and adult services is explored by both Helms (Chapter 8) and by McDonagh (Chapter 9), but the problem is broader than that. For young adults in full- or part-time education, services need to be designed so that they are accessible and appropriate, staffed by health professionals with understanding and expertise in the problems of this age group. We will return to this issue later in the chapter.

New Thinking on Risk

There have been many references to the notion of risk throughout this book. We have explored the belief that young people are exposing themselves to greater and greater risk, through increased drinking, cannabis use, or engaging in unsafe sex. It is this belief that underlies the gloomy predictions about adolescent health expressed in the BMA report on adolescent health (Nathanson, 2003). However, we have also seen that taking risks may be viewed as part of a learning process. Without experiencing behaviours that are risky, young people cannot develop notions of what is safe and healthy for them. If all behaviours that have potential risks for health are avoided, then the young person cannot learn how to manage obstacles and challenges, or how to develop coping resources. As we have argued in Chapter 1 when discussing the Lifespan Model of Developmental Challenge, a healthy lifestyle is anything that adds to the individual's dynamic resource pool, and acquiring skills in preparation for adulthood can facilitate such resources.

In a thoughtful article about risk Michaud (2006) points out that there is a close association between a general negative stereotype of young people, and the belief that they are likely to engage in high risk behaviours. He argues that the negative stereotype is damaging to relationships between the generations, and that it is something we need to question at every opportunity. In fact risk behaviour in adolescence is not universal. Not all young people engage in risky behaviours. These behaviours are most likely to be seen in adolescents who experience disadvantage, poverty and deprivation. Thus, Michaud suggests, we need to address the causes of disadvantage as much as we need to develop good quality health education.

This viewpoint leads on to the idea that alcohol or substance use is not necessarily a threat to health, but should rather be seen as part of a phase of exploration or experimentation. This argument fits closely with the conclusions drawn by Engels and van den Eijnden (Chapter 6), who show that drinking and cigarette smoking have what they call facilitating functions for young people. Thus they point out that drinking alcohol helps adolescents deal with social situations and develop important social skills. This is very close to the argument we developed in Chapter 1 concerning a healthy lifestyle. This, we believe, can only develop in the context of a situation where a young person is being helped to engage with health and health issues. This engagement may sometimes involve risk behaviours.

Of course there is a fine line to be drawn here, for some risk behaviours are clearly unsafe and damaging to health. How do we distinguish, and how do we help young people distinguish, between experimentation and dangerous behaviour? Furthermore, will adults and young people agree about this? Or will they have differing views of what is safe and what is unsafe, what is dangerous and what is not?

Here are some quotes from a study of young people and 'risky' drinking (Coleman and Cater, 2005a).

> *"We was out on some scaffolding …. When you're drunk everything is all over the place, and then, then all of a sudden it hits you that you're up on a high place and you're drunk. Very dangerous things like that, like just being silly and running around, just doing stupid stuff."*
> *(Male, 16)*
> *"We just got absolutely wasted and drunk. And then because it seemed an idea to go down the cliff going down the beach, because we couldn't be bothered to walk around the footpath … But then it pissed down with rain, and the cliff was made out of clay, and we had to get back up the cliff. And I don't know what the hell I was doing, because I was completely wankered."*
> *(Female, 17)*

In both these cases young people are putting themselves at risk of injury or even death, so we can have little doubt that this is dangerous behaviour. While adults cannot prevent such behaviours, there are many things that can be done to reduce the likelihood of such behaviours occurring, as L. Coleman (Chapter 5) and Mackinnon (Chapter 10) point out. The authors writing in this book are unanimous in believing that there is a need for a greater focus on the development of resilience and coping skills in the health education curriculum. We would also like to see a greater recognition that harm minimization is a more productive strategy than prohibition. We should recognize that young people themselves can take responsibility, and are more aware of how to manage risk than adults give them credit for. The following quotes from the study by Coleman and Cater (2005a) make this clear.

> *"People think 'oh god, look, alcoholic children on the streets'. But we were more sensible than they think we were. They sit there going 'yeah, you don't eat your dinner' – yes, we do. We eat our dinner, most of the boys drink six pints of milk, full fat milk, before they go out, because they don't want to be sick."(Female, 15)*

> *"We're all quite good like, we don't ever drink drinks that we leave on the bar for too long, or make sure, because we were quite conscious that drugs can be put in your drinks and stuff .... And we were quite good like that...."*
> *(Female, 17)*
> *"There's usually one or two people who aren't as drunk as everyone else .... If you were doing something they would just kind of come up and be like 'What were you doing? Were you ok?' And stuff like that."*
> *(Female, 15)*

There are many different ways that risk can be understood. The point here is that not all risk-taking is bad. In some situations, and in particular where young people are developing new skills and exploring new sensations, risk-taking has positive benefits. However, it is essential that health education and health promotion encourage adolescents to learn about the different outcomes of risk behaviours, as noted by Mackinnon (Chapter 10). In the view of most of the authors in this book, just saying no is not helpful. Young people will explore and experiment whatever adults say. In light of this we strongly advocate a harm minimization approach, linked with the development of a curriculum which has within it a focus on resilience, social skills and coping strategies.

Young People, Health and Public Policy

In the first few years of the 21st century there has been an increasing focus on public policy issues relating to adolescent health (Coleman, 2001). Many of the chapters in this book have referred to a publication which stemmed from a working party representing all the medical Royal Colleges and entitled *Bridging the gaps: health care for adolescents* (2003). This was an important step forward, and was the first time in the United Kingdom that such a consensus of views had been incorporated in a policy document. The report contained a number of key recommendations.

In the first place the report made it clear that adolescents have specific needs in relation to health services. These needs may overlap with younger children or with adults, but they are different in significant ways. The needs of young people identified in the report are:

- having access to services at times that are convenient, and that do not conflict with the school day, or with training timetables;
- a guarantee of confidentiality;
- services sited at locations that are accessible for young people, and that take into account transport difficulties;
- having health service staff with a knowledge of young people and their circumstances.

The second point made by this report is that adolescents receive less attention from health service planners than any other age group. There is a manifest gap in service provision for those who are no longer children but are not yet independent adults. We have noted above the social changes relating to delayed entry into the labour market, and these contribute to the creation of an age cohort which is almost invisible to planners and commissioners. This situation needs to change.

Thirdly, the report argues that more attention needs to be paid to the transition between paediatric and adult services. This issue is one that has received considerable attention in this book, from both Helms (Chapter 8) and McDonagh (Chapter 9), and we do not need to say any more about it here. Fourthly, the report argues for a greater involvement of young people in service planning, and we will return to this point in the next section. Finally, the report underlines the urgent need for better training in adolescent health. Again we will discuss this in more detail below.

The report *Bridging the gaps: health care for adolescents* is not the only policy publication that has appeared in Britain addressing adolescent health care. Macfarlane and McPherson (Chapter 7) make reference to a number of other policy initiatives, including the 'You're welcome' standards published by the Department of Health, and the National Service Framework for Children, Young People and Maternity Services. The Green Paper *Youth matters* (2005) has also had an impact, highlighting the importance of emotional health for young people, and signposting the development of four innovative Young People's Health Demonstration sites, located across the country and offering a high quality comprehensive service for young people. These sites were in place from autumn 2006.

In addition to government publications, other writers have taken up the task of arguing for better health care provision for this age group. We have mentioned the article by Michaud (2006), as well as the one written by Viner and Barker (2005). This latter paper contains a number of proposals that have implications for health care policy. We will outline some of these proposals briefly here.

- In the first place it is argued that a single issue approach to adolescent health is not helpful. By concentrating only on drugs, smoking, contraception or other single issues the health professional is likely to miss the probable links between various aspects of health, and to underestimate the degree of coexistence of risk behaviours. What is needed, argue Viner and Barker (2005), is an approach that is holistic, and one which focuses on common predisposing and protective factors.
- A second suggestion in this paper is that the age banding of national data is revised. At present most data sets provide age bandings of 5–15 and 16–44. This age banding does not allow us to look closely at older adolescents or the young adult population, and is not helpful if we wish to design more appropriate services for these age cohorts.
- The authors of this article argue strongly for new research programmes on adolescent health, as well as professional networks to encourage and support social scientists and health professionals who have an interest in adolescent health.
- Lastly, it is suggested that the Healthy Schools Programme (discussed in Chapter 3) has considerable potential to make a difference to the health of young people. However, there is currently little funding available for the development of this programme. Viner and Barker (2005) argue for a redesign of the school curriculum so that health promotion is embedded in all aspects of secondary school teaching.

As has been mentioned, one aspect of policy which is invariably mentioned as being of primary importance in achieving better health services for young people is the training of health professionals. This is an issue which is given prominence in virtually all policy documents on the subject of adolescent health, as well as being mentioned in most of the chapters of this book. In the UK there is presently no formal training in adolescent health outside mental health, nursing and general practice. Even in these specialities only a minority of trainees have any substantive training in adolescence, and for the most part those working in nursing, mental health or general practice have little knowledge of young people and their particular health needs. What can be done to alter this situation?

In the first place it should be mandatory that all undergraduates and all graduates of the Royal Colleges who are involved in any way in the care of adolescents should have some training in this field. In order for this to be achieved a concerted effort by the Department of Health, the universities and the Royal Colleges is necessary. In addition there are a variety of avenues that could lead to an improvement of the present situation. For example, the Royal College of General Practitioners in London has an Adolescent Task Group, dedicated to providing better training opportunities for those working in primary care. Macfarlane and McPherson (Chapter 7) draw attention to the EuTEACH initiative, a pan-European group of paediatricians and other professionals who collaborate to provide a common training in adolescent health care. Finally, there is currently no academic centre specializing in adolescent health in the United Kingdom. In both the United States and in Australia centres of excellence in adolescent health have been established in medical schools, and have made a considerable difference to the field. It is to be hoped that before too long something similar will be established in Britain.

Engaging Young People in Clinical Services

It is appropriate that we end this chapter with a section on the engagement of young people in clinical services. If we wish to improve the health of young people we must seek to offer services that appeal to this age group. There are many ways in which this can be done, and it is encouraging that over the last decade there appears to be a growing commitment to this objective (see Coleman, 2001; Viner and Barker, 2005). The first and most obvious goal is to have more adolescent clinics in both primary and secondary care settings. The establishment of such clinics will almost inevitably raise issues of accessibility, confidentiality, and professional training. It is these issues that are addressed in the publication of the 'You're welcome' standards outlined in Chapter 7.

A further element which can contribute to the engagement of young people in clinical services is to have them involved in service planning and delivery. While it is easy to pay lip service to this notion, in reality health professionals have to make a genuine commitment to the objective if it is to have an impact on service delivery. Research on innovative services for young people (e.g. Cater and Coleman (J.), 2006) shows that having a token adolescent on the management committee is not sufficient to make a difference. The services that have given thought to this issue have come up with a variety of imaginative ways to engage young people. Here are some examples.

• Ask young people to work on the publicity for the service. Designing leaflets, looking for ways to publicize the service, and being ambassadors within their own peer groups can be very effective ways of making adolescents feel some sense of ownership;

- Involve young people in the design, decoration and layout of the rooms or buildings which are used for the service;
- Seek the help of young people in the evaluation process. Adolescents can design questionnaires or carry out interviews with service users. This is an activity that is very popular. Some services ask young people to take part in 'mystery shopper' activities, for example phoning up a service to ask about its opening times or policy on confidentiality;
- Make it clear that the service welcomes the attendance of a friend at clinic appointments. This has proved to be an important issue for some young people, who feel embarrassed or awkward when disclosing information about their health. Services that welcome friends get high levels of attendance;
- Finally, as has already been mentioned, accessibility of the service is a key factor in engaging young people. Services that are on school premises, or in city centres, are likely to be seen as 'user-friendly'. Transport is also an issue, and mobile services can play a key role in rural areas.

Many of the topics discussed in the previous section will also make a difference in engaging young people. Thus, services that have a holistic approach, and do not just see themselves as single issue services, are likely to appeal to young people. The training of staff is obviously extremely important, and as McDonagh (Chapter 9) makes clear, professionals who have paid attention to communication skills in work with young people are more likely to be able to offer helpful consultations. The age factor is also important. It is critical that services do not offer one facility for 'children' and then move abruptly at 16 or 18 to an 'adult' service. Most of the innovative services reviewed by Cater and Coleman (J.) (2006) had a more flexible approach, opening their doors to adolescents and young adults with no restriction according to age. This is also the approach being taken by the four Young People's Health Demonstration sites (Department of Health, 2006).

We must also recognize the importance of new technologies. There are many ways in which the power of mobile phones and the Internet can be harnessed to engage young people. Good examples of web sites for young people are given in Chapters 7 and 9. There is also a suggestion (noted in Viner and Barker, 2005) that 'smart' cards may be introduced in the UK, which could be linked to the introduction of user-held health records. This is another way in which young people might become more engaged with their health. Involving adolescents in the design of a web site for their own service could also be attractive, and provide a further sense of ownership.

To conclude, throughout this book we have discussed the difficulties surrounding the definitions of health and risk, and hope to have pointed out to the reader that there are no simple solutions. Health is a multilevel and multifaceted life process, involving the interaction of hereditary, somatic, psychosocial, cultural and individual factors which can best be understood from the perspective of an interactive, systemic framework. Furthermore, we have emphasized that, however defined, health is more than the absence of illness. Thus, health promotion should capture the importance of enabling young people to create their own positive development.

We have in this final chapter looked briefly at four overarching themes that have application to the subjects covered by this book. These themes include the impact of social change on adolescent health, some new thinking on the concept of risk, important policy initiatives relating to adolescent health, and lastly some thoughts about how to engage young people in clinical services. The goals of this book have been to raise awareness of adolescent health, to offer a clearer understanding of some of the key questions and concerns relating to this field, and most important of all, to find ways of offering better services and thus improving the health of all our young people.

Glossary

Aetiology – is the science that deals with the causes or origin of disease, the factors which produce or predispose toward a certain disease or disorder.

Amenorrhœa – the absence of a reproductive woman's menstrual period. This condition is associated with females who exercise excessively (such as elite athletes) or those who are restricting their diet as is the case in anorexia nervosa. This occurs as the normal levels of sex hormones such as oestrogen are affected by the increase in activity-related chemicals (endorphins).

Amotivation – this is characterized by an absence of motivation or interest in participation. The activity has little or no value or importance to the individual.

Anaemia – is a deficiency of red blood cells, which can lead to a lack of oxygen-carrying ability, causing unusual tiredness and other symptoms.

Anxiolytic effects – term used to describe the reduction of anxiety symptoms. Traditionally, drugs including anti-depressants and beta-receptor blockers have been used, alternative therapies range from St John's Wort, cognitive or behavioural therapy to exercise.

ASE model – decision-making model that states that intentions and behaviours are determined by Attitudes, perceived Social norms and self-Efficacy.

Asymptomatic – without detectable symptoms.

Attachment problems – normal attachment develops during the child's first two to three years of life. Problems with the mother–child relationship during that time interfere with the normal development of a healthy and secure attachment. The ability to trust and form reciprocal relationships will affect the emotional health and behaviours of the child, as well as the child's development and future interpersonal relationships.

Attention deficit hyperactivity disorder (ADHD) – is a condition that becomes apparent in some children in the preschool and early school years. It is hard for these children to control their behaviour and/or pay attention.

Autistic spectrum disorder (ASD) – autism is a lifelong disability which affects the development of social, communication and imagination skills. Children with autistic spectrum disorder have difficulty understanding what other people are saying and need help to play.

Cardiovascular fitness – the ability of the respiratory and circulatory system to maintain an effective supply of oxygen to the body's muscles during prolonged exercise.

Cerebral palsy – is most commonly the result of failure of a part of the brain to develop, either before birth or in early childhood. The main effect of cerebral palsy is difficulty in movement. Many people with cerebral palsy are hardly affected, others have problems walking, feeding, talking or using their hands. Some people are unable to sit up without support and need constant enabling.

Chlamydia – is a common sexually transmitted disease caused by a bacterium, which can damage a woman's reproductive organs. Even though symptoms of chlamydia are usually mild or absent, serious complications that cause irreversible damage, including infertility, can occur "silently" before a woman ever recognizes the problem. Chlamydia also can cause discharge from the penis of an infected man.

Clinical depression – when an individual is diagnosed by a clinician (psychologist or psychiatrist) as suffering from a number of depressive symptoms classified on a diagnostic scale. The person will typically have an inability to function in daily life for a sustained period.

Cohort – is a group of people from a given population defined by experiencing an event (typically birth) in a particular time span.

Conduct disorders – refers to a group of behavioural and emotional problems in youngsters. Children and adolescents with this disorder have great difficulty following rules and behaving in a socially acceptable way.

Congenital abnormalities – birth defects.

Corrective feedback – this type of feedback provides the participants with information on how to improve their performance. Feedback is used to help reinforce correct behaviour and shape improving competence. Corrective feedback focuses not only on giving the participant specific information on how to correct errors but also to improve performance.

Cross-sectional data – refers to data collected by observing many subjects (such as individuals, firms or countries/regions) at the same point of time. Analysis of cross-sectional data usually consists of comparing the differences among the subject groups. For example, a group of 16 year-olds is compared to a group of 18 year-olds.

Curriculum – course of study, series of lectures.

Curvilinear relationship – one variable is associated with another variable, but the relationship is described by a curve rather than a straight line.

Cystic fibrosis (CF) – is an inherited condition. It can have many symptoms, affecting different parts of the body, particularly the lungs and digestive system. In a healthy person, there is a constant flow of mucus over the surfaces of the air passages in the lungs. This removes debris and bacteria. In someone with CF, the mucus is excessively sticky and cannot perform this role properly. In fact, the sticky mucus provides an ideal environment for bacterial growth. Children born with CF do not have a normal life expectancy.

Delphi study – is based on a structured process for collecting knowledge from a group of experts by means of a series of questionnaires interspersed with controlled opinion feedback. It has been developed to make discussion between experts possible without a normal group discussion that might influence opinion forming.

Demographic – a statistic characterizing human populations (or segments of human populations broken down by age or sex or income etc.).

Disease remission – is the state of absence of disease activity in patients with known chronic illness.

Ectopic pregnancy – occurs when the fertilized egg attaches itself outside the cavity of the uterus.

Endocrinologist – is a physician who specializes in treating disorders of the endocrine system, such as diabetes and hyperthyroidism.

Etanercept – a drug used for treating rheumatoid arthritis.

Extrinsic motivation – this type of motivation can be seen when a person looks to the environment or others for incentives or rewards to reinforce their participation in an activity.

Flow – a conceptual explanation of arousal. The skill of an individual needs to match the demands of the activity to provide a challenge which should result in optimal performance. If the person's skill exceeds the demands of the activity then boredom is likely to occur; in contrast, if the demands of the activity exceed the skill of the individual then anxiety is likely.

Gender stereotyping – stereotyping is concerned with the thoughts held about another individual on the basis of their membership of a particular group. These cognitions are often resistant to change and are used to make generalizations. This term is closely related to behavioural acts of discrimination and prejudiced feelings or emotions held. Typically women are portrayed as nurturing, sensitive and less assertive whereas men are portrayed as dominant, independent and controlling.

Group cohesion – often described as team spirit or bonding. This term is used to describe the strength of interconnectedness or integration of individuals who make up a group or team. This can be in relation to the task the group has to complete or the social connections within the group.

GUM-clinic – is an NHS-run clinic for all aspects of sexual health (genito-urinary medicine).

Haemoglobinopathies – refers to a range of genetically inherited disorders of red blood cell haemoglobin and includes sickle cell disease.

Health education – a process of informing people how to achieve and maintain good health, of motivating them to do so and of promoting environmental and lifestyle changes to help them in their objective.

Health promotion – the process of enabling people to increase their control over their health and to improve it.

Holistic – dealing with or treating the whole of something or someone and not just a part.

Homogeneity – consisting of elements with similar characteristics, in contrast to heterogeneity, which means consisting of elements with a variety of different characteristics.

Hydrotherapy – is the use of water, either internally or externally, to maintain health and prevent disease.

Hypertension – high blood pressure.

Identity formation – process of finding a sense of self in terms of commitment to certain values, for instance, professional, social, religious and political values.

Informal curriculum – areas and aspects of school life located outside of the formal teaching in the classroom, including extra-curricular activities, school trips, discipline policies and the school environment, such as the staffroom and playground.

Intoxication – poisoning.

Intrinsic motivation – this type of motivation can be seen when a person finds the activity in which they are participating rewarding in itself (enjoyment, satisfaction, curiosity).

Juvenile idiopathic arthritis (JIA) – refers to a number of different conditions, all of which strike children, and all of which have immune-mediated joint inflammation as their major manifestation.

Malignancy – a clinical course that progresses rapidly to death, often a cancerous tumour.

Mental disorder – severe and persistent mental illness that affects the brain.

Mentoring – when a role model, or mentor, offers support to another person. A mentor has knowledge and experience in an area and acts as a guide to the person being mentored.

Metabolic disease – is a group of more than a thousand inherited disorders in which there is a genetic fault in the body's chemistry. The effect on the patient is varied and not always predictable. Many defects cause severe illness and death whilst others seem to cause no problems.

Methotrexate – is used to treat several different types of rheumatic disease.

Mnemonic – is a device, such as a formula or rhyme, used as an aid in remembering.

Moral panic – a mass perception that some individual or group, frequently a minority group or a subculture, is dangerously deviant and poses a threat to society. These panics are generally fuelled by media coverage of social issues.

Morbidity – the degree or severity of a disease.

Motivational climate – this term is used to describe the individual's perception of the environment in terms of the emphasis placed upon achievement in particular settings (such as school or physical activity). A climate can be created by individuals such as parents, peers, teachers, coaches or by the structure (standards, teaching methods, assessment and recognition). A task-involved climate emphasizes self-referenced progress and competence whereas an ego-involved climate emphasizes normative standards and competition.

Muscle dysmorphia – one of the sub-types of the body dysmorphic disorder (BDD). The individual displays a pathological obsession with the whole body, viewing their bodies as less muscular than is desired. This can lead to excessive exercise and anxiety when not exercising. Other behaviours can include modifications to diet, abuse of drugs and checking appearance.

Muscular dystrophy – a group of more than 30 genetic diseases characterized by progressive weakness and degeneration of the skeletal muscles that control movement.

Nephrologist – is a physician who has been educated and trained in kidney diseases, kidney transplantation and dialysis therapy.

NHS – the National Health Service in Britain.

Normative changes – changes that occur to individuals in a certain society at a given time, prescribed by laws or norms, such as the legal age of beginning school. Non-normative changes occur in the lifespan due to reasons other than societal norms, and thus do not happen to all individuals in that society (e. g. winning a lottery, having a car accident).

Obesity – occurs as a result of excessive fatty tissue and is derived from the Latin word *obedere* (devour). It is typically measured by calculating a person's weight in relation to their height (taking age and gender into consideration) to give a value (body mass index, BMI) which is then converted into a score. Obesity forms a category that falls between overweight and clinical obesity.

Obstetrician – is a physician who deals principally with the management of pregnancy and childbirth.

Osteoporosis – is a disease in which bones become fragile and more likely to break.

Overtraining – can occur in individuals who physically train to a level (frequency, intensity, duration) that exceeds their capacity to recover adequately. The individual then fails to make gains in their fitness (power and stamina).

Palliative care – is the active holistic care of patients with advanced progressive illness. Management of pain and other symptoms and provision of psychological, social and spiritual support is paramount. The goal of palliative care is achievement of the best quality of life for patients and their families.

Pathology – is the study of the processes underlying disease and other forms of illness.

Peer education – education offered by trained people, who are members of the same group (or at least fit similar criteria, such as age and educational level) as the relatively homogeneous group they are educating. A key aim is to increase the acceptance of educational messages through avoiding a hierarchical situation.

Pelvic inflammatory disease – is a general term that refers to infection and inflammation of the upper genital tract in women. It can affect the uterus (womb), fallopian tubes (tubes that carry eggs from the ovaries to the uterus), ovaries and other organs related to reproduction. The scarring that results on these organs can lead to infertility, ectopic pregnancy, chronic pelvic pain, abscesses, and other serious problems.

Perceptual-motor – involving perceptions (hearing, seeing, tasting, feeling) and movement concurrently, emphasizing the interactions between sensory input and motoric output.

Pilot programme – preliminary trial run of a programme to try out instruments and/or procedures.

Pituitary gland – a small gland at the base of the brain involved with the regulation of hormones.

Positive psychology – is a whole new field of scientific inquiry. Since the Second World War, psychologists have focused almost exclusively on the study and repair of negative behaviour and mental illness. In doing so, psychology has neglected how to make lives more fulfilling. In an attempt to restore a balance, positive psychology focuses on human strengths rather than weaknesses, and how lives can go well rather than wrong.

Prednisolone – a drug used to treat inflammatory conditions such as arthritis.

Primary health care – all health services provided outside hospital.

Prospective study – in a prospective study, investigators follow participants forward in time for weeks, months, or even years and record what happens to them.

PSHE – Personal, Social and Health Education.

Qualitative investigation – an investigation that uses qualitative methods, i.e. interviews, texts, observations, in order to understand rather than measure a phenomenon statistically.

Quasi-experimental design – the word "quasi" means *as if* or *almost*, so a quasi-experiment means almost a true experiment. However, the researcher cannot control or vary the independent variables.

Renal transplant –is a surgical procedure to implant a healthy kidney into a patient with kidney failure.

Resilience – the ability to recover quickly from illness, change, or misfortune.

Respiratory – involving an organ concerned in breathing.

Scoliosis – is a lateral curvature of the spine.

Secondary care – service provided in or by hospitals.

Self-efficacy – people's beliefs about their capabilities to influence events that affect their lives. Self-efficacy beliefs determine how people feel, think, motivate themselves and behave.

Self-esteem – also called self-worth, concerns how an individual evaluates their self-schemas (athlete, student, attractive, fun) and possible selves (loved, successful, famous). Low self-esteem is associated with depression, anxiety, eating disorders, inactivity, dropout from exercise, drug abuse and some forms of delinquency.

Separation-individuation process – psychodynamic theory describing the process by which a baby separates from the mother and develops a sense of self. Adolescence is sometimes called a 'second separation-individuation process', because young people become independent of their parents and develop their own identity.

Sickle cell disease – is an inherited blood disorder that affects red blood cells. People with sickle cell disease have red blood cells that contain an abnormal type of haemoglobin. Sometimes these red blood cells become sickle-shaped (crescent-shaped) and have difficulty passing through small blood vessels. Sickle cells are destroyed rapidly in the body of people with the disease, causing anaemia, jaundice and the formation of gallstones. The sickle cells also block the flow of blood through vessels resulting in lung tissue damage, pain episodes, stroke and damage to most organs.

Social-physique anxiety – a specific form of anxiety that is created when an individual's physique is under public inspection (such as in the gym, at the swimming pool, on the beach). This can lead to an avoidance of situations where anxiety might be heightened, and to alterations in diet.

Somatic – relating to the body.

Spina bifida – the backbone usually provides a protective tube of bones with the nerves (spinal cord) running down the middle. In spina bifida, the bones do not close round the spinal cord and the nerves can bulge out on the unborn baby's back and become damaged. This happens very early on in pregnancy – often before the woman even knows she is pregnant.

SRE – Sex and Relationship Education.

Steroid – a hormone derived from cholesterol. Steroids exhibit a variety of biological functions, from participation in cell membrane structure to regulation of physiological events. Synthetic steroids that mimic an action of progesterone are widely used oral contraceptive agents. Other synthetic steroids are designed to mimic the stimulation of protein synthesis and muscle-building action of naturally occurring androgens.

STI – sexually transmitted infection.

Teratogenicity – The capability of producing malformation in an unborn child.

Tertiary care – specialized consultative care, usually on referral from primary or secondary medical care personnel, by specialists working in a centre that has personnel and facilities for special investigation and treatment.

WHO – World Health Organization.

References

Aas, H.N., Leigh, B.C., Anderssen, N. and Jakobsen, R. (1998) Two-year longitudinal study of alcohol expectancies and drinking among Norwegian adolescents. *Addiction*, 93, 373–384.

Adams, J. and Painter, C. (2004) *Explore, dream, discover: a resource and training pack on the flower holistic models of sexual health and sexuality, self-esteem and mental health, with guidance on their use in practice*, Centre for HIV and Sexual Health, Sheffield.

Aggleton, P. (1996) *Health promotion and young people*, Health Education Authority, London.

Aggleton, P., Whitty, G., Knight, A. *et al.* (1996) *Promoting young people's health: the health concerns and needs of young people*, Health Education Authority, London.

Aggleton, P., Whitty, G., Knight, A. *et al.* (1998) Promoting young people's health: the health concerns and needs of young people. *Health Education*, 6, 213–219.

Ajzen, I. (1988) *Attitudes, personality and behaviour*, Open University Press, Milton Keynes.

Alexander, T. (2002) *A bright future for all: promoting mental health in education*, Mental Health Foundation, London.

Alfermann, D. and Stoll, O. (2000) Effects of physical exercise on self-concept and well-being. *International Journal of Sport Psychology*, 30, 47–65.

Allbutt, H., Amos, A. and Cunningham-Burley, S. (1995) The social image of smoking among young people in Scotland. *Health Education Research*, 10, 4, 443–454.

Allen, J.B. and Howe, B.L. (1998) Player ability, coach feedback, and female adolescent athletes' perceived competence and satisfaction. *Journal of Sport and Exercise Psychology*, 20, 280–299.

American Psychiatric Association (1994) *Diagnostic and statistical manual*, 4th edn, American Psychiatric Association, Washington DC.

Anderson, A.R. and Henry, C.S. (1994) Family system characteristics and parental behaviours as predictors of adolescent substance use. *Adolescence*, 29, 405–420.

Anderson, B.J. and Wolpert, H.A. (2004) A developmental perspective on the challenges of diabetes education and care during the young adult period. *Patient Education and Counselling*, 53, 347–352.

Anderson, J.C., Funk, J.B., Elliott, R. and Hull Smith, P. (2003) Parental support and pressure and children's extracurricular activities: relationships with amount of involvement and affective experience of participation. *Applied Developmental Psychology*, 24, 241–257.

Arena, B. (1997) Hormonal problems in young female athletes. *Sports Exercise and Injuries*, 2, 122–125.

Arnett, J. (2004) *Emerging adulthood: the winding road for the late teens through the twenties*, Oxford University Press, Oxford.

Babkes, M.L. and Weiss, M.R. (1999) Parental influence on children's cognitive and affective responses to competitive soccer participation. *Pediatric Exercise Science*, 11, 44–62.

Backett, K. and Davison, C. (1992) Rational or reasonable? Perceptions of health at different stages of life. *Journal of Health Education*, 51, 55–59.

Balding, J (2004) *Young people in 2003*, Schools Health Education Unit. Exeter.

Bandura, A. (1977) Self-efficacy: Toward a unifying theory of behavioral change. *Psychological Review*, 84, 191–212.

Bearman, P. and Bruckner, H. (2004) *Rules, behaviors and networks that influence STD prevention among adolescents*, National STD Prevention Conference, Philadelphia, United States.

Beck, K.H., Thombs, D.L. and Summons, T.G. (1993) The social context of drinking scales: construct validation and relationships to indicants of abuse in an adolescent population. *Addictive Behaviours*, 18, 159–169.

Beresford, B. (2004) On the road to nowhere? Young disabled people and transition. *Child: Care, Health and Development*, 30, 6, 581–587.

Beresford, B. and Sloper, P. (2003) Chronically ill adolescents' experiences of communicating with doctors: a qualitative study. *Journal of Adolescent Health*, 33, 172–179.

Biddle, S.J.H., Fox, K.R. and Boutcher, S.H. (eds) (2000) *Physical activity and psychological well-being*, Routledge, London.

Biddle, S.J.H and Mutrie, N. (2001) *Psychology of physical activity: determinants, well-being and interventions*, Routledge, London.

Blake, S. and Frances, G. (2001) *Just say no! to abstinence education: lessons learnt from a sex education study tour of the United States,* National Children's Bureau, London.

Blamey, A., Mutrie, N. and Aitchison, T. (1995) Health promotion by encouraged use of stairs. *British Medical Journal*, 311, 289–290.

Bland, J. H. and Colby, J. (1999) *The complete mall walker's handbook*, Fairview Press, Minneapolis.

Blaxter, M. (1987) Attitudes to health, in Cox, B. (ed.) *The health and lifestyle survey*, Health Promotion Research Trust, London.

Blum R. (1995) Transition to adult healthcare: setting the stage. *Journal of Adolescent Health*, 17, 3–5

Bone, J. and Gardiner, J. (2002) *Speaking up, speaking out: 20/20 vision programme*, Industrial Society, London.

Boreham, R. and Blenkinsop, S. (2004) *Drug use, smoking and drinking among young people in England, 2003*, The Stationery Office, London.

Boreham, C. and Riddoch. C. (2001) The physical activity, fitness and health of children. *Journal of Sports Sciences*, 19, 915–929.

Botting, B., Rosato, M. and Wood, R. (1998) Teenage mothers and the health of their children. *Population Trends*, 93, 19–28. [www.statistics.gov.uk/downloads/theme_population/].

Boyd, M. P. and Yin, Z. (1996) Cognitive-affective sources of sport enjoyment in adolescent sport participants. *Adolescence,* 31, 383–395.

Boyle, M.P., Farukhi, Z., and Nosky, M.L. (2001) Strategies for improving transition to adult cystic fibrosis care, based on patient and parent views. *Pediatric Pulmonology*, 32, 428–436.

Breslau, N. Kilbey, M. M. and Andreski, P. (1993) Nicotine dependence and major depression: New evidence from a prospective investigation. *Archives of General Psychiatry*, 50, 31–35.

British Medical Association (BMA) (2003) *Adolescent health* [www.bma.org.uk].

Brown C., Rowley S. and Helms P. (1994) Symptoms, health and illness behaviour in cystic fibrosis. *Social Science and Medicine*, 39, 375–379.

Bruch, H. (1974) *Eating disorders: obesity, anorexia and the person within*, Basic Books, New York.

Bruch, H. (1985) Four decades of eating disorders, in Garner, D.M. and Garfinkel, P.E. (eds) *Handbook of Psychotherapy for Anorexia Nervosa and Bulimia*, Guilford Press, New York.

Bryant-Waugh, R. and Lask, B. (1995) Eating disorders in children. *Journal of Child Psychology and Psychiatry*, 6, 2.

Buckworth, J. and Dishman, R.K. (2002) *Exercise psychology*, Human Kinetics, Champaign, IL.

Buonamano, R., Cei, A. and Mussino, A. (1995) Participation motivation in Italian youth sport. *The Sport Psychologist*, 9, 265–281.

Burchardt, T. (2005) *The education and employment of disabled young people: frustrated ambition*, The Policy Press, Marston Book Services, Oxon, UK.

Burtney, E. and Duffy, M. (eds) (2004) *Young people and sexual health: individual, social and policy contexts*, Palgrave Macmillan, Basingstoke.

Carron, A.V. (1982) Cohesion in sports: interpretations and considerations. *Journal of Sport Psychology*, 4, 123–138.

Carron, A.V. and Dennis, P.W. (1998) The sport team as an effective group, in Williams, J.M. (ed.) *Applied Sport Psychology: Personal Growth to Peak Performance*, 3rd edn, Mayfield, Mountain View, CA, 127–141.

Cash, T.F. and Deagle, E.A. (1997) The nature and extent of body image disturbance in anorexia and bulimia nervosa. A meta-analysis. *International Journal of Eating Disorders*, 22, 107–125.

Casper, R.C. (1993) Exercise and mood. *World review of nutrition and dietetics*, 1, 115–143.

Cater, S. and Coleman, J. (2006) *Adolescent health provision: factors facilitating the provision of young people's health services*. Report for the Department of Health. Available at the Trust for the Study of Adolescence [www.tsa.uk.com].

Cater, S. and Coleman, L.M. (2006) *'Planned' teenage pregnancy: perspectives of young parents from disadvantaged backgrounds*, Joseph Rowntree Foundation, York.

Churchill, R., Allen, J., Denman, S. *et al.* (2000) Do the attitudes and beliefs of young teenagers towards general practice influence actual consultation behaviour? *British Journal of General Practice*, 50, 953–957.

Coakley, J.J. and White, A. (1992) Making decisions: gender and sport participation among British adolescents. *Sociology of Sport Journal*, 9, 20–35.

Coffield, F. (1992) *Young people and illicit drugs*, Northern Regional Health Authority and Durham University, Durham.

Colby, S.M., Tiffany, S.T., Shiffman, S. and Niaura, R.S. (2000) Are adolescent smokers dependent on nicotine? A review of the evidence. *Drug and Alcohol Dependence*, 59, S83–S95.

Coleman, J.C. (2001) Meeting the health needs of young people. *Journal of Epidemiology and Community Health*, 55, 532–533.

Coleman, J.C. (2002) Into adulthood, in Lotherington, J. (ed.) *The seven stages of life*, Centre for Reform, London.

Coleman, J.C. and Hendry, L.B. (1999) *The nature of adolescence*, 3rd edn, Routledge, London.

Coleman, J.C. and Schofield, J. (2005) *Key data on adolescence*, 5th edn, Trust for the Study of Adolescence, Brighton.

Coleman, L.M. (1999) Comparing contraceptive use surveys of young people in the UK: what can we learn from such a review? *Archives of Sexual Behavior*, 28, 225–264.

Coleman, L.M. and Cater, S. (2005a) *Underage "risky" drinking: motivations and outcomes*, Joseph Rowntree Foundation, York.

Coleman, L.M. and Cater, S. (2005b) Exploring the relationship between adolescent alcohol consumption and risky sexual behaviour. *Archives of Sexual Behavior*, 34, 649–661.

Coleman, L.M. and Coleman, J.C. (2002) The measurement of puberty: a review. *Journal of Adolescence*, 25, 535–550.

Coleman, L.M. and Ingham, R. (1999) Exploring young people's difficulties in talking about contraception: how can we encourage more discussion between partners? *Health Education Research: Theory and Practice*, 14, 741–750.

Collishaw, S., Maughan, B., Goodman, R. and Pickles, A. (2004) Time trends in adolescent well-being. *Journal of Child Psychology and Psychiatry*, 45, 1350–1362.

Copp, A. (2005) An overview of children's health, in Horton, C. (ed.) *Working with children 2006/2007*, Society Guardian and Sage Publications, London.

Council of Europe (1993) *European Sports Charter. Recommendation No. R (92) 13*, Sports Council, London.

Cowie, H., Boardman, C., Dawkins, J. and Jennifer, D. (2004) *Emotional health and well-being: a practical guide for schools*, Paul Chapman Publishing, London.

Crabbe, J. B., Smith, J. C. and Dishman, R. K. (1999) EEG and emotional response after cycling exercise. *Medicine and Science in Sports and Exercise*, 31, S173.

Crisp A. (1980) *Anorexia nervosa – let me be*, Academic Press, New York.

Csikszentmihalyi, M. (1990) *Flow: the psychology of optimal exercise*, Harper and Row, New York.

Currie C., Roberts, C., Morgan, A. *et al.* (eds) (2004) *Young people's health in context: international report from the HBSC 2001/02 survey*. WHO Policy Series: Health Policy for Children and Adolescents, Issue 4, WHO Regional Office for Europe, Copenhagen.

Davis, C. (1999) Excessive exercise and anorexia nervosa: addictive and compulsive behaviors. *Psychiatric Annals*, 29, 221–224.

Dawson, D.A. (2000) The link between family history and early onset alcoholism: earlier initiation of drinking or more rapid development of dependence? *Journal of Studies on Alcohol*, 61, 637–646.

Deci, E.L. and Ryan, R.M. (1985) Intrinsic motivation and self-determination in human behavior, cited by Frederick, C.M. and Ryan, R.M. (1995) Self–determination in sport: A review using cognitive evaluation theory. *International Journal of Sport Psychology*, 26, 5–23.

Deci, E.L., and Ryan, R.M. (1991) A motivational approach to self: integration in personality, in Dienstbier, R. (ed.) *Nebraska symposium on motivation: Vol. 38. Perspectives on motivation*, University of Nebraska Press, Lincoln, NE, 237–288.

De Knop, P., Wylleman, P., Theeboom M. *et al.* (1999) The role of contextual factors in youth participation in organized sport. *European Physical Education Review*, 5, 153–168.

Denman, S. (1998) The health promoting school: reflections on school-parent links. *Health Education*, 2, 55–58.

Dennison, C. (2004) *Teenage pregnancy: an overview of the research evidence*, Health Development Agency, London.

Department for Education and Employment (DfEE) (2000) *Sex and Relationships Education guidance*. Reference: Department for Education and Employment 0116/2000.

Department for Education and Skills (2005) *Youth matters*, The Stationery Office, London.

Department of Health (2001) *The National Strategy for Sexual Health and HIV*, Department of Health.

Department of Health (2004) *At least five times a week: evidence on the impact of physical activity and its relationship to health*, Department of Health, London. Retrieved on 7 March 2006, from http://www.dh.gov.uk/PublicationsAndStatistics/Publications/Publicatios PolicyAndGuidance/PublicationsPolicyAndGuidanceArticle/fs/en?CONTENT_ID = 4080994andchk = 1FtlOf

Department of Health (2005a) *Young People's Health Demonstration Sites: guidance*, Department of Health, London.

Department of Health (2005b) *'You're welcome' quality criteria: making health services young people friendly: guidance document*, Department of Health, London [www.dh.gov.uk].

Department of Health (2006) *Our health, our care, our say*, Government White Paper, The Stationery Office, London.

Department of Health and Department for Education and Skills (2004) *The National Service Framework for Children, Young People and Maternity Services*, The Stationery Office, London.

Dickinson, P., Neilson, G. and Agee, M. (2004) The sustainability of mentally healthy schools initiatives: insights from the experiences of a co-educational secondary school in Aotearoa/New Zealand. *International Journal of Mental Health Promotion*, 6, 27–34.

Dishman, R. K. (2001) The problem of exercise adherence: fighting sloth in nations with market economies. *Quest*, 53, 279–294.

Donovan, D., Suckling, H., Walker, Z. *et al.* (2004) *Difficult consultations with adolescents*, Radcliffe Medical Press, Oxford.

Dovey-Pearce, G., Hurrell, R., May, C. *et al.* (2005) Young adults' (16–25 years) suggestions for providing developmentally appropriate diabetes services: a qualitative study. *Health and Social Care in the Community*, 13, 409–419.

Duffy, M., Wimbush, E., Reece, J. and Eadie, D. (2003) Net profits? Web site development and health improvement. *Health Education*, 103, 5, 278–285.

Duncan, S.C. (1993) The role of cognitive appraisal and friendship provisions in adolescents' affect and motivation toward activity in physical education. *Research Quarterly for Exercise and Sport,* 64, 314–323.

Duncan, S.C., Duncan, T.E., Biglan, A. and Ary, D. (1998) Contributions of the social context to the development of adolescent substance use: a multivariate latent growth modeling approach. *Drug and Alcohol Dependence,* 50, 57–71.

Durkin, S.J. and Paxton, S.J. (2002) Predictors of vulnerability to reduced body image satisfaction and psychological well-being in response to exposure to idealised female media images in adolescent girls. *Journal of Psychosomatic Research,* 53, 995–100.

Durlack, J. and Wells, A. (1997) Primary prevention mental health programmes: the future is exciting. *American Journal of Community Psychology,* 25, 233–243.

Eating Disorders Association (2006) [www.edauk.com].

Eccles, J., Flanagan, C. and Lord, S. (1996) Schools, families and early adolescents: what are we doing wrong, and what can we do instead? *Developmental and Behavioural Paediatrics,* 17, 267–276.

Edwards, L. (2003) *Promoting young people's well-being: a review of research on emotional health,* SCRE Centre, University of Glasgow.

Elkins, W.L., Cohen, D.A., Koralewicz, L.M. and Taylor, S.N. (2004) After school activities, overweight, and obesity among inner city youth. *Journal of Adolescence,* 27, 181–189.

Ellis, S. and Grey, A. (2004) Prevention of sexually transmitted infections: a review of reviews into the effectiveness of non-clinical interventions, Health Development Agency, London.

Engels, R.C.M.E. (2003) Beneficial functions of alcohol use for adolescents: theory and implications for prevention. *Nutrition Today,* 38, 25–30.

Engels, R.C.M.E., Finkenauer, C., Kerr, M. and Stattin, H. (2005) Illusions of parental control: parenting and smoking onset in Swedish and Dutch adolescents. *Journal of Applied Social Psychology.*

Engels, R.C.M.E. and Knibbe, R.A. (2000) Alcohol use and intimate relationships in adolescence: when love comes to town. *Addictive Behaviours,* 25, 435–439.

Engels, R.M.E., Knibbe, R.A. and Drop, M.J. (1999a) Visiting public drinking places: an explorative study into the functions of pub-going for late adolescents. *Substance Use and Misuse,* 34, 1061–1080.

Engels, R.C.M.E., Knibbe, R.A. and Drop, M.J. (1999b) Why do late adolescents drink at home? A study on psychological well-being, social integration and drinking context. *Addiction Research,* 7, 31–46.

Engels, R.C.M.E., Scholte, R., Van Lieshout, C.F.M. *et al.* (2005) Peer group reputation and alcohol and cigarette use. *Addictive Behaviours.*

Engels, R.C.M.E., and Ter Bogt, T. (2001) Influences of risk behaviours on the quality of peer relations in adolescence. *Journal of Youth and Adolescence,* 30, 675–695.

Epstein, R., Rice, P. and Wallace, P. (1989) Teenage health concerns: implications for primary health care professionals. *Journal of the Royal College of General Practitioners,* 39, 247–249.

Fairburn C.G. and Brownell, K.D. (eds) (2002) *Eating disorders and obesity: a comprehensive handbook,* 2nd edn, The Guilford Press, New York.

Fairburn, C.G., Cooper, Z. and Shafran, R. (2003) Cognitive behaviour therapy for eating disorders: a transdiagnostic theory and treatment. *Behaviour Research and Therapy,* 41, 509–529.

Fairburn C.G., Doll, H.A., Welch, S.L. *et al.* (1998) Risk factors for binge eating disorder. *Archives of General Psychiatry,* 55, 425–432.

Fairburn, C.G., Shafran, R. and Cooper, Z. (1999) A cognitive behavioural theory of anorexia nervosa. *Behaviour Research and Therapy,* 37, 1, 1–13.

Farrell, C. (1978) *My mother said... the way young people learn about sex and birth control,* Routledge and Kegan Paul, London.

Fenton, K.A. and Hughes, G. (2003) Sexual behaviour in Britain: why sexually transmitted infections are common. *Clinical Medicine,* 3, 199–202.

Fox, K.R. (2000) The influence of exercise on self-perceptions and self-esteem, in Biddle, S.J.H., Fox, K.R. and Boutcher, S.H. (eds) *Physical activity and mental well-being,* Routledge, London, 78–111.

Fox, K., Goudas, M., Biddle, S. *et al.* (1994) Children's task and ego goal profiles in sport. *British Journal of Educational Psychology,* 64, 253–261.

France, C., Thomas, K., Slack, R. and James, N. (2001) Psychosocial impacts of chlamydia testing are important. *British Medical Journal,* 322, 1245–1246.

Franzoi, S.L. (1995) The body-as-object versus the body-as-process: gender differences and gender considerations. *Sex Roles,* 33, 417–437.

Frederick, C.M. and Morrison, C.S. (1996) Social physique anxiety: personality constructs, motivations, exercise attitudes and behaviour. *Perceptual and Motor Skills,* 82, 963–972.

Frederick, C.M. and Ryan, R.M. (1993) Differences in motivation for sport and exercise and the relationships with participation and mental health. *Journal of Sport Behavior,* 16, 125–145.

Frederick C.M. and Shaw, S.M. (1995) Body image as a leisure constraint: Examining the experience of aerobic exercise classes for young women. *Leisure Science,* 17, 57–73.

Friedli, L. (1997) *Mental health promotion: a quality framework,* Mental Health Foundation, London.

Furlong, A. and Cartmel, F. (1997) *Young People and Social Change: Individualization in Late Modernity,* Open University Press, Buckinghamshire.

Garn, S.M., Bailey, S.M., Solomon, M.A. and Hopkins, P.J. (1981) Effects of remaining family members on fatness prediction. *American Journal of Clinical Nutrition,* 43, 148–153.

Garner, D.M. and Bemis, K.M. (1982) A cognitive-behavioral approach to anorexia nervosa. *Cognitive Therapy and Research,* 6, 123–150.

Garner, D.M. and Bemis, K.M. (1985) Cognitive therapy for anorexia nervosa, in Garner, D.M. and Garfinkel, P.E. (eds), *Handbook of psychotherapy for anorexia nervosa and bulimia,* Guilford Press, New York, 107–146.

Garner, D.M. and Garfinkel, P.E. (1980) Sociocultural factors in the development of anorexia nervosa. *Psychological Medicine,* 10, 647.

Geenen, S.J., Powers, L.E., and Sells, W. (2003) Understanding the role of health care providers during transition of adolescents with disabilities and special health care needs. *Journal of Adolescent Health,* 32, 225–233.

Glendinning, A. (1998) Family life, health and lifestyles in rural areas: the role of self-esteem. *Health Education,* 2, 59–68.

Glendinning, A., Love, J., Shucksmith, J. and Hendry, L.B. (1992) Adolescence and health inequalities: extensions to McIntyre and West. *Social Science and Medicine,* 35, 5, 679–687.

Goleman, D. (1996) *Emotional intelligence,* Bloomsbury, London.

Gordon, J. and Turner, K. (2001) School staff as exemplars – where is the potential? *Health Education,* 101, 6, 283–291.

Gould, D. (1987) Understanding attrition in children's sport, in Gould, D. and Weiss, M.R. (eds) *Advances in paediatric sciences (Vol. 2): Behavioral issues,* Human Kinetics, Champaign, IL, 61–85.

Gould, D. and Petlichkoff, L. (1988) Participation motivation and attrition in young athletes, in Smoll, F.L., Magill, R.A. and Ash, M.J. (eds) *Children in sport,* Human Kinetics, Champaign IL, 161–178.

Grant, T. (ed.) (2000) *Physical activity and mental health: national consensus statements and guidelines for practice,* Health Education Authority, London.

Gray, N.J., Klein, J.D., Noyce, P.R. *et al.* (2005) Health information seeking behaviour in adolescence: the place of the internet. *Social Science and Medicine,* 60, 7, 1467–1478.

Green, H., McGinnity, A., Meltzer, H. *et al.* (2005) *Mental health of children and young people in Britain, 2004,* Office for National Statistics, London.

Greendorfer, S.L., Lewko, J.H. and Rosengren, K.S. (2002) Family and gender-based influences in sport socialization of children and adolescents, in Smoll, F.L. and Smith, R.E. (eds) *Children and youth in sport: a biopsychosocial perspective,* 2nd edn, Kendall Hunt Publishing, Dubuque, IW, 153–186.

Hagell, A. (2002) *The mental health of young offenders,* Mental Health Foundation, London.

Harden, A., Rees, A., Shepherd, J., *et al.* (2001) *Young people and mental health: a systematic review of research on barriers and facilitators,* EPPI-Centre, University of London.

Harden, A., Weston, R. and Oakley, A. (1999) *A review of the effectiveness and appropriateness of peer-delivered health promotion for young people,* EPI-Centre, Social Science Research Unit, London.

Hart, R. (1992) *Child's participation: from tokenism to citizenship,* UNICEF International Child Development Centre.

Hart, R (1997) *Children's participation: the theory and practice of involving young citizens in community development and environmental care,* UNICEF, Earthscan.

Hawton, K., Hall, S., Simkin, S. *et al.* (2003) Deliberate self-harm in adolescents: a study of the characteristics and trends in Oxford 1990–2000. *Journal of Child Psychology and Psychiatry,* 44, 1101–1198.

Hawton, K., Rodham, K., Evans, E. and Weatherall, R. (2002) Deliberate self-harm in adolescents: self-report survey in schools in England. *British Medical Journal,* 325, 1207–1211.

HPA (Health Protection Agency) (2005) *Diagnoses and rates of selected STIs seen at GUM clinics,* 2000–2004, Health Protection Agency, United Kingdom.

Heinberg, L.J., Thompson, J.K. and Stormer, S. (1995) Development and validation of the sociocultural attitudes towards appearance questionnaire. *International Journal of Eating Disorders,* 17, 81–89.

Hendry, L., Glendinning, A., Reid, M. and Wood, S. (1998) *Lifestyles, health and health concerns of rural youth, 1996–1998,* Department of Health, Scottish Office, Edinburgh.

Hendry, L.B. and Kloep, M. (1999) Adolescence in Europe: an important life phase? in Messer, D. and Millar, S. (eds) *Exploring developmental psychology,* Arnold, London.

Hendry, L. and Kloep, M. (2002) *Life-span development: resources, challenges and risks,* Thomson Learning, London.

Hendry, L.B. and Kloep, M. (2006) Youth and leisure: a European perspective, in Jackson, S. and Goossens, L. (eds) *Handbook of adolescent development,* Psychology Press, London.

Hendry, L.B. and Reid, L. (2001) Social relationships and health: the meaning of social 'connectedness' and how it relates to health concerns for rural Scottish adolescents. *Journal of Adolescence,* 23, 705–719.

Hendry, L.B., Shucksmith, M., Love,. G. and Glendinning, A. (1993) *Young people's leisure and lifestyles,* Routledge, London.

Hendry, L. and Singer, F. (1981) Sport and the adolescent girl: a case study of one comprehensive school. *Scottish Journal of Physical Education,* 9, 18–22.

Hermus, R.J. (ed.) (1983) *Alcohol, health and society,* CIVO/TNO, Zeist.

Herzog, R. (1991) Measurement of vitality in America's changing life study. *Proceedings of the International Symposium on Aging.* Series 5. No. 6. DHSS Publication No. 91–1482, US Dept of Health and Human Services, Hyattsville.

Hill, G.M. (1993) Youth sport participation of professional baseball players. *Sociology of Sport Journal,* 10, 107–114.

Hill A.J., Oliver S. and Rogers P.J. (1992) Eating in an adult world: the rise of dieting in childhood and adolescence. *Br J Clin Psychol,* 31, 95–105.

Holland, J., Ramazanoglu, C., Sharpe, S. and Thomson, R. (1998) *The male in the head: young people, heterosexuality and power,* Tufnell Press, London.

Horn, T.S. and Amorose, A.J. (1998) Sources of competence information, in Duda, J.L. (ed.) *Advances in sport and exercise measurement,* Fitness Information Technology, Morgantown, WA, 49–63.

Howlett, M., McClelland, L. and Crisp. A.H. (1995) The cost of illness that defies. *Postgraduate Medical Journal,* 71, 842, 705–706.

Index Mundi [www.indexmundi.com].

Ingham, R. (2001) Survey commissioned by Channel Four for the series 'Generation Sex', presented 16 October 2001.

Ingham, R. and van Zessen, G. (1998) From cultural contexts to international competencies: a European comparative study. *Paper presented at AIDS in Europe, Social and Behavioural Dimensions,* 1998.

Jacobsen, L., Mellanby, A., Donovan, C. *et al.* (2000) Teenagers' views on general practice consultations and other medical advice. *Family Practice*, 17, 156–158.

Jambor, E.A. (1999) Parents as children's socialising agents in youth soccer. *Journal of Sport Behavior*, 22, 350–359.

Jenks, C. (2003) *Transgressions*, Routledge, London.

Jessor, R. (1987) Problem-Behaviour Theory, psychosocial development, and adolescent problem drinking. *British Journal of Addiction*, 82, 331–342.

Johnsgard, K.W. (1989) *The exercise prescription for depression and anxiety*, Plenum Press, New York.

Johnson, A., Mercer, C., Erens, B. *et al.* (2001) Sexual behaviour in Britain: partnerships, practices and HIV risk behaviours. *The Lancet*, 358, 1835–1842.

Johnson, A., Wadsworth, J., Wellings, K. and Field, J. (1994) *Sexual attitudes and lifestyles*, Blackwell Scientific Press, Oxford.

Johnston, O. (2001) Eating, exercise and body regulation across the lifespan: a qualitative approach. Unpublished doctoral dissertation, School of Psychology, The Queen's University of Belfast.

Jones, B.T., Corbin, W. and Fromme, K. (2001) A review of expectancy theory and alcohol consumption. *Addiction*, 91, 57–72.

Jones, R., Finlay, F., Simpson, N. and Kreitman, T. (1997) How can adolescent's health needs and concerns best be met? *British Journal of General Practice*, 47, 631–634.

Kaarsgaren, R.J., Zulstra, R.F., Helms, P. (1994) Asthma medication in children 1991. *Respiratory Medicine*, 88, 383–386.

Kahn, E.B., Ramsey, L.T., Brownson, R.C. *et al.* (2002) The effectiveness of interventions to increase physical activity: a systematic review. *American Journal of Preventive Medicine*, 22, 73–107.

Kalnins, I., McQueen, D., Backett, K. and Currie, C. (1992) Children, empowerment and health promotion: some new directions in research and practice. *Health Promotion International*, 7, 53–59.

Kendall, K.A. and Danish, S.J. (1994) The development of preliminary validation of a measure of parental influence on youth participation in organized sports. Paper presented at the *Annual conference of the Association for the Advancement of Applied Sport Psychology*, Lake Tahoe, NV.

Kipps, S., Bahu, T., Ong, K., *et al.* (2002) Current methods of transfer of young people with type 1 diabetes to adult services. *Diabetic Medicine*, 19, 649–654.

Kirtland, K.A., Porter, D.E., Addy, C.L. *et al.* (2003) Environmental measures of physical activity supports: perception versus reality. *American Journal of Preventive Medicine*, 24, 323–331.

Kloep, M. and Hendry, L.B. (1999) Challenges, risks and coping in adolescence, in: Messer, D. and Millar, S. (eds) *Exploring developmental psychology from infancy to adolescence*, Arnold, London, 400–416.

Kloep, M. Hendry, L.B., Ingebrigtsen, J. E. *et al.* (2001) Young people in 'drinking' societies: Norwegian, Scottish and Swedish adolescents' perceptions of alcohol use. *Health Education Research*, 16, 279–291.

Klosterman, B.K., Slap, G.B., Nebrig, D.M. *et al.* (2005) Earning trust and losing it: adolescents' views on trusting physicians. *Journal of Family Practice*, 54, 679–687.

Klump, K.L. and Gobrogge, K.L. (2005) A review and primer of molecular genetic studies of anorexia nervosa. *International Journal of Eating Disorders*, 37, S43–S48.

Koff, E. and Bauman, C. (1997) Effects of wellness, fitness and sport skills programs on body image and lifestyle behaviors. *Perceptual Motor Skills*, 84, 55–62.

Kopelman, P. (1999) Aetiology of obesity II: genetics, in *Obesity: the report of the British Nutrition Foundation Task Force*, Blackwell Science, Oxford, 39–44.

Kremer, J. (1997) Introduction, in Kremer, J. Trew, K. and Ogle, S. (eds) *Young people's involvement in sport*, Routledge, London.

Kremer, J., Trew, K. and Ogle, S. (eds) (1997) *Young people's involvement in sport*, Routledge, London.

Kumpfer, K.L. and Turner, C.W. (1990) The social ecology model of adolescent substance abuse: implications for prevention. *International Journal of the Addictions*, 25, 435–463.

Kuntsche, E., Knibbe, R.A., Gmel, G. and Engels, R.C.M.E. (2005) Why do young people drink? A review of drinking motives. *Clinical Psychology Review*, 25, 841–861.

Lam, P.Y., Fitzgerald, B.B. and Sawyer, S.M. (2005) Young adults in children's hospitals: why are they there? *Medical Journal of Australia*, 182, 8, 381–384.

Lasheras, L., Aznar, S., Merino, B. and Lopez, E. G. (2001) Factors associated with physical activity among Spanish youth through the national survey. *Preventive Medicine*, 32, 455–464.

Lask, B. and Bryant-Waugh, R. (eds) (2000) *Anorexia nervosa and related eating disorders in childhood and adolescence*, Psychology Press Ltd, Hove.

Lawrence, M. (1989) *Fed up and hungry: women, oppression and food*, The Women's Press, London.

Lee, E., Clements, S., Ingham, R. and Stone, N. (2004) *A matter of choice? Explaining national variation in teenage abortion and motherhood*, University of Southampton.

Leff, S.S. and Hoyle, R.H. (1995) Young athletes' perceptions of parental support and pressure. *Journal of Youth and Adolescence*, 24, 187–203.

Lerner, R. (1998) Theories of human development, in Damon, W. and Lerner, R. (eds) *Handbook of Child Psychology*, 5th edn, John Wiley & Sons, Inc. New York.

Lerner, R. (2002) *Concepts and theories of human development*, 3rd edn, Erlbaum, Mahwah, New Jersey.

Lloyd, B. and Lucas, K. (1998) *Smoking in adolescence: images and identities*, Routledge, London.

Long, B.C. and Stavel, R.V. (1995) Effects of exercise training on anxiety: a meta-analysis. *Journal of Applied Sport Psychology*, 7, 167–189.

Lotstein, D.S., McPherson, M., Strickland, B. and Newacheck, P.W. (2005) Transition planning for youth with special health care needs: results from the national survey of children with special health care needs. *Pediatrics*, 115, 1562–1568.

Loumidis, K.S. and Roxborough, H. (1995) A cognitive-behavioural approach to excessive exercising, in Annett, J., Cripps, B. and Steinberg, H. (eds), *Exercise addiction: motivation for participation in sport and exercise*, British Psychological Society, Leicester, 45–53.

Lowry, R.G. and Kremer, J. (2004) Exploring intrinsic and extrinsic motivational differences according to choice of physical activity. *Journal of Sport and Exercise Psychology*, 26, S127–S127 Suppl.

Macfarlane, A. and McPherson, A. (2002) *The diary of a teenage health freak*, Oxford University Press, Oxford.

Mackinnon, D. (2005) Becoming an adult in rural Scotland. Unpublished PhD thesis, University of Glasgow, Glasgow.

Mackinnon, D. and Soloman, S. (2003) Delivering health information online: What do young people currently use the Internet for and what do they want? *Scottish Youth Issues Journal*, 6, 115–126.

Maggs, J.L. and Hurrelmann, K. (1998) Do substance use and delinquency have differential associations with adolescents' peer relations? *International Journal of Behavioral Development*, 22, 367–388.

Malina, R.M. (1996) Tracking of physical activity and physical fitness across the lifespan. *Research Quarterly for Exercise and Sport*, 67, 48–57.

Markham, A. Thompson, T. and Bowling, A. (2005) Determinants of body image shame. *Personality and Individual Differences*, 38, 1529–1541.

Martinsen, E.W. (1994) Physical activity and depression: clinical experience. *Acta Psychiatrica Scandinavica*, 89, 23–27.

McAuley, E., Bane, S.M., Rudolph, D.L. and Lox, C. (1995) Physique anxiety and exercise in middle-aged adults. *Journal of Gerontology: Psychological Sciences and Social Sciences*, 50, 229–235.

McDonagh, J.E. (2005) Growing up and moving on. Transition from pediatric to adult care. *Pediatric Transplantation*, June 9, 3, 364–72.

McDonagh, J.E., Foster, H., Hall, M.A. and Chamberlain, M.A. (2000) Audit of rheumatology services for adolescents and young adults in the UK. *Rheumatology*, 39, 596–602.

McDonagh, J.E., Minnaar, G., Kelly, K. *et al.*, (2006) Unmet education and training needs in adolescent health of health professionals in a UK children's hospital. *Acta Paediatrica* 95 (6), 715–719.

McDonagh, J.E., Southwood, T.R. and Shaw, K.L. (2004) Unmet adolescent health training needs for rheumatology health professionals. *Rheumatology*, 43, 737–743.

McDonagh, J.E., Southwood, T.R. and Shaw, K.L. (2006a) Growing up and moving on in rheumatology: development and preliminary evaluation of a transitional care programme for a multicentre cohort of adolescents with juvenile idiopathic arthritis. *Journal of Child Health Care*, 10, 1, 22–42.

McDonagh, J.E., Southwood, T.R. and Shaw, K.L. (2006b) The impact of a coordinated transitional care programme on adolescents with juvenile idiopathic arthritis. *Rheumatology* 46(1): 161–168.

McCamish-Svennsson, C., Samuelsson, G., Hagberg, B. *et al.* (1999) Social relationships and health as predictors of life satisfaction in advanced old age. *International Journal of Aging and Human Development*, 48, 301–324.

McNeish, D. (1999) *From rhetoric to reality: participatory approaches to health promotion with young people,* Health Education Authority, London.

Meltzer, H., Gatward, R., Corbin, T. *et al.* (2003) *The mental health of young people looked after by local authorities in England*, Office for National Statistics, The Stationery Office, London.

Meltzer, H., Gatwood, R., Goodman, R. and Ford, T. (2000) *Mental health of children and adolescents in Great Britain*, Office for National Statistics, The Stationery Office, London.

Mental Health Foundation (2002) *Peer support: someone to turn to. An evaluation report of the Mental Health Foundation*, Mental Health Foundation, London.

Michaud, P.-A. (2006) Adolescents and risk: why not change our paradigm? *Journal of Adolescent Health*, 38, 481–483.

Milburn, K. (1995) A critical review of peer education with young people with special reference to sexual health. *Health Education Research,* 10, 4, 407–420.

Minuchin, S., Rosman, B. L. and Baker, L. (1978). *Psychosomatic families: Anorexia nervosa in context.* Harvard University Press Cambridge, MA.

Morgan, W.P. and Dishman, M. L. (2001) Adherence to exercise and physical activity: Preface. *Quest*, 53, 277–278.

MORI (2001) *Get off the couch!* Report prepared for BUPA, London.

Nathanson, V. (ed.) (2003) *Adolescent health*, British Medical Association, London.

Neumark-Sztainer, D., Wall, M., Guo, J. and Story, M. (2006) Obesity, disordered eating and eating disorders in a longitudinal study of adolescents: How do dieters fare 5 years later? *Journal of the American Dietetic Association*, 106, 4, 559–568.

Newman, T. (2002) *Promoting resilience: a review of effective strategies for child care services*, Centre for Evidence-Based Social Services, University of Exeter.

Nicholas, B. and Broadstock, M. (1999) *Effectiveness of early interventions for preventing mental illness in young people*, New Zealand Health Technology Assessment Clearing House, Auckland, New Zealand.

Nicholls, J.C. (1978) The development of concepts of effort and ability, perception of attainment, and the understanding that difficult tasks require more ability. *Child Development*, 49, 800–814.

Nicholls, J.G. (1984) Achievement motivation: Conceptions of ability, subjective experience, task choice, and performance. *Psychological Review*, 91, 328–346.

Nichter, M. and Nichter, M. (1991) Hype and weight. *Medical Anthropology.* 13, 135, 621–634.

Norman, G.J., Schmid, B.A., Sallis, J.F. *et al.* (2005) Psychosocial and environmental correlates of adolescent sedentary behaviours. *Pediatrics*, 116, 908–916.

Ntoumanis, N. and Biddle, S.J.H. (1999) A review of motivational climate in physical activity. *Journal of Sport Science,* 17, 643 – 665.

Ofsted (2005) *Healthy minds: Promoting emotional health and well-being in schools*, Department for Education and Skills, HMSO, London.

Ogden J. and Wardle, J. (1990) Cognitive restraint and sensitivity to cues for hunger and satiety. *Physiology and Behaviour*, 47, 3, 477–481.

Olivardia, R. and Pope, H.G. (2002) Muscle dysmorphia in male weightlifters: a case control study. *American Journal of Psychiatry*, 157, 1291–1296.

Olsson, C.A., Bond, L., Burns, J.M., *et al.* (2003) Adolescent resilience: a concept analysis. *Journal of Adolescence*, 26, 1–11.

ONS (Office for National Statistics) (2001–2003) *Mortality statistics*, Statbase, London.

ONS (Office for National Statistics) (2005) *Conception statistics: conceptions for women resident in England and Wales, 2003*, London.

Orbach, S. (1986) *Hunger strike*, Penguin, Harmondsworth, UK.

Orr, D.P., Fineberg, N.S. and Gray, D.L. (1996) Glycaemic control and transfer of health care among adolescents with insulin dependent diabetes mellitus. *Journal of Adolescent Health*, 18, 44–47.

Pacaud, D., McConnell, B., Huot, C. *et al.* (1996) Transition from pediatric care to adult care for insulin-dependent diabetes patients. *Canadian Journal of Diabetes Care*, 20, 4, 14–20.

Palazolli, M.S. (1974) *Self-starvation: from intrapsychic to the transpersonal approach to anorexia nervosa*, Human Context Books, Chaucer Publishing Company, London.

Palmer, R.L. (1989) *Anorexia nervosa – a guide for sufferers and their families*, Penguin, Harmondsworth.

Papaioannou, A. and Theodorakis, Y. (1996) A test of three models for the prediction of intention for participation in physical education lessons. *International Journal of Sport Psychology*, 27, 383–399.

Pape, H. (1997) Drinking, getting stoned or staying sober: a general population study of alcohol consumption, cannabis use, drinking-related problems and sobriety among young men and women. Doctoral dissertation, NOVA, Oslo.

Pape, H. and Hammer, T. (1996) Sober adolescence: Predictor of psychosocial maladjustment in young adulthood? *Scandinavian Journal of Psychology*, 37, 362–377.

Pate, R.P., Trost, S.G., Mullis, R. *et al.* (2000) Community interventions to promote proper nutrition and physical activity among youth. *Preventive Medicine*, 31, S138–S149.

Patterson, J. and Blum, R.J. (1996) Risk and resilience among children and youth with disabilities. *Archives of Pediatric and Adolescent Medicine*, 150, 692–698.

Patton, G.C., Selzer, R., Coffey, C. *et al.* (1999) Onset of adolescent eating disorders: population based cohort study over 3 years. *British Medical Journal*, 318, 765.

Peersman, G. (1996) *A descriptive mapping of health promotion studies in young people*, EPI-Centre, Social Science Research Unit, London.

Petraitis, J., Flay, B.R. and Miller, T.Q. (1995) Reviewing theories of adolescent substance use: Organizing pieces in the puzzle. *Psychological Bulletin*, 117, 67–86.

Philip, K. and Hendry, L.B. (1996) Young people and mentoring: towards a typology. *Journal of Adolescence*, 9, 43–62.

Philip, K., Shucksmith, J. and King, C. (2004) *Sharing a laugh? A qualitative study of mentoring interventions with young people*, Joseph Rowntree Foundation, York.

Poag, K., and McAuley, E. (1992) Goal setting, self-efficacy, and exercise behavior. *Journal of Sport and Exercise Psychology*, 14, 352–360.

Potter, K. and Hodgkiss, F. (2002) *Consultation with children and young people on the Scottish Executive's Plan for Action on alcohol misuse*, Stationery Office, Edinburgh.

Prentice, A.M., Black, A.E., Murgatroyd, P.R. *et al.* (1989) Metabolism or appetite: questions of energy balance with particular reference to obesity. *Journal of Human Nutrition and Dietetics*, 2, 95–104.

Prentice, A.M. and Jebb, S.A. (1995) Obesity in Britain: gluttony or sloth? *British Medical Journal*, 311, 437–439.

Prescott, C.A. and Kendler, K.S. (1999) Age at first drink and risk for alcoholism: A noncausal association. *Alcoholism: Clinical and Experimental Research*, 23, 101–107.

Prokhorov, A.V., Pallonen, U. E., Fava, J. L. *et al.* (1996) Measuring nicotine dependence among high-risk adolescent smokers. *Addictive Behaviours*, 21, 117–127.

Pyle, R.l., Halvorson, P.A., Neuman, P.A. and Mitchell, J.E. (1986) The increasing prevalence of bulimia in freshman college students. *The International Journal of Eating Disorders*, 5, 4, 631–647.

Radia, K. (1996) *Housing and mental health care of Asians*, Joseph Rowntree Foundation, York.

Raglin, J.S. (1997) Anxiolytic effects of physical activity, in Morgan, W.P. (ed.) *Physical activity and mental health,* Taylor & Francis, Washington DC, 107–126.

Reid, G.J., Irvine, M.J., McCrindle, B.W. *et al.* (2004) Prevalence and correlates of successful transfer from pediatric to adult health care among a cohort of young adults with complex congenital heart defects. *Pediatrics*, 113, 3, 197–205.

Richardson, L.P., Davis, R., Poulton, R. *et al.* (2003) A longitudinal evaluation of adolescent depression and adult obesity. *Archives of Pediatric and Adolescent Medicine*, 157, 739–745.

Roberts, G.C. (2001) Understanding the dynamics of motivation in physical activity: the influence of achievement goals on motivational processes, in Roberts, G.C. (ed.) *Advances in motivation in sport and exercise,* Human Kinetics, Champaign, IL, 1–50.

Robertson, L.P., McDonagh, J.E., Southwood, T.R. and Shaw, K.L. (2006) Growing up and moving on. A multicentre UK audit of the transfer of adolescents with Juvenile Idiopathic Arthritis (JIA) from paediatric to adult centred care. *Annals of the Rheumatic Diseases*, 65, 74–80.

Roker, D (1998) *Worth more than this: young people growing up in family poverty*, Trust for the Study of Adolescence, Brighton.

Royal College of Paediatrics and Child Health (2003) *Bridging the gaps: health care for adolescents*, RCPCH, London [available on www.rcpch.ac.uk/publications/recent_publications/bridging_the_gaps.pdf].

Rutter, M. (1996) Psychosocial adversity: risk, resilience and recovery, in Verhofstadt-Deneve, L., Kienhorst, I and Breat, C. (eds) *Conflict and development in adolescence,* DSWO Press, Leiden.

Rutter, M. and Smith, D. (1995) *Psychosocial disorders of youth*, John Wiley & Sons, Ltd, Chichester.

Ryan, R. M., Frederick, C. M., Lepes, D. *et al.* (1997) Intrinsic motivation and exercise adherence. *International Journal of Sport Psychology,* 28, 335–354.

Sanci, L., Coffey, C., Patton, G. and Bowes, G. (2005) Sustainability of change with quality general practitioner education in adolescent health: a 5-year follow-up. *Medical Education*, 39, 557–560.

Sanci, L., Coffey, C. and Veit, F. (2000) Evaluation of the effectiveness of an educational intervention for general practitioners in adolescent health care: a randomised control trial. *British Medical Journal*, 320, 224–230.

Sarrazin, P. and Famose, J-P. (1999) Children's goals and motivation in physical education, in Vanden Auweele, Y., Bakker, F., Biddle, S.J.H., Durand, M. and Seiler, R. (eds), *Psychology for physical educators,* Human Kinetics, FEPSAC, Champaign IL, 27–50.

Scanlan, T.K., Carpenter, P.J., Lobel, M. and Simons, J.P. (1993) Sources of enjoyment for youth sport. *Pediatric Exercise Science,* 5, 275–285.

Scanlan, T.K. and Lewthwaite, R. (1986) Social psychological aspects of the competitive sport experience for male youth sport participants: IV predictors of enjoyment. *Journal of Sport Psychology,* 8, 25–35.

Schachter, S. and Rodin, J. (1974) *Obese Humans and Rats*, Erlbaum, Potomac, MD.

Schofield, M. (1965) *The sexual behaviour of young people*, Longmans, London.

Schwarzer, R. (1992) Self efficacy in the adoption and maintenance of health behaviours: theoretical approaches and a new model, in Schwarzer, R. (ed.) *Self-efficacy: thought control of action*, Hemisphere, Washington DC, 217–243.

Scriven, A. and Stiddard, L. (2003) Empowering schools: translating health promotion principles into practice. *Health Education*, 2, 3, 20–31.

Scully, D. and Clarke, J. (1997) Gender issues in sport participation, in Kremer, J., Trew, K. and Ogle, S. (eds) (1997) *Young people's involvement in sport*, Routledge, London.

Scully, D., Kremer, J., Meade, M., Graham, R. and Dudgeon, K. (1998) Exercise and psychological well-being: a critical review. *British Journal of Sports Medicine*, 32, 111–120.

Scully, D., Reilly, J. and Clarke, J. (1998) Perspectives on gender in sport and exercise. *Irish Journal of Psychology*, 19, 424–438.

Seifriz, J.J., Duda, J.L. and Chi, L. (1992) The relationship of perceived motivational climate to intrinsic motivation and beliefs about success in basketball. *Journal of Sport and Exercise Psychology*, 14, 375–391.

Shaw, K.L., Southwood, T.R. and McDonagh, J.E. (2004a) Users' perspectives of transitional care for adolescents with juvenile idiopathic arthritis. *Rheumatology*, 43, 770–778.

Shaw, K.L., Southwood, T.R. and McDonagh, J.E. (2004b) Transitional care for adolescents with juvenile idiopathic arthritis: results of a Delphi study. *Rheumatology*, 43, 1000–1006.

Shaw, K.L, Southwood, T.R. and McDonagh, J.E. (2004c) Developing a programme of transitional care for adolescents with juvenile idiopathic arthritis: results of a postal survey. *Rheumatology*, 43, 211–219.

Shaw, K.L., Southwood, T.R. and McDonagh, J.E. (2006) Growing up and moving on in rheumatology: parents as proxies of adolescents with juvenile idiopathic arthritis. *Arthritis Care Research*, 55, 2, 189–198.

Shedler, J. and Block, J. (1990) Adolescent drug use and psychological health: a longitudinal inquiry. *American Psychologist*, 45, 612–630.

Shepherd, J., Garcia, J., Oliver, S. *et al.* (2002) *Barriers to, and facilitators of the health of young people: a systematic review of evidence on young people's views and on interventions in mental health, physical activity and healthy eating*, EPPI-Centre, Social Science Research Unit, London.

Shucksmith, J. and Hendry, L.B. (1998) *Health issues and adolescents: growing up and speaking out*, Routledge, London.

Shucksmith, J., Hendry, L.B. and Glendinning, A. (1995) Models of parenting: implications for adolescent well-being within different types of family context. *Journal of Adolescence*, 18, 253–270.

Shucksmith, J. and Spratt, J. (2002) *Young people's self-identified health needs*, HEBS, Edinburgh.

Shucksmith, J. and Spratt, J. (2003) Young people's self-identified health needs. *Scottish Youth Issues Journal*, 6, 47–62.

Siersted, H.C., Boldsen, J., Hansen, H.S., Mostgaard, G. and Hyldebrandt, N. (1998) Population-based study of risk factors for underdiagnosis of asthma in adolescence: Odense schoolchild study. *British Medical Journal*, 316, 651–655.

Silbereisen, R.K. and Noack, P. (1988) On the constructive role of problem behaviour in adolescence, in Bolger, N. (ed.), *Persons in context: developmental processes*, Cambridge University Press, Cambridge, 153–180.

Smith, J., Cunningham-Burley, S. and Backett-Milburn, K. (2003) Young people, health and health information: a scoping study of youth organisations and their views. *Scottish Youth Issues Journal*, 6, 27–46.

Social Exclusion Unit (1999) *Teenage pregnancy*, HMSO, London.

Spijkerman, R., van den Eijnden, R.J.J.M., Vitale, S. and Engels, R.C.M.E. (2004) Explaining adolescents' smoking and drinking behaviour: the concept of smoker and drinker prototypes in relation to variables of the theory of planned behaviour. *Addictive Behaviours*, 1615–1622.

Spink, K.S. and Carron, A.V. (1992) Group cohesion and adherence in exercise classes. *Journal of Sport and Exercise Psychology*, 14, 78–86.

Spink, K.S. and Carron, A.V. (1993) The effects of team building on the adherence patterns of female exercise participants. *Journal of Sport and Exercise Psychology*, 15, 39–49.

Sport England (2003a). *Young people and sport in England: trends in participation 1994–2002*, SE/2218/P/02/03, Sport England, London.

Sport England (2003b) *Young people and sport: national survey 2002*, SE/2220/P/02/03, Sport England, London.

Stanton, W. (1995) The Dunedin study of childhood and adolescent smoking: selected findings, in Slama, K. (ed.) *Tobacco and health*, Plenum Press, New York.

Stewart-Brown, S. (2005) Mental health promotion: childhood holds the key. *Public Health Medicine* 5(3) 96–104 .

Stone, E.J., McKenzie, T.L., Welk, G.J. and Booth, M. (1998) Effects of physical activity interventions in youth: review and synthesis. *American Journal of Preventive Medicine*, 15, 298–315.

Stone, G. (1987) The scope of health psychology, in Stone, G., Weiss, S., Matarazzo, G. and Singer, G. (eds) *Health psychology: a discipline and a profession*, University of Chicago Press, Chicago.

Strober, M., Freeman R., Lampert C., Diamond J. and Kaye W. (2000) Controlled family study of anorexia nervosa and bulimia nervosa: Evidence of shared liability and transmission of partial syndromes. *American Journal of Psychiatry*, 157(3), 393–401.

Suris, J.C., Parera, N. (2005) Sex, drugs and chronic illness: health behaviours among chronically ill youth. *European Journal of Public Health*, 15, 5, 484–8.

Suris, J.C., Resnick, M.D., Cassuto, N., Blum, R.W.M. (1996) Sexual behaviour of adolescents with chronic disease and disability. *Journal of Adolescent Health*, 19, 124–131.

Swann, C., Bowe, K., McCormik, G. and Kosmin, M. (2003) *Teenage pregnancy and parenthood: a review of reviews*, Health Development Agency, London.

Tchanturia, K., Anderluh, B., Morris, R.G. *et al.* (2004) Cognitive flexibility in anorexia and bulimia nervosa. *Journal of the International Neuropsychological Society*, 10, 413–520.

Teenage Pregnancy Unit (TPU) (2000) *Best practice guidance on the provision of effective contraception and advice services for young people*, Teenage Pregnancy Unit, London.

Telfair, J., Alexander, L.R., Loosier, P.S. *et al.* (2004) Providers' perspectives and beliefs regarding transition to adult care for adolescents with sickle cell disease. *Journal of Health Care for the Poor and Underserved*, 15, 443–461.

Temple M.T. and Fillmore, K.M. (1986) The variability of drinking patterns and problems among young men, age 16–31: a longitudinal study. *International Journal of the Addictions*, 20, 1595–1620.

Testa, A. and Coleman, L.M. (2006) *Sexual health knowledge, attitudes and behaviours among Black and minority ethnic youth in London*, Trust for the Study of Adolescence, Brighton.

Tilford, S., Delaney, F. and Vogels, M. (1997) *Effectiveness of mental health promotion interventions: a review*, Health Education Authority, London.

Timperio, A., Crawford, D., Telford, A. and Salmon, J. (2004) Perceptions about the local neighbourhood and walking and cycling among children. *Preventive Medicine*, 38, 39–47.

Tisdall, K. (2002) *Constructing the problem, constructing the solution: Young people's health in Scottish executive policies*, HEBS, Edinburgh.

Tobler, N.S., Roona, M. R., Ochshorn, P. *et al.* (2000) School-based adolescent drug prevention programs: 1998 meta-analysis. *Journal of Primary Prevention*, 20, 275–336.

Tofler, I.R., Knapp, P.K. & Drell, M.J. (1998). The achievement by proxy spectrum in youth sports: Historical perspective and clinnical approach to pressured and high-achieving children and adolescents. *Child and Adolescent Psychiatric Clinics of North America*, 7(4), 803–820.

Tomlinson, P. and Sugarman, I.D. (1995) Complications with shunts in adults with spina bifida. *British Medical Journal*, 311, 286–287.

Treasure, J. and Holland, A. (1995) Genetic factors in eating disorders, in Szmuckler G. Dare C. and Treasure J., (eds) *Handbook of Eating Disorders: Theory, Treatment and Research*, John Wiley and Sons, Inc., New York, 65–81.

Turtle, J., Jones, A. and Hickman, M. (1997) *Young people and health: the health behaviour of school-aged children*, Health Education Authority, London.

UNICEF (2001) A league table of teenage births in rich nations. Innocenti Report Card no. 3, UNICEF Innocenti Research Centre, Florence [www.unicef-icdc.org/publications/index.html].

Valencia, L.S. and Cromer, B.A. (2000) Sexual activity and other high-risk behaviours in adolescents with chronic illness: a review. *Journal of Pediatric and Adolescent Gynecology*, 13, 2, 53–64.

Vallerand, R.J. and Losier, G.F. (1999) An integrative analysis of intrinsic and extrinsic motivation in sport. *Journal of Applied Sport Psychology,* 11, 142–196.

Van Der Vorst, H., Engels, R.C.M.E., Deković, M., Vermulst, A.A. and Meeus, W. (2004) Attachment, parental control and alcohol initiation in adolescence. Revision submitted to *Psychology of Addictive Behaviours*.

Viner, R. (1999) Politics, power, and pediatrics. *The Lancet*, 353, 232–234.

Viner, R. (2001) National survey of use of hospital beds by adolescents aged 12–19 in the United Kingdom. *British Medical Journal*, 322, 957–958.

Viner, R. (ed.) (2005) *The ABC of adolescence*. British Medical Journal Books, London.

Viner, R. and Barker, M. (2005) Young people's health: the need for action. *British Medical Journal*, 330, 901–903.

Wackerhausen, S. (1994) Et åbent sundhetsbegreb – mellem fundamentalisme og relativisme, in Jensen, U.J. and Andersen, P.F. (eds) *Sundhetsbegreber – filosofi og praksis*, Philosophia, Århus, 43–73.

Walker, J.L. (2001) A qualitative study of parents' experiences of providing sex education for their children: the implications for health education. *Health Education Journal*, 60, 2, 132–146.

Waters, E., Stewart-Brown, S. and Fitzpatrick, R. (2003) Agreement between adolescent self-report and parent reports of health and well-being: results of an epidemiological study. *Child: Care, Health and Development*, 29, 501–509.

Watson, A.R. (2000) Non-compliance and transfer from paediatric to adult transplant unit. *Pediatric Nephrology*, 14, 469–472.

Weare, K. (2004) *Developing the emotionally literate school*, Paul Chapman Publishing, London.

Wechsler, H., Devereaux, R.S., Davis, M. and Collins, J. (2000) Using the school environment to promote physical activity and healthy eating. *Preventive Medicine*, 31, S121–137.

Weiss, M.R. and Hayashi, C.T. (1995) All in the family: parent–child influences in competitive youth gymnastics. *Pediatric Exercise Science*, 7, 36–48.

Wells, J., Barlow, J. and Stewart-Brown, S. (2003) A systematic review of universal approaches to mental health promotion in schools. *Health Education*, 103, 197–220.

West, P. and Sweeting, H. (1997) 'Lost souls' and 'rebels': a challenge to the assumption that low self-esteem and unhealthy lifestyles are related. *Health Education*, 5, 161–167.

West, P. and Sweeting, H. (2002) *The health of young people in Scotland: quantitative dimensions*, Health Education Board for Scotland, Edinburgh.

West, P. and Sweeting, H. (2003) Fifteen, female and stressed: changing patterns of psychological distress over time. *Journal of Child Psychology and Psychiatry*, 44, 399–411.

West, P., Sweeting, H. and Leyland, A. (2004) School effects on pupils' health behaviours: evidence in support of the health promoting school. *Research Papers in Education*, 19, 3, 261–291.

While, A., Forbes, A., Ullman, R. *et al.* 2004. Good practices that address continuity during transition from child to adult care: syntheses of the evidence. *Child: Care, Health and Development*, 30, 5, 439–452.

White, P.H., Gussek, D.G. and Fisher, B. (1990) Career maturity in adolescents with chronic illness. *Journal of Adolescent Health Care*, 1, 72

White, S.A. and Duda, J.L. (1994) The relationship of gender, level of sport involvement and participation motivation to task and ego orientation. *International Journal of Sport Psychology*, 25, 4–18.

WHO (World Health Organization) (1946) *Constitution of the World Health Organization*, WHO, Geneva.

WHO (World Health Organization) (1980) *International classification of impairments, disabilities and handicaps: a manual of classification relating to the consequences of disease*, WHO, Geneva.

WHO (World Health Organization) (1992) *The ICD-10 classification of mental and behavioural disorders. Clinical descriptions and diagnostic guidelines*, WHO, Geneva.

WHO (World Health Organization) (1999) STI rates comparisons across Europe – global prevalence and incidence of selected curable sexually transmitted infections [www.who.int/docstore/hiv/GRSTI/002.htm].

WHO (World Health Organization) (2000) *Health and health behaviour among young people*, WHO Policy Series: Health Policy for Children and Adolescents, Issue 1, International Report, WHO, Copenhagen.

WHO (World Health Organization) (2004) Draft working definition of sexual health, October 2002 [www.who.int/reproductive-health/gender/glossary.html]

Wight, D., Raab, G.M., Henderson, M. *et al.* (2002) Limits of teacher delivered sex education: interim behavioural outcomes from randomised trial. *British Medical Journal*, 324, 1430–1435.

Wilkinson, V.A. (1981) Juvenile chronic arthritis in adolescence: facing the reality. *International Rehabilitative Medicine*, 3, 11–17.

Williamson, D.F., Madans, J., Anda, R.F. *et al.* (1993) Recreational physical activity and 10-year weight change in US national cohort. *International Journal of Obesity*, 17, 115–126.

Windle, M. and Windle, R.C. (1996) Coping strategies, drinking motives, and stressful life events among middle adolescents: Associations with emotional and behavioural problems and with academic functioning. *Journal of Abnormal Psychology*, 105, 551–560.

Wits, E., Spijkerman, R. and Bongers, I (1999) *Als je alleen blowt, ist niet leuk man,* IVO, Rotterdam.

Wolf, N. (1991) *The Beauty Myth*, Doubleday, New York.

Young, I. (2004) Exploring the role of schools in sexual health promotion, in Burtney, E. and Duffy, M. *Young people and sexual health: individual, social and policy contexts,* Palgrave Macmillan, Basingstoke.

Youngstedt, S.D., Dishman, R.K., Cureton, K.J. and Peacock, L.J. (1993) Does body temperature mediate anxiolytic effects of acute exercise? *Journal of Applied Physiology*, 74, 825–831.

Zack, J., Jacobs, C.P., Keenan, P.M. *et al.* (2003) Perspectives of patients with cystic fibrosis on preventive counselling and transition to adult care. *Pediatric Pulmonology*, 36, 5, 376–383.

Zuckerman, M. (1994) *Behavioral expressions and biosocial bases of sensation seeking*, Cambridge University Press, New York.

Index